AFRICAN STRUGGLES TODAY

AFRICAN STRUGGLES TODAY

SOCIAL MOVEMENTS SINCE INDEPENDENCE

Peter Dwyer and Leo Zeilig

Haymarket Books
Chicago, Illinois

Published in 2012 by
Haymarket Books
P.O. Box 180165
Chicago, IL 60618
info@haymarketbooks.org
773-583-7884
www.haymarketbooks.org

ISBN: 978-1-60846-120-2

Cover design by Amy Balkan. Cover photo of a 10,000-strong march for political, economic, and environmental justice outside the 2002 US World Summit on Sustainable
Development in Johannesburg, South Africa. ©Saurabh Das. Associated Press photo.

Trade distribution:
In the US, Consortium Book Sales and Distribution, www.cbsd.com
In Canada, Publishers Group Canada, www.pgcbooks.ca
In the UK, Turnaround Publisher Services, www.turnaround-uk.com
In Australia, Palgrave Macmillan, www.palgravemacmillan.com.au
All other countries, Publishers Group Worldwide, www.pgw.com

Published with the generous support of Lannan Foundation and the Wallace Global Fund.

Printed in the United States by union labor on FSC certified stock.

Library of Congress Cataloging-in-Publication Data is available.

10 9 8 7 6 5 4 3 2 1

SUSTAINABLE FORESTRY INITIATIVE

Certified Sourcing
www.sfiprogram.org
SFI-01234

CONTENTS

Acknowledgments   ix

1 Introduction   1

2 Social Movements and the Working Class
  in Africa   18

3 An Epoch of Uprisings: 50
  Social Movements in Postcolonial Africa,
  1945–98

4 Cracks in the Monolith: 92
  Social Movements in Post-Apartheid
  South Africa

5 Social Movements after the Transition: 129
  Choiceless Democracies?

6 Frustrated Transitions: 166
  Social Movements, Protest, and Repression
  in the Democratic Republic of Congo,
  Zimbabwe, and Swaziland

7 Social Forums and the World Social Forum
  in Africa   204

8 Conclusion   237

  List of Acronyms   255

  Notes   258

  Index   285

"Social movements of the world, let us advance towards a global unity to shatter the capitalist system!"

—Final Declaration of the Social Movements Assembly
World Social Forum, February 10, 2011, Dakar, Senegal

ACKNOWLEDGMENTS

This book is a reflection of our interest in the resistance to oppression and exploitation by the peoples of Africa. We have been writing, working, living, and visiting in parts of Africa for twenty years and we draw many lessons and much inspiration from its extraordinary history of struggle. A fundamental premise of this book is a recognition that social change is about more than just "great leaders"; change is often driven "from below" by those who are excluded from the pages of academic and historical books. This book is a story about the puzzled, disillusioned, well-organized, and angry men and women who continue the struggle to transform their lives and societies for the better.

The roots of this book go back to our attendance at two workshops in Johannesburg. The first was conducted by the Southern Africa Centre for Economic Justice and the other by the Congress of South African Trade Unions (COSATU). It struck us that among a group of progressive academics, researchers, activists, and nongovernmental organizations (NGOs) from Southern Africa, little was collectively known about the condition and political role of progressive civil society organizations (CSOs) in the region. At the two-day planning workshop on political education, the fifteen or so participants admitted they knew little about the state of civil society in Africa. There was a practical gap in knowledge within Africa and between movements in the global south and north. There was also a tendency to uncritically romanticize nationalist movements, while in the north and at various social forums there was much talk of one united anticapitalist movement. We have sought to integrate an analysis of the complexities of the continent's recent history with an understanding of really existing movements.

We owe an enduring debt to Miles Larmer for undertaking much of this research with us. The book would never have been completed were it not for his involvement, his research, and the lengthy discussions (and comradely disagreements) we had with him. If he did not agree with the conclusions the book reached, this only serves to illustrate what complex and important work this is.

We must also thank Anthony Arnove and Julie Fain at Haymarket Books, who have encouraged and supported us with the book from the start. David Whitehouse has been central to the painful process of completing the book. He read and edited various drafts very closely and provided invaluable advice and criticism. Sarah Grey deserves thanks as well for her painstaking work on the completed manuscript. Thanks to Emily Albarillo for proofreading.

The book also, in part, reflects an ongoing working relationship with David Seddon, who has so often shared with us his passion and deep understanding of the issues that have long preoccupied us. We have also benefited from the long-standing solidarity and comradeship of Femi Aborisade, Tafadzwa Choto, and Andy Wynne. We have both been inspired and influenced for years by Alex Callinicos and Colin Barker; their influence on us can be found in these pages. Colin's own research on social movements, which manages to be both highly original and grounded in Marx's writing and method, has helped shape many ideas in this book.

Peter Dwyer, Oxford
Leo Zeilig, London
April 2012

CHAPTER 1

INTRODUCTION

This book is about the role of social movements in contemporary Africa. Its core argument is that social movements—popular movements of the working class, the poor, and other oppressed and marginalized sections of African society—have played a central role in shaping Africa's contemporary history.[1] In the twentieth century, social movements were central to challenging the material exploitations of Western imperialism and bringing an end to formal European control of the continent. Similarly, they resisted dictatorial and military rule in postcolonial Africa, and in the late 1980s and early 1990s paved the way for the return of democracy to much of the continent. In the last two decades, social movements have critiqued and resisted the imposition of economic liberalization across the continent by the international financial institutions and their allies among African rulers. Despite this extraordinary record, African social movements have not been the subject of systematic analysis. While there has been a considerable proliferation of modern history books on Africa, none focus on popular struggles.[2] Although many individual case studies of particular movements have been carried out, the wider impact of those movements has often been neglected, with popular movements consigned to condescending footnotes in broader imposed narratives of the transfer of state power and the triumph of liberal democracy. It is the aim of this study to place social movements at the center of the analysis of postcolonial African political change, capturing both their exciting diversity and their capacity to unite as temporary "coalitions of the discontent" in periods of rapid social change. In such circumstances, they have the potential to play a leading role in progressive political and social change, as they did during the struggle for independence in the 1950s and early 1960s and again in the pro-democracy movements of the early 1990s.

The book is thus designed as a corrective to the tendency to see Africa's postcolonial half-century as one dominated by political repression, economic decline, and ethnic conflict. Africans have constantly struggled in difficult circumstances to improve their lot, using collective forms of action to challenge unjust and unaccountable systems of political and economic power. This book documents many of those struggles during the post-1945 period in general, and those that took place in southern Africa in the 1990s and 2000s in particular. However, it is also acknowledged that these movements, formidable though they have been, have not ultimately coalesced into a sustained force for social change akin to the labor movements of late nineteenth- and early twentieth-century western Europe, which permanently transformed the lives of that continent's working class. Africans, in contrast, have seen their living standards decline and many of their societies deteriorate into political repression and, in some cases, virtual anarchy.

As well as celebrating the successes of these movements, much of the book therefore asks the implicit question "What went wrong?" If social protest has been at the heart of Africa's politics, then why is much of the continent so resolutely undemocratic, authoritarian, and poor? How have vibrant movements of the sort analyzed here failed to develop into broader political forces for radical social and political change? Why have their achievements been so consistently hijacked by economic and political elites, both Western and indigenous? Answering this question certainly necessitates a critique of the politics of African nationalism and the nature of postcolonial African elites. It also requires a critical analysis of the politics and composition of social movements themselves. By addressing these concerns, it is the authors' hope that this book will make a modest contribution to strengthening the activists and movements currently active on the continent

This analysis is rooted in the authors' extensive research on the continent, particularly in southern and central Africa. It draws on dozens of interviews with social movement activists and a decade of observation and participation in the debates and activities of movements and organizations that are themselves grappling with many of the questions raised above. The resultant analysis shows the experience of African social movements to be varied, complex, and often contradictory. They have often sought to utilize the democratic "space" they have helped win, only to find their activities hampered by elected governments that replicate the authoritarianism of their predecessors. Their efforts to speak for the "masses" or the "people" are limited by the profound inequalities (of resources, power, and social capital) that pervade their structures. They seek to operate in a global context, but their local grievances are subordinated to the liberal agenda of Western civil society, even in parts of the anticapitalist movement (which is the focus of chapter 7). In portraying the difficult relationships between the African poor and working class and the organizations that seek to represent them, we reject both the tendency to reify these movements as authentically "of the people" and the equal tendency to reject such movements as the puppets of their Western funders. These issues are further elaborated in chapter 2.

The view from below

Our orientation in this book is toward social forces that frequently lie hidden in the official historical accounts that dominate both academic studies and the media. We seek to understand historical and political change in a way that reflects the aspirations, grievances, and worldview of the majority of the African people. Social change, we argue, is created in the popular resistance of which social movements are increasingly an important element. This approach to a "politics from below" is of course not particularly original, nor particular to Africa. The model of political transformation in this book is developed from an approach to historical writing forged in the 1950s and 1960s. E. P. Thompson's famous study *The Making of the English Working Class* wrote consciously "against the weight of prevailing orthodoxies" which "tend to obscure the agency of working people, the degree to which they contributed by conscious efforts, to the making of history. . . . Only the successful . . . are remembered. The blind alleys, the lost causes, and the losers themselves are forgotten."[3]

History from below is not a new phenomenon in Africa. This approach to Africa's past, present, and future was popularized in the annual History Workshop at South Africa's University of the Witwatersrand. Drawing on the work of Thompson, these studies emphasized the importance of the agency of the "poors" and stressed the vibrancy of the experiences of popular classes.[4] In the 1970s, pioneering labor studies were carried out across the continent, employing an empirical "change from below" perspective to shed light on the consciousness of workers in Ghana, Nigeria, Kenya, and Zambia, among other countries.[5] Some more recent studies of Zimbabwe have continued this pioneering work.[6] More generally, however, there has been a shift away from agency-oriented studies of social movements; political change in Africa tends to be interpreted primarily in terms of the machinations of elites and their interactions with international institutions. Politics is reduced to "governance" and social movements to "civil society." The "masses," in such analyses, are passive electoral fodder, easily manipulated by appeals to narrow ethnic solidarities and/or the trickle down of neo-patrimonial recompense.

This book is, then, an attempt to restore the agency of social movements to the center of democratic transformation and change on the continent. It is a sustained attempt against forgetting, for example, the general strikes that gave birth to mass nationalist politics in Senegal and Zimbabwe, or the demonstrations more than forty years later by students at the University of Lubumbashi that helped to trigger the "democratic transition" and the period of Congo's "second revolution."[7] These histories are told against a frequently hostile and seemingly unbending social world. The ideological tools (organizations, initiatives, and leadership) that social movements used in the democratic transitions were one of the ways they were able to exercise agency and achieve successful transformation.

Ideological tools

These ideas are linked explicitly to central concerns of this book. It should be clear that the "activism" to which we refer is not simply a topic of research, but an important element in social and economic transformation. Political change without the intervention of ideological and social struggle (political activism) can lead to stagnation or worse: "the common ruin of struggling classes."[8] Therefore to make and remake history requires, in Chris Harman's words, a social group with "its own ideas, its own organization and eventually its own . . . leadership. Where its most determined elements managed to create such things, the new society took root. Where it failed . . . stagnation and decay were the result."[9]

Harman stressed in 2004 the centrality of political and ideological structures in the historical process: "Economic development never took place on its own, in a vacuum. It was carried forward by human beings, living in certain societies whose political and ideological structures had an impact on their actions."[10] In turn, these structures were the products of a confrontation between social groups.

Social transformation is therefore propelled by ideological and political conflict between rival social groups, not simply economics.

The resolution of these conflicts "is never resolved in advance, but depends upon initiative, organization, and leadership,"[11] the raw material through which human beings are able to make history, but not on a level playing field (or in a vacuum). We do not choose the circumstances in which these struggles take place.[12]

Historical progress proceeds in these unchosen circumstances. Samir Amin argued in 1990 that it was the economic backwardness of western Europe that gave it an advantage in the development of capitalism. Other Eurasian and African societies had experienced similar developments in production, but these were ultimately suffocated by existing state structures. The Chinese empire—the most economically advanced in the "Middle Ages"—was able to block these developments, while in the least advanced areas of western Europe the social forces unleashed by these changes could break down the old superstructures.[13] The capacity to "break down" old institutions was not simply a matter of economics, but crucially of politics and ideology. It was not only a question of struggling against the economic control by old social groups but also the prevailing worldview. Where the social forces associated to the new forms of production were unsuccessful, or too closely connected to the old states and institutions, "they were defeated and the old orders hung on for a few more centuries until the battleships and cheap goods of Europe's capitalists brought it tumbling down."[14]

In the democratic transitions examined in this book a multitude of organizations and "social groups" generated their own programs and ideas for the "transition," but the "initiative, organization, and leadership" that came to dominate these movements hailed from NGOs, now-excluded members of the previous ruling class, and trade union bureaucrats who saw no alternative to liberalization and the free market agenda of the Washington consensus. Though there *were* individuals, trade unionists, militants, and occasionally organizations that tried to drive the movements to the left, these were ultimately unable to lead and grow sufficiently to counter the politics and "ideological tools" of a recycled elite. For much of the continent's recent history, that politics has been dominated by a hegemonic nationalism, linked inextricably to the interests and parties of a particular social group but claiming to speak for the whole of society.

Understanding the faces of nationalism

Historically, nationalism tends to be the chosen ideology (and the state the central political focus) of members of a specific social group seeking to govern a politically defined nation. The political manifestation of this social group is often embodied in the leadership of the dominant hegemonic organization that provides intellectual and moral leadership in a national liberation movement and expresses particular material interests. However, leaders of a national movement do not always recognize themselves as a specific social group, expressing themselves instead as a *national* liberation movement speaking for all the people.

Colonial oppression, by subjugating people on a racialized basis, had the unintended consequence of uniting the subjugated peoples within particular colonial territories. The broad political objective of national liberation movements was therefore to secure the independence of their "country" from foreign domination—"national oppression." Revolutionary national liberation movements were composed of different social groups temporarily united under the banner of national liberation. Indeed, the term "movement" implies an amalgam of groups—political, economic, social, and cultural—working more or less collectively to bring about the goal of national liberation. While such movements develop in differing contexts, it is still possible to identify common characteristics they embody. One of these is that there is usually a group of people—often sharing similar material interests—in "leadership" positions with a specific, if not fixed, political strategy that, although seldom unchallenged, becomes hegemonic and leads a movement that strategically draws on different social groups. Consequently, it is important to interrogate the character of national liberation by defining nationalism as a particular set of ideas and by examining how, as a distinct political ideology, nationalism expresses particular material interests.

It is worth examining these arguments in more detail. Colonial oppression creates material incentives for resistance among all members of the oppressed nationality, but it also violates the particular material interests of various classes and strata in different ways. The material injuries that are experienced by *all* members of the oppressed nationality may actually constitute a relatively narrow band of common grievances against the colonial occupiers, while the most consistent and most particularly felt oppression— and thereby the oppression that motivates the sharpest resistance— may be particular to each social class or stratum.

For example, peasants may experience grievances against colonial landlords that can be successfully articulated within a "national" framework, but also against local landlords which cannot— as they did in India, where Gandhi approved rent strikes against the British landlords but not their Indian equivalents, the zamindars. Both classes, peasant and landlord, may be anti-colonial, but for different reasons. The unity of people who share a common enemy is essentially a "negative" quality—they both seek to remove the colonial regime, but disagree on what they would want from a successor regime. Therefore, we could say that classes diverge on their positive social goals.[15] Through such divergences, the "material basis" for a national liberation movement is thus *fragmented* into multiple material bases, which need to be fully analyzed if such movements are to be adequately understood.

Nationalists generally fail, unsurprisingly, to interrogate the material and historical bases of their own movements. Nationalists do not deny that other conflicts or forms of oppression exist, but maintain that they are secondary to the shared identity of all the peoples of a nation, irrespective of their gender, religion, and so on. The implication is that nationalism has no specific material and social basis. Nationalism, especially non-Western nationalism, is popularly understood as an essentially "natural" response by oppressed peoples to their oppression by an external force, for example colonial settlers. The corollary is nationalism understood as a distinct political force, disconnected from any particular social group or specific material conditions.

The "nationalist project" in sub-Saharan Africa has been historically tied to the role played by what we term the "student-intelligentsia." Often described as a petit bourgeoisie, at independence this class was without its own capital and sought national liberation and state power as a way of securing control of such capital. They presented themselves as above class antagonism, portrayed colonialism as the sole initiator of class divisions inherently foreign to African society, and developed political ideas—African socialism and African unity—that sought to justify the goal of a liberated nation, free of class division. Their project, however, was driven by their own interests, and they succeeded in constraining wider demands for political and economic transformation. In the period after independence the intelligentsia continued to play a leading role, often in the context of the political weaknesses of other social groups. A more detailed exploration of the postcolonial period is provided in chapter 3.

Social movements and NGOism

In the last twenty years, the capacity of the postcolonial state to ensure the interests of this elite and to manage the demands of the wider populace has been seriously weakened by the impact of economic liberalization. In this context, a plethora of civil society organizations (CSOs) and non-governmental organizations (NGOs), have emerged to fill the gaps created by the negative impact of structural adjustment and neoliberalism on state-provided social services, often using the language of "empowerment" and "community participation." The general result has been the massive distortion of social resistance by the introduction of "donor syndrome," the distribution of donor money to activist groups and NGOs.

This phenomenon is linked to the political disillusionment of the left in the 1980s and 1990s. The collapse of the Eastern Bloc led many radically minded civil society activists to retreat from the notion of a confrontation with global capitalism, and to turn instead to single-issue campaigns and substitute the voluntarist provision of welfare services for demands on the state. This explains the proclivity of single-issue campaigns among NGO activists, who saw new possibilities of "empowering" communities through donor funds. In this context, NGO approaches and donor funding ingratiated themselves into some of the social movements and campaigns that we describe in the book. As John Bomba, a Zimbabwean activist, commented, NGO funds can "disarm the movement that was emerging from the ground and shift people's focus from the real battles to some very fantastical arenas."[16]

Indeed, one of the underlying tensions within the social movements analyzed in this book is that between an activist orientation and a tendency towards NGO-ization and a focus on the provision of welfare-oriented services that might otherwise be provided by the state. We do not, however, dismiss any organization engaged in service provision as an NGO that can easily be counterposed to more activist-oriented social movements. Rather, social movements exist on a spectrum of orientations; any single movement may contain diverse (and even contradictory) elements of bureaucratization and activism. This issue is explored in more detail in chapter 2.

The structure of this book

While this is a study of social movements, it is based on the authors' understanding that no history is complete if its focus is solely on the movements from below. As subsequent chapters will show, the relationship between popular politics, organizations, and leadership is extremely complex, involving a dialectical connection that draws forces together in particular times and places. Central to this analysis, therefore, is the relationship between classes and movements, and the tensions between leadership and organizations that shape social change. This requires both the assertion of the agency of the poor and the detailed empirical investigation of the politics of both "below" and "above." Yet this interaction does not take place in a vacuum that can be freshly made by each generation. Agency is constrained (and facilitated) by structures that are inherited or born into. Karl Marx's well-known but still relevant axiom suggests that humans make "their own history, but do not make it just as they please, they do not make it under circumstances chosen by themselves, but under circumstances directly encountered, given and transmitted from the past."[17] These unchosen circumstances are not simply the existing institutions, government systems, and the judiciary, but also the experiences of previous struggles and movement and the successes, defeats, and memories of political action transmitted from the past.

These concerns, which form the backbone of our study, demand a direct connection with real events. These theoretical issues describe a relationship between movements, levels of political action, and leadership that operate within directly encountered circumstances. Any relationship can only be examined in its movement and development, as it evolves through the course of events. In Thompson's words, "like any other relationship, it is a fluency which evades analysis if we attempt to stop it dead at any given moment and anatomize its structure . . . the relationship must always be embodied in real people and in a real context."[18] In this context, we seek to elaborate the particular way in which we understand the social movement concept and how we apply it to complex African realities in chapter 2.

Chapter 3 sets out the historical background to more recent struggles. In our view, it is necessary to examine the history of protest and resistance over the last six decades—as manifested in strikes, marches, demonstrations, and riots—if we are to understand and be able to explain the process of struggle and popular politics in Africa, both to celebrate its successes and to understand its failures and limitations. While the primary focus of the book is the most recent period of protest and political action since the democratic revolutions of the early 1990s, our story properly starts in 1945. As already indicated, the awakening of national consciousness in the third quarter of the twentieth century was not a singular event, but one which enabled—despite the ultimate success of nationalist leadership and the consequent limits placed on social reforms—the economic and social grievances of ordinary Africans to be articulated. The promise of "independence" was not simply one in which European rulers were replaced with indigenous ones. For most involved, it implicitly or explicitly necessitated a radical reorganization of the political and economic order in ways that would improve the political rights and living standards of the mass of ordinary Africans. The process of decolonization involved a dialectical interaction of forces in which the nationalist leadership often promoted struggle by the colonial poor while also seeking to direct and constrain them. Despite these efforts, however, the overthrow of colonialism continued to carry expectations of transformative change for the wider populace. Asse Lilombo, a Congolese activist, depicts what decolonization in 1960 meant to him: "It was not only a party of independence; it was a party of liberation."[19]

When such transformation did not occur in the years after formal independence, social movements engaged in activities designed to ensure that their dreams of a more just and equal society were realized. Although independent labor and civil organizations were repressed and incorporated during the rise of one-party states and military regimes, grassroots activists continued to challenge the betrayal of their dreams of independence, albeit in deeply problematic circumstances.

Most African countries emerged from colonialism with their economies dependent on the export of one or two primary products.

Independent African countries could grow, and even promote certain reforms, as long as there was a steady market and price for their commodities. The postwar boom, which established a seemingly permanent international consensus in support of state-led models of development, began to break up in the late 1960s. By the mid-1970s, commodity prices were collapsing and pulling into the vortex those newly independent states that had a precarious dependence on cotton, groundnuts, copper, or a number of other primary products. The crisis of postwar Keynesian capitalism, the rise in oil prices, the collapse in commodity prices, and the debt crisis that followed destroyed the state-led developmental project implemented by postcolonial African regimes. By the late 1970s, the global economic downturn had radically altered the terrain of grassroots contestation. Increasing international competition compelled many African rulers to enforce budgetary restraints, call for austerity, and eventually abolish what were now deplored as "restrictive" protectionist practices.

The economic status of most Africans worsened significantly, but the attempts of the International Monetary Fund (IMF) and World Bank to make Africans pay the price for a crisis that was not of their making led to a new wave of resistance, taking the concrete form of "food riots" that were in fact just the tip of an iceberg of social and economic discontent. These protests have been described as the "first wave" of resistance to structural adjustment: expressing early and unorganized (to a certain extent) fury at the devastating cuts and attacks to state provisions.[20] When some apparently hegemonic African states proved vulnerable to such pressures, delaying and even reversing the economic reforms demanded by the international financial institutions (IFIs), popular resistance was emboldened and began to take a more proactive form in the 1980s. Economic discontent combined with political demands, finding expression in labor organizations, churches, and less organizationally specific expressions of protest. In the late 1980s and early 1990s a second wave of protests was born. Inspired in part by the political changes in Eastern Europe, Africa experienced a new political revolution. This wave was more explicitly and organizationally political. One-party states were swept away by popular movements often led by trade unions and national conferences, so that by the mid-1990s, most of the continent had returned to democratic forms of government. However, just as in the movement for independence thirty years earlier, the unity of the pro-democracy movements masked profound differences over the future orientation of the new political system. In the context of the collapse of the Eastern Bloc, models which linked political liberalization to economic liberalization were hegemonic—and the ongoing debt crisis left African governments with little choice but to implement more radical versions of the economic liberalization programs that had helped generate the movements that led to the removal of their predecessors.

As already mentioned, the main focus of this book is the subsequent period of nearly two decades, up to the present day. Chapter 4 is devoted to the particular experience of social movements in South Africa. While the literature on South Africa is well developed, it is striking, in comparison, how little primary research has been carried out on the activities and perspectives of social movements in the rest of the continent. This study aims to help fill that gap. Chapter 5 examines the experience of social movements in countries that achieved at least a limited form of democracy by the 1990s, and chapter 6 looks at others that have experienced a relapse into dictatorship or, with the repression of pro-democracy movements, remain highly undemocratic systems. In these three chapters, we explore in detail the experiences of social movements and civil society organizations as they have sought to achieve goals of greater social and economic justice and more effective forms of political accountability and democracy. Each chapter is based on a detailed analysis of the situation of the countries under study, drawing on relevant literature and, in chapters 5 and 6, interviews with dozens of civil society organizers and social movement activists. Key themes in these chapters are relations between social movements and African states; the ways in which social movements have been able to resist the implementation of economic liberalization programs; the extent to which such civil society organizations are themselves representative of the masses they claim to speak for; and to what extent they are themselves subject to the influence of Western donor agencies and NGOs that have at times provided a significant part of their funding.

Chapter 7 explores the anticapitalist movement that hit the headlines after the November demonstrations at the Seattle World Trade Organization meeting in November 1999. This was, until the revolutions in North Africa (the "Arab Spring" that began in January 2011), the most important development in international "politics from below" in the last fifteen years. This movement of movements began to challenge the gross inequities of the neoliberal Western-dominated capitalism that has been largely hegemonic since the end of the Cold War. It also presented profound challenges to older left and radical analyses of the nature of capitalism, of how progressive change is to be achieved, and, in particular, the structures necessary to do so. In this context it was a courageous attempt to generate political alternatives, even if these efforts have not been successful. Still, a generation of activists have been inspired and educated politically through involvement in the anticapitalist movement. In its organizational form—the Social Forums held since 2001 on a global, national, and local basis—the anticapitalist movement has both challenged the inequities of the present world system and articulated a compelling vision that "another world is possible."

African social movements have been active participants in this global anticapitalist movement. Its analysis of modern global capitalism's capacity to undermine state sovereignty and commodify the "commons" resonates with Africans' firsthand experience of imposed economic liberalization and choiceless democracies, as well as the continent's long history of globalization in the forms of the Atlantic slave trade and forced integration into the empires of

European powers. Many African activists have found in the anti-capitalist movement not only established networks of campaigns, advocates, and comrades, but also an international framework that enables them to break from a purely national or local analysis. However, this chapter also suggests limits to the relevance of the anticapitalist movement to the African context. It details the experiences of Social Forums held in Africa and attended by the authors, focusing in particular on the World Social Forum held in Nairobi, Kenya, in January 2007. Drawing on personal experience as well as interviews with participants, the authors argue that the inequalities and contradictions inherent in the global anticapitalist movement find their clearest expression in the African context, where its inability to fully incorporate African experiences and analyses arises directly from the very structures of this apparently structureless movement.

The January 2011 revolutionary upsurge has, among many things, posed much more urgently some of the practical questions with which activists had begun to grapple in the Social Forum milieu; the "who are we, who are they, what can we do about it" questions that go to the heart of any of the discussions about strategy and tactics that swirl inside social movements. The answers cannot be prefigured in advance or through abstract contemplation but can be found only in the cut and thrust of movements in motion. Yet we believe that the movements and issues discussed here offer lessons from the sharp jostle of experience.

The book concludes in chapter 8 with a comparative analysis of the role of social movements in Africa, both historically and in the contemporary period. It identifies important lessons drawn from the findings of the study and suggests ways in which social movement approaches may strengthen the activities of civil society and non-governmental organizations on the continent as well as internationally. The revolutionary process that is still developing in North Africa and igniting movements in parts of the Middle East is testament to the continued vibrancy of social movements across the continent. Indeed, one of the primary reasons for writing this book was to insist that we cast our gaze on the continuing organic development of these movements that demand our attention, solidarity, and celebration. This book seeks to develop and deepen the search for political alternatives for those who want to see a world not dominated by neoliberalism, austerity, and underdevelopment.

CHAPTER 2

SOCIAL MOVEMENTS
AND THE WORKING CLASS IN AFRICA

This chapter seeks to establish the analytical framework that will be utilized in the more empirical chapters that follow. Drawing on some of the most important analyses of social movements within and outside the continent, it explores how a social movement approach can shed new light on the nature of popular struggles and resistance to state power, social and economic injustice, and exploitation in Africa. It critiques the ways in which popular movements have been understood—and misunderstood—by analysts of postcolonial African politics and society. Finally, it seeks to locate the role of social movements in broader movements for political change in Africa, and more widely, against the worst manifestations of neoliberal capitalism and for a deeper democracy and greater social justice—ultimately raising, in the words of the anticapitalist movement, the possibility of another world.

Conceptualizing social movements

The idea of understanding societal and political change through the prism of social movements is not a new one, but it has been applied more commonly to Western society than to Africa, and is generally linked to the development of modern nation-states.

What do we understand by "social movements"? In much of the scholarship, social movements are perceived as a series of largely unconnected and distinct campaigns, civil society organizations (CSOs), and pressure groups.[1] In contrast, we see social movements as both a unified and differentiated totality. While there are distinct "movements" and different and competing layers within social movements, these continually interact, connect, and conflict. Social movements may start out with distinct and limited goals but be drawn into broader struggles that change societies. We see working-class politics as an important component in social movements both internationally and in Africa. In this chapter, and the book more generally, we explore the historical and contemporary development of a politics that derives from the working class and the wider African urban and rural poor. At the same time, we understand and explore the serious constraints on the development of such a politics within social movements, specifically an unpromising political and economic structural context. Our "social movements" approach stresses the agency of the popular classes' subalterns in shaping their own future, while not in any sense neglecting or playing down the powerful structural factors which militate against their capacity to do so.

In the early nineteenth century, a qualitatively new form of protest movement developed in Europe. Charles Tilly demonstrates how, with urbanization, industrialization, mass literacy, the extension of the franchise, and the development of states ostensibly committed for the first time to the improvement of their peoples, new social movements mobilized in relation to both that commitment and to grievances that arose from the rapid processes of social change that were taking place. Through a range of tactics focused on displaying their numbers, such as demonstrations, petitioning, and protests, these new social movements, which claimed to speak for some or all of the people, asserted themselves towards the new states. These were not generally movements that aimed to overthrow or replace the new states or their rulers, but rather to influence their policies or practices. Although social movements did sometimes find themselves in conflictual or confrontational relationships with rulers, modern political systems were supposedly characterized by their capacity to incorporate dissenting movements and enable them to influence policy. Social movements should, according to Tilly, therefore be understood as part of the panoply of the modern state, with its burgeoning democratic spaces and opportunities.[2]

Karl Marx and Friedrich Engels provided a broader concept of social movements. They used the concept to describe revolutions, trade unionism, the struggle for suffrage, resistance to imperial occupation, and the emergence of alternative and utopian projects and ideas. These processes of revolt and protest could be conceptualized as a single totality that included the working classes, but also "plebs," the "poor," and others engaged in the "social question"— that is, the struggles and lived experiences of the exploited and the oppressed in their entirety. "Social movement" thus described an entire space of political and social contestation involving trade unionism, labor politics, national independence, and "localized" forms of oppression. Marx and Engels privileged the politics of the working class as holding the potential to solve the social question by challenging capitalist exploitation, but they saw class struggle as only one element of a differentiated social movement.[3]

Marx and Engels were in this respect consistent in their support of any group that fought oppression, including in what they regarded as feudal or "backward" societies. Both wrote extensively on the revolt of indigenous communities against imperial and national oppression. Their support for struggles in India is typical. During the Indian Revolt of 1857, Marx praised the "great revolt" and Engels wrote at length on the military tactics that the insurgents might use to defeat the British.[4] This resistance to colonialism was "celebrated in the same lyrical cadences as they would deploy in celebrating the Parisian communards."[5] The struggle in India and the emancipation of the English working class, for example, were therefore both part of the "social movement in general."

It should already be clear from analyses of such movements that the social forces that existed within them, the ideas and activities they generated, and the outcomes they brought about varied enormously. This clearly demonstrated that social movements were and are inherently heterogeneous and contradictory, tending to incorporate a number of movements or elements as part of a differentiated totality. Similarly, social movements contain differentiated potentials. A number of theorists have argued that because such movements are inherently contradictory, they are unable to develop an ideology that would unite their varying strands. Colin Barker argues that groups within social movements are misguided if they seek to substitute their understandings for those of the entire movement. Rather, Barker reminds us, social movements are a muddle of competing and shifting layers and tendencies, working occasionally in harmony, often in striking opposition.[6]

Jeff Goodwin's comparative analysis of revolutionary movements complements these arguments. He states that social movements are not the actions of classes, but coalitions, and that it is these coalitions that drive change and comprise new systems of government. Radical change in society is, Goodwin suggests, commonly achieved by coalitions of social interests rather than distinct classes. Any such coalition, however, involves cooperation and compromise between different interest groups, depending on the structural context in which they arise. The question of which interests come to dominate any such movement and which see their interests as subordinated is central to understanding the degree or type of social change they achieve. Goodwin argues that the success of any movement will be, in part, dependent on political ideas and that it "simply may not possess the sufficient leverage or 'hegemony' . . . that is necessary to take advantage of (or create its own) political opportunities."[7] This is particularly germane to the study of social movements in Africa: for example, when analyzing the influence of the popular classes in broader nationalist or pro-democracy coalitions (see chapter 3).

There is, then, a permanent contest between ideas and arguments within social movements. The outcome of such contests depends on both the actual and potential actions of the political and social forces in a particular social movement. The social movement is therefore the field in which struggle takes place and political hegemony is constantly contested. Implicit in the study of social movements are two questions: What is the potential for different, more radical projects to emerge? Could their outcome have been different from that which occurred? Unless analysts ask these questions, we can grasp little sense of the evolution of social movements or the import of their actual achievements. It also necessitates an open approach to the study of social movements that adopts a broad perspective as to what is and is not a "social movement," rather than a strict definition that seeks to identify in advance what is and is not an authentic movement "of the people."

Clearly, such a conceptualization rejects a narrow definition of social movements based on a functionalist model of pressure group politics, which enable the state to make limited policy reforms in response to specific demands by legitimate political actors. "Social movements" is a broader and less normative concept than liberal concepts of "civil society" or the more institutional notion of "interest groups," both of which assume (tacitly or overtly) the desirability of containing conflict within existing political frameworks. Scholarship that limits social movement analysis to particular campaigns for (for example) civil rights, democratization, or peace needlessly limits its own capacity to understand both the broader context and the underlying nature of typically disparate and contradictory social movements. For example, while the civil rights movement in the United States originated largely as a respectable, non-violent movement located primarily in southern Black churches, it developed through student politics and organizations via the anti–Vietnam War movement, eventually incorporating a significant rise in trade union militancy in the late 1960s and 1970s.[8] Central to these developments was a constant debate within the civil rights movement around a range of general and specific questions and issues. Such debates and movement trajectories need to be understood in their totality so as to analyze particular outcomes and whether they might have turned out differently.

Social movements, it should be understood, can manifest themselves in overt institutional and organizational forms—but they commonly take more amorphous and temporary forms, for example protest movements which coalesce briefly around a particular issue or initiative before dissolving into wider society. They may, of course, involve both such tendencies. Studying such movements therefore requires an understanding of social movements as relationships. As E. P. Thompson reminds us: "Like any other relationship it is a fluency which evades analysis if we attempt to stop it dead at any given moment and anatomise its structure. . . . The relationship must always be embodied in real people and in a real context."[9] The conclusion is clear: if we are conscious of the contested, disparate, and contradictory nature of the "social movement in general," it becomes possible to identify the potential for more radical liberatory tendencies implicit (and sometimes explicit) in the social movements we analyze and study. We do not argue that all social movements evolve towards revolutionary transformation, but that only by understanding social movements as a differentiated and contested totality can we see the conflicts and potentials within them that can lead to revolutionary change.

Social movements are inevitably authors of their own construction, within pre-existing limitations. Intention and agency are not, however, simply at the mercy of determining "structural" forces. The core of social movement action is more complex and nuanced. As Barker has observed, certain revolutionary situations are concluded with the reassertion of existing power, others end in a stalemate, and some may actually become revolutions. Nevertheless, whatever the conclusion—retreat, stalemate, or revolution—it will have come about through conscious and organized effort.[10]

An important area of investigation is therefore the circumstances in which the aims and achievements of particular social movements are restricted to partial reforms by existing states, and where these develop into more radical transformative demands. In what circumstances do such movements evolve beyond the reformist aims of elites and develop the capacity for radical change? An essential, but by no means determining, factor in the capacity of social movements to envisage and develop emancipatory alternatives is the agency and intention of the classes operating inside these movements. How do particular social forces achieve political hegemony within the social movement? In the case of sub-Saharan Africa, we argue that the failure to develop and assert effective political alternatives to dominant nationalist and neoliberal ideas has helped to determine the shape, form, politics, and outcomes of the social movements studied in this book. Various circumstances have constrained the ability of these movements to realize radical or deeper change, but among them is the nature of the ideological tools available to and wielded by classes within social movements.

Movements may contain many contradictory intentions, but in certain situations, the common class membership of (at least some of) the movement's participants confers a unifying material interest that leads them to organize together, provide united intent, and lead the broader movement to articulate an emancipatory alternative. What it is about *classes,* and not other groupings, that allows them to play this kind of role in a broader movement? It is not simply a matter of shared material interests, but rather that some classes, by virtue of their position in the production process, can lead a fight that can potentially reorganize the social relations of production (the ways in which a society organizes to meet its needs), thereby laying the basis to reconstitute society's whole structure—including non-class relations such as family, caste, sectarian, or communal relations. These classes thus have the capacity, rooted in production relations, to attract allies for a broad struggle over all the conditions of subordination that make up the broad social question. However, a class can fail to live up to its potential in this regard, because the social and political context may prevent it from discovering what role(s) it can play. In that sense, the *actual* role that a class plays in a given movement is not structurally *determined*.

Therefore, we wish in particular to reject any attempt to identify social movements which are (and are not) authentically representative of "the people" or of a particular class: such a tendency is redolent of older structurally determined positions which prescribed to the working class or the "peasantry" a role in a preconceived revolutionary movement. Equally, we reject any attempts, fashionable though they are in social movement scholarship, to limit the potentialities of social movements to specific reforms and campaigns. It is evident that there is no such thing as a pre-formed radical social movement that is authentically "of the people." In practice, such movements exist along a spectrum that reflects their origins, sources of funding, links to particular nation-states, ideological bases, and divergent social forces. While they may reflect or articulate in some way the aspirations of some of the poor and help structure and shape the *potential* of social movements, their capacity to do this should be assessed through empirical research—as we seek to do in this volume.

Transformative moments in African history

Although social movement authors such as Goodwin do not write directly about Africa, their concerns and assertions have direct relevance to the continent. Goodwin, like most other observers, sees revolutionary struggles on the wane. Today the battles are more modest ones for democratization. Accordingly, social movements remain an active feature of the modern world, but their role is limited to Tilly's notions of pressure group influence within an otherwise relatively stable liberal democracy. Whether this is true or untrue in the Western world, the evidence presented in chapters 4, 5, and 6 demonstrates the continuing instability of liberal democracies in Africa and, in particular, that efforts by elites (both indigenous and Western) to achieve their vision of liberal democracy have often involved authoritarian initiatives that have themselves generated opposition from below. Such opposition is by no means limited to demands for particular policy reforms, but challenges the very assumptions on which those societies have been based.

It is evidently true, of course, that not every protest (in Africa or elsewhere) is a social movement, and not every social movement is a revolution-in-waiting. A useful way of interpreting the periods of social movement radicalization and direct action examined in chapter 3 is as "protest cycles," which can be regarded as successive periods of intensified (and less intense) struggle. Sidney Tarrow sees protest cycles as periods of intensified conflict across society, operating as "crucibles" in which a "repertoire" of collective action can expand.[11] Protest cycles pull in new layers of society which have not been active before, or reenergize those battered by earlier experiences of defeat. New organizations emerge, or older ones are regenerated by activists and new members. It is within the cycle of protest that new forms of organizing society emerge, and fresh organizations, movements, and parties develop. The central experience of these protest cycles is the transformation in people's ideas of what is possible. Old authorities are questioned, new forms of decision-making emerge, and fresh layers of younger activists are drawn into a widening repertoire of mass action.[12] New movements then interact with established political forces (parties, for example, or more formally constituted civil society organizations) and, as noted above, often form coalitions of interests to bring about change of a greater or lesser extent. Understanding these cycles—and how they have unfolded in practice in recent sub-Saharan African history—requires understanding that such coalitions, in which the participation of classes is an element, contain within themselves an ongoing battle for political hegemony between competing social forces, the outcome of which is never certain and which depends on (among other factors): the extent of mass involvement in their activities and organizations; the openness of their internal debates; and the permanent contest for hegemony between different forces. Social movements have the potential in such circumstances to construct, from their struggles, new institutions and democratic practices that can become the basis for alternative forms of power. Their capacity to do this, however, depends on the extent to which popular and working-class forces are able to challenge elites, who will generally seek a more limited level of social transformation.

In Africa, the leadership of the struggles for independence and post-independence political movements has of course not generally rested in the hands of the working class or popular forces. Other groups assumed control, leading, frustrating, and in some cases subverting the potential militancy of these movements. This reality illustrated a twin problem. One was the inherent limitation of nationalist politics that sought freedom from colonial tyranny, but that limited political change to the establishment of nation-states inherently constrained by the preexisting domination of the globe by powerful Western states and the forces of the global economy they largely controlled. The second problem was the weaknesses of the African working class, its organizations, leadership, and (more recently) its damaging reconfiguration on the anvil of economic liberalization.

This book identifies three major cycles of protest in recent African history, when social movements played a vital role in challenging injustice and exploitation and raised the possibility of radical social change. The first was the movement for political independence in post–World War II Africa, which led to the establishment of new nation-states across most of the continent by the 1960s. The second was triggered by the first wave of structural adjustment programs imposed by the IMF and World Bank but often implemented "voluntarily" by African governments from the late 1970s onwards. By the late 1980s, this wave developed into a third protest cycle across the continent that was more explicitly oppositional, pulling in new and old social forces alike. The third wave, which extended into the late 1990s, broadened economic grievances into political ones and can be credited with the most thorough political transformation of the continent since the 1960s independence movements. The first and third wave of protests contained within them the potential for revolutionary change, involving a process in which mass movements overthrow an old power (rather than seizing existing state machinery) and implement democratic institutions that have the potential to become the foundations of a new society.[13] We explore the dynamics of each of these cycles of protest in much greater detail in chapter 3.

The cage of independence: Nationalism and social movements

The popular struggle for African independence, often understood as unified movements to establish self-rule of nation-states, consisted in fact of diverse social forces that achieved temporary unity under the banner of nationalism, but that also had particular social and economic aims their supporters believed could be realized through the achievement of an independent nation-state. African elites had long appealed for colonial reforms that would deliver improvements for the tiny minority of "educated" or "civilized" Africans, with little success. Only with the emergence of mass African movements in the post–World War II period was the capacity of colonial authorities to govern their territories effectively undermined to the point that the process of substantial reform, ultimately leading to self-rule, could begin. The popular expression of economic and social grievances, particularly in the forms of strike action and rural unrest, was crucial in accelerating the process of decolonization in virtually every African colony.

This was widely recognized during the nationalist period itself. Thomas Hodgkin, in his famous book of 1956, made the point that the very term "African nationalism" "tends to conceal the 'mixed-up' character of African political movements. . . . Most of these various types of organisation possessed links, formal or informal, with one another. Many of them were not concerned, overtly or primarily, with achieving national independence or stimulating a sense of . . . nationhood."[14] However, there has ever since been a tendency to see such movements as essentially "parochial" in relation to the wider aim of the nation-state. This, as Frederick Cooper has argued, distracted attention from the full extent and significance of these popular mobilizations, which were primarily anti-colonial, rather than essentially nationalist in character:

> It is tempting to read the history of the period from 1945 to 1960 as the inevitable triumph of nationalism and to see each social movement taking place within a colony—be it by peasants, women, by workers, or by religious groups—as another piece to be integrated into the coming together of a nation. What is lost in such a reading are the ways in which different groups within colonies mobilized for concrete ends. . . . Whether such efforts fed into the attempts of nationalist parties to build anti-colonial coalitions needs to be investigated, not assumed.[15]

What is most important to stress here, however, is that this period of mass nationalism depended on the belief among large sections of the African population that achieving independence would lead in short order to the improvement of their material conditions and measures to address their grievances. Nationalist politicians made promises to their supporters that implied a transformative post-independence project. In the Congo, for example, Asse Lilombo remembers independence as "a big feast, a party of liberation. We had been liberated from slavery. The women were dressed up. There was goat and beer. The party lasted days. . . . We would be responsible for ourselves. We would manage our country ourselves."[16] Notwithstanding the extent to which these promises were dismissed by outside observers as "unrealistic," they crucially informed the positions adopted by social movements in the run-up to and in the aftermath of the transition to self-rule. Postcolonial labor and independent social movements needed to be suppressed and incorporated precisely because they articulated relatively transformational understandings of independence—and therefore posed a threat to the unity of nationalist parties after they took control of their respective states.

The role of ideology

The ideology of nationalism was the domain of the intelligentsia and the middle-class leaders of these movements. These were in many cases the product of colonial metropolitan universities, colleges, and scholarships. They tended therefore to adopt an approach to governance that was not dissimilar to their colonial predecessors during the mid-twentieth century. State power, historically centralized in the position of the colonial governor, was now transferred to the president and his ruling party. The assumption of a national, technically conceived developmental project resulted in the denial of political autonomy for either opposition parties or social movements and created a continued reliance on foreign advisors. Constructing a nation and determining its identity and priorities ceased to be the task of a broad movement and became dominated by the nationalist party and, more particularly, its leader. These parties, particularly after the advent of one-party states, not only suppressed dissent but also retreated in most cases from their engagement with the wider population, particularly in rural areas. Simultaneously, Africa's postcolonial rulers tacitly accepted the subordinate position of their countries in the international economic and political system and thereby effectively ruled out support for any project that would seek to alter the global system of Western-driven capitalism that had rendered the continent poor and undeveloped in the first place.

For many new African leaders, the most relevant model of national development was the Soviet Union, a country that had transformed itself in a few decades from a backwater of underdevelopment into an industrial superpower of global importance. Kwame Nkrumah stated: "In a little over thirty years [it] has built up an industrial machine so strong and advanced as to be able to launch the Sputnik. . . . I pose it as an example for Africa."[17] The

Stalinist model of state-capitalist development reigned supreme in the minds of this new ruling class: all that was necessary was to lay one's hands on the levers of state power. The developmental model promoted by the Comintern that was so influential across the "Third World" was also rooted in a two-stage transition to socialism, effectively postponing any political formulation that would directly address class contradictions within African societies.[18]

Other leaders adopted versions of "African socialism" supposedly rooted in the "unity" of pre-colonial African society, something which served to deny the expression of diverse or localized demands. In either case, national independence and development was the primary task; all questions of social transformation had to be postponed. In reality, this not only hampered social movements' capacity to address their immediate concerns, it also placed in the hands of their new rulers the right to determine the pace and direction with which such social questions were addressed. In such a national context, the rights or aspirations of any particular section of society could thereby be dismissed as "sectional" or "parochial."

While labor movements in a number of countries were able to resist their total incorporation into the nationalist project, their biggest problem was their inability to generate intellectual or ideological alternatives to the developmentalist-Stalinist framework that dominated nationalist thinking. In this context, trade unions sometimes adopted syndicalist or economistic approaches, rejecting nationalist or new state ideologies by arguing that their role was "non-political." This unfortunately dovetailed with the (in our view, incorrect) accusation that organized workers represented, in an African context, a "labor aristocracy" whose selfish defense of its privileges came at the expense of other, particularly rural, sections of society.[19] The curtailment of multi-party democracy during the first decade of independence as the logical extension of unified nationalism in the postcolonial context also prevented the emergence of new political parties that might represent particular social classes or forces. More generally, however, African social movements tended not to develop their own independent intellectual explanations of their own subordination.

Helpful insight into the postcolonial reality was, however, provided by Frantz Fanon. Writing in the period when the first wave of newly independent states were asserting themselves, Fanon, himself a leading figure in the Algerian revolutionary movement, was among the first to see the dangers of a "nationalist consciousness."[20] He identified how the national bourgeoisie—the nationalist elites and intelligentsia—evolved after independence into the very exploiting class that it had supplanted: it became "a sort of little caste, avid and voracious . . . only too glad to accept the dividends that the former colonial power hands out to it."[21] Fanon's *The Wretched of the Earth* grasped the predicament that independence presented to the movements and leadership of national liberation. Postcolonial power was caught between an enfeebled national bourgeoisie and the global limitations imposed on any newly developing nation in the modern world. In this context, it was inevitable that these new national bourgeoisies would act to suppress those in their own societies whose demands could not be met within the existing economic and political system. Fanon, like many thinkers of his time, was influenced by Maoist interpretations of socialism and by the successful revolution in Cuba, which emphasized the central role of the peasantry in revolutionary struggle. Fanon accepted the widespread argument that the organized African working class had been effectively "bought off" with the profits of imperialist exploitation, and that revolutionary action against the new African ruling classes would only come from the poorest African rural masses.

Further insight into the failures of independence came from national liberation leaders whose fight for self-rule was frustrated by settler colonialism. As they observed the realities of actually existing independence in other African countries, some analyzed the pitfalls of nationalism and developed political positions that sought to repeat their mistakes. Amílcar Cabral, who led the Partido Africano da

Independência da Guiné e Cabo Verde against Portuguese colonial rule, initially focused his political activity on Guinea's urbanized coastal areas. This changed in 1959, however, when a group of strikers were shot at the Pijiguiti docks in the port of Bissau. Like Fanon, Cabral's orientation then shifted to the countryside and agitation amongst the peasantry. During the struggle for independence, he sought to establish "organs of popular power," local organizations providing health and education services that would demonstrate the link between the seizure of political power and material improvements in the lives of ordinary Africans.[22]

Like Fanon, Cabral was dismissive of "African socialism" and its characterization of a static and classless Africa, believing that cultural change occurred in the process of revolutionary struggle. He argued for the preeminence of class over ethnicity; although his party organized primarily among the peasantry, Cabral believed this movement would eventually combine with the country's small urban working class. Cabral also thought the revolution would require what he termed an "ideal proletariat," which he saw as constituted of the radical elements of the petit bourgeoisie. They would help create unity between the oppressed classes and combat ethnic divisions. Out of the specificity of the anti-imperialist struggle, Cabral developed a critical analysis of a new African culture, fulfilling the "historical personality of the people."[23] This was what Cabral meant by his much-misinterpreted slogan "return to the source"—not a return to tradition, but a critical engagement with African history.

Cabral did not therefore regard nationhood as equivalent to liberation: "We accept the principle that the liberation struggle is a revolution and that it does not finish at the moment when the national flag is raised and the national anthem played."[24] Yet his criticisms of independent African states conceal a more general tension in the politics of nationalist Third Worldism (the idea that the central division in the world was between developed countries and the "Third World," or developing, bloc). The question "What is to be done with the state after independence?"—the fundamental question for Cabral and the key to Fanon's "curse of independence"—was acknowledged but never satisfactorily answered by those who identified the limitations of the "flag independence" of the 1950s and 1960s. As Cabral wrote before he was murdered by the Portuguese in 1973, the year before Cape Verde and Guinea-Bissau finally achieved independence: "The problem of the nature of the state created after independence is perhaps the *secret* of the failure of African independence."[25]

How does this relate to the social movements described in this book? Fanon's critique and the practice advocated by Cabral were important attempts to grapple with the realities of the postcolonial world and the challenge of constructing emancipatory alternatives that could challenge the failures of independence. The social movements celebrated in this book do not display Patrick Chabal's "illusions of civil society," but are in fact real movements that demonstrate the vibrancy of a politics from below.[26] However, they certainly do illustrate the tensions and contradictions inherent in social movements. Nevertheless, the traditions of radical political alternatives on the continent are important to study, because they raised and sought to address questions that are still of fundamental importance to African social movement activists today.

Global downturn, globalization, and resistance

By the time Cabral issued his warning about the nature of the African state, the assumptions underlying state-led developmental nationalism were being undermined by the onset of the global recession of the mid-1970s. The recession, which affected the world unevenly, was most severe in the recently independent countries of the Third World. The sudden rise in the price of oil hit most African economies hard, as did the collapse of international commodity prices. Most of sub-Saharan Africa was, as a legacy of colonialism, economically dependent on the export of raw materials, cash crops, and the production of single minerals. The price of such goods was determined by Western institutions such as the London Metal Exchange, and the collapse in the value of commodities devastated the earning power of many African states. For example, the collapse in the price of copper halved the Gross Domestic Product (GDP) of Zambia in the space of a few years. This decisively exposed national developmentalism as largely dependent on international factors beyond the control of supposedly sovereign African states. Many governments dealt with this problem by short-term borrowing, creating the long-term debt burden that, notwithstanding the real achievements of the Jubilee movement, is still with us today.

The period saw a major shift to what we describe today as neoliberalism. For governments and policy makers, neoliberalism was an important ideological challenge to the supremacy of the state in decision-making. Many now argued that "the time had come for the state to play a less important role in shaping the economy, that the private sector should play a very much larger part in economic policy-making, and that the market should be left to operate as freely as possible."[27] The move toward neoliberalism affected every corner of the continent. Even in South Africa, the continent's largest economy, P. W. Botha took over from John Vorster as leader of the ruling National Party in September 1978, promising to revitalize the free-market economy and transfer resources from the state to the private sector. He pushed through policies to reduce the colossal state spending that had grown by an average of 10 percent per year between 1973 and 1976.

From the late 1970s onwards, indebted African states were no longer in a position to borrow commercially and were forced on the mercies of the IMF, World Bank, and Western governments. Donors used increasingly severe conditions on loans to impose economic reforms on African governments. In particular, governments seeking to borrow money were forced to remove price controls on basic foodstuffs, a measure which disproportionately affected the growing urban population—the millions of poor Africans who had migrated to the cities in the decade after independence. As detailed in chapter 3, the removal of these controls prompted a series of revolts in the late 1970s and early 1980s against donor-imposed increases in basic food prices.

These protests brought the urban African poor onto the streets, often informally led by the working classes; street protests were often supplemented by strike action, sometimes organized by trade union leaders but more usually initiated by rank-and-file union members or shop stewards. These were not simply revolts of the "urban crowd"; in Zambia, for example, local union officials on the Copperbelt helped shape the direction of the uprisings in 1986, reflecting the verbal criticisms by national union leaders of the removal of subsidies. The protestors looted state-owned stores, but also targeted government and ruling party offices.[28] This wave of revolts, initially relatively disorganized, began to germinate ideas of more organized resistance towards incumbent regimes (leading, for example, to the overthrow of Sudanese President Nimeiri in 1985) and notions of social justice deployed against the regimes' complicity with IMF loan conditions.

Some analysts nevertheless referred to such actions as "desperate IMF riots" taking place in "wretched Third World cities," suggesting an absence of organization, politics, and democratic traditions.[29] Others unhelpfully contrasted "workers' struggles" with "populist forms of socio-political movement."[30] A few years later, others claimed that the distinct weaknesses of African civil society made it impossible for it to lead the type of movements that had transformed Eastern Europe in 1989. Chabal argued at the time that there was little "scope in contemporary Africa for the type of civil society that, as happened in Eastern Europe in the 1980s, could play a decisive role in the substantive transformation of the political system."[31] The tendency to label these events "IMF riots," "food riots," or illustrative of the "illusions of civil society" significantly understates the extent of social movement coordination and organization involved.

The organizers of such protests, through their actions, gained a clearer sense of the very limited sovereignty of their countries, which were peripheral to the global economy and dependent on international factors. This had real consequences for social movement strategies. Activists were increasingly aware that their actions and protests needed to be directed toward both national governments and the international bodies that significantly influenced government policies. African movements, it can be argued, thus experienced globalization and the need to respond to it at an earlier stage than their Western counterparts. From this time, trade unions, church groups, and women's organizations sought to strengthen their coordination with international counterparts, both in Africa and more widely. In the repressive context of one-party states and military regimes, there were significant restrictions on the practicality of such linkages. Nevertheless, the failure of the national development model had significant consequences: it led to the reversal of the limited social and economic gains of postcolonial states, increasing popular unrest against African governments, and it exposed the hollowness of the supposed hegemonic authority of those states, encouraging popular debate regarding the link between economic justice and political accountability. The internationalization of protest movements and the complex relationship between social movements, states, and international organizations is explored further in chapter 7.

Democracy and new social movements

The link between economic grievances of the type discussed above and the need for a return to democratic political systems grew increasingly urgent in the late 1980s. Whereas earlier economic protests had often avoided questioning the political legitimacy of African regimes, now the right of those regimes to govern came more strongly under question, as different social forces converged around the linked questions of economic and political rights.

Previously distinct groups struggling against sectionally specific cuts began to identify a commonality in the diverse protests. Student movements played a particular role in this regard. Previously privileged student bodies experienced drastic reductions in their living standards and the quality of their education as IMF-imposed public sector spending cuts threatened the very survival of higher education in many African countries. Student bodies, no longer an isolated elite, now linked their activism to wider social change.[32]

As chapter 3 details, between 1990 and 1994, popular protest movements and strikes brought down more than thirty African regimes, with multi-party elections held for the first time in a generation. This period saw the convergence of social movements, frequently drawn together by the organizing strength and militancy of organized labor. As one observer remarked shortly after this period, trade unions "sought not simply to protect the work-place interests of their members but have endeavoured to bring about a restructuring of the political system."[33] This was arguably the most important show of collective and organizational power in the history of the continent's social movements, in general, and of trade unions in particular.

There were nevertheless significant problems with the opposition movements that emerged and the processes of democratic transition they initiated. As David Harvey identifies, these movements were galvanized by resistance to structural adjustment or the neoliberal counterrevolution.[34] Despite this, the solutions put forward by trade union–led movements were general and amorphous, speaking ubiquitously of "change": for example, in French, changement politique; in Senegalese Wolof, sopi; and in Zimbabwean Shona, chinja. Such slogans helped pull together the disparate cords of opposition forces, but they did not express the widespread demand for economic and social redress that provided much of the popular impetus for "change."

As the movements converged and grew into powerful opposition forces, other changes of global significance were taking place.

The East European revolutions in 1989–90 brought a paradoxical wave of hope and despair. They showed that one-party states could be toppled by popular democratic movements from below, but also that "communism" no longer constituted a meaningful political alternative to global capitalism.[35] A generation of students, trade union militants, and intellectuals across the world and in Africa lost their ideological moorings.[36] Thus, the struggles fought on the continent against both repressive one-party regimes and the IMF and World Bank policies they had implemented failed to construct programmatic alternatives. The street demand for "change" could easily become a useful but vacuous basis for middle class–dominated opposition movements to gain or regain power amid the disarray or absence of radical alternatives. New governments were elected and, in the context of the enduring debt burden, usually followed the same policy prescriptions dictated by international agencies. We explore the impact of such policies, and social movement responses to them, in the remainder of this volume. It will suffice to state here that, amid the brief international hegemony of neoliberalism in the 1990s, social movements in general and trade unions in particular failed to articulate any ideological alternative to such policies. Their capacity to respond effectively to new waves of economic liberalization was hampered both by this and by the significant decline in trade union membership and formal-sector employment that was the result of the implementation of these policies.

This supposed "end of history" ended with the emergence of the international antiglobalization movement, its birth marked by the "Battle of Seattle" against the World Trade Organization (WTO) in November 1999.[37] This movement attempted to express an alternative global politics, often simply by stating that an "alternative" was possible. It had impressive advocates and a diversity of political ideas.[38] It developed unevenly in the global north, achieving its high points in regional mobilizations against international organizations and in bringing activists together at World Social

Forums. In Africa, however, "anticapitalism" was both more deeply rooted—in long-standing revolts against international agencies and national governments—and less developed, in the sense that there was *less* explicit emphasis on politics and a lack of political ideas that could be labeled anticapitalist. The antiglobalization movement nevertheless provided a great opportunity for African social movements: a new way of constructing alternatives to neoliberalism and a new form of international activism that, in stressing local agency and diversity, was a step forward from the restrictive Stalinism and state capitalism (presented as "African socialism") that most Africans had previously experienced. However, as chapter 7 will explore, this "movement of movements" contained its own contradictions, hierarchies, and inequalities, especially from an African perspective.

Modernism and postmodernism in African scholarship

There are many reasons why an alternative politics struggled to emerge even after Seattle and particularly in Africa. The capacity of social movements to develop independent analysis and a critique of the IFIs and national development models was crippled both by the retreat of the left internationally and by the intellectual predominance of postmodernism. If neoliberalism was the policy prescription of restructuring in the developing world, postmodernism was its philosophical bedfellow. While the shift away from more structural and deterministic approaches to the role of class in society practiced in the 1970s (for example, the "labor aristocracy" argument or the reification of the peasantry as the predetermined vanguard class) was a positive development, there evolved a tendency (which is still significant today) to focus instead on "multiple identities," claiming ethnic, youth, and religious identities as categories for analysis without seeking to situate them in a wider political economy.[39]

The effects of postmodernism and the consequent reduction in class-based analysis thoroughly permeated research on African social realities. Recent academic writing on Africa has stressed that political movements cannot fit into the "narrow" constraints of class, stressing in its place such multiple identities. This focus on "identity," "indeterminacy," "complexity," and "performance," in which the "discourse" or "symbolism" of social movements becomes the primary frame of analysis, leads inexorably to neglecting the content of those movements.[40] Much writing in this area, indeed, eschews any interest in or commitment to progressive political and social change.[41] There is, in the use of the term "postcolony" and the (in many ways sensible) rejection of earlier projects of "modernization" and "development," a widespread skepticism about any attempt to improve the lives of ordinary Africans through progressive politics.[42] As Graham Harrison summarizes, "attention is paid . . . to the ways in which social power is *constructed* rather than *structured*. Here, African states are seen as decentralised forms of authority which permeate local social relations, producing an almost subterranean power which is not invested in formal state institutions as much as constructed by local élites and chieftaincies."[43]

Jean-François Bayart is one of the most important representatives of these trends. His work rightly rejects analysis of Africa through models of development and dependency and opposes older structuralist categories that saw African people as the victims of extraneous forces beyond their control. In so doing, however, Bayart dispenses with useful universal frames of analysis, such as class, imperialism, and the state:[44]

> The social groups involved in the invention of politics in Africa . . . have their own historicity, which should prevent them from being assimilated too hastily into categories evolving from Western experiences of inequality, even when they do qualify for the category of "social class." Thus the working class in sub-Saharan Africa is run through with divisions from traditional societies, especially the cleavages between elders and juniors or between nobles and inferiors.[45]

Many poststructural studies describe important cultural processes and reveal the complexity and intricacies of locally constructed relations and social forms. It is certainly the case that the particular dynamics of class in African societies (as in all others) need to be properly researched and examined, not assumed; class has in practice always interacted with other categories and divisions in society that are equally worthy of analysis. However, it is equally important to avoid a different form of reductionism in which all societies are believed to be so culturally particular that no adequate comparative analysis can be made between human experience in Africa and elsewhere. The interaction between global structures and local African specificities is at the heart of the approach adopted to study social movements in this volume.

From a different perspective, Achille Mbembe utilizes diffuse and Foucaultian conceptions of power to analyze the complex "composite" nature of the postcolony.[46] He demonstrates that the cultural expression of Cameroonian protest, in the forms of lampooning, "irony," and the playing of games is performative, a theatrical event that ultimately enables the repetition of subordination; an unchallenged institutional structure leaves the people, having internalized the system they blame for their ills, to "protest its loyalty and confirm the existence of an undoubted institution."[47] Yet Mbembe's analysis disregards the genuinely subversive power of such linguistic forms of protest. For example, Pascal Bianchini describes how students at the University of Dakar have created their own linguistic tools for describing their predicament: *cartouchard* is a term used by students to describe a student who has exhausted his or her chances (literally "cartridges"), forcing him or her to succeed in end-of-year exams or face expulsion from the university.[48] Frequently, slogans are recast to ridicule dominant political and economic policies: in South Africa, the Growth and Employment and Redistribution Programme (GEAR) was widely referred to as "reverse GEAR."[49] In Cameroon, student activists at the University of Yaoundé adopt inventive and intentionally ironic nicknames such as Savimbi, Fidel Castro, and Thatcher[50] as forms of cultural and linguistic resistance—commonly produced as part of the concrete experience of struggle, not as an alternative to it.

Class and social movements in Africa

Given our analysis, it is necessary to explore the particular meaning of class relations and their interaction with social movements in Africa. The emphasis of this study is on the diversity of social movement activism and organization on the continent. There is perhaps a tension between this and the authors' assertion that the African urban working class has been central to the historical development of social movement activity on the continent. The question immediately arises as to how this class relates to labor organizations such as trade unions, particularly given the decline in formal-sector employment in many countries in the last two decades. Recent studies arising from or influenced by the anticapitalist movement have sought to replace the Marxist idea of working-class agency with alternative formations based on broader or less defined movements or coalitions for progressive or radical change.

This study's account of how the African working class should be understood corresponds to what Hal Draper called "the main body of the proletariat *plus* those sections of the population whose life situations in society tend to be similar."[51] The reason for distinguishing between these two categories is that the distinct work situation of the proletariat (strictly, its relation to the means of production) tends to put it in a position to provide leadership to other allied social strata. This is because the work done by the proletariat provides a form of collective organization and puts in its hands economic levers that are crucial to the functioning of society.

Marx also described "the communal revolution as the representative of all classes of society not living upon foreign [alienated] labor"—in short, all those do not live by exploiting others.[52] This corresponds closely to those we identify as the popular classes—a wide "African crowd" including the lumpenproletariat of the shantytowns, unemployed youth, elements of the new petit bourgeoisie, laid-off workers, and university students.

It is among these popular classes that the strictly defined working class, for the reasons already stated, has the potential to provide leadership. As Claire Ceruti and Leo Zeilig argued in 2007, "The dynamic reality of class struggle on the continent reveals a working class, albeit reformulated, playing a central role both in the movement for democratic change and in the narrowly defined 'economic' struggles that punctuate daily life on the continent."[53]

Other studies of class in Africa also draw attention to this important distinction between the working class and its popular allies:

> Let us consider the composition of these "popular forces" to which we allude in our discussion of class struggle in contemporary Africa. They may include not only the urban and rural working classes (consisting of those who have little or no control or ownership of the means of production and only their labor to sell, whether in the formal or the informal sector) but also other categories, including on the one hand those whom Marx referred to as "paupers" and on the other small peasants and tenant farmers, "independent" craftsmen and artisans, small retailers and petty commodity producers, and members of the "new petty bourgeoisie" (sometimes called "the new middle classes") generally including the lower echelons of the public sector. Not only do these various social categories constitute, in effect, the relative surplus population . . . they often share a consciousness of their interdependency and common vulnerability.[54]

Such an analysis allows for a constantly shifting constellation of popular forces that nevertheless frequently relies on the organizational capacity and political hegemony of the more "classic" African working class. Of course this class has itself been transformed, along with the political economy of Africa, but transformation does not necessarily mean defeat or redundancy.[55]

E. P. Thompson makes a similar distinction that is rarely highlighted in accounts of his work: "Class happens when some men, as a result of common experiences (inherited or shared), feel and articulate the identity of their interests as between themselves, and as against other men whose interests are different from (and usually opposed to) theirs." But even here, where Thompson is talking about the subjective formation of class consciousness, he is quite clear about *which* "common experiences" he is discussing: "The class experience is largely determined by the productive relations into which men are born—or enter involuntarily."[56] Without the reference to productive relations, there is no way to develop a stable notion of class—since, after all, people's consciousness or loyalties may fluctuate drastically.

It is possible to maintain a dynamic view in which the working class is continually formed and reshaped along with its "penumbra" of other popular classes, all the while developing a unique consciousness and tradition rooted in its experiences of these changes. Indeed, this cross-sectional view is crucial to understanding the longitudinal and historical dynamics of interaction among all these popular forces.

It is of course true that many observers now see the possibility of the African working class achieving or leading emancipatory change—or limited social reform—as slight or even extinguished. Mike Davis's study of the apparently fragmented and broken proletariat of the global south, *Planet of Slums,* raises germane questions about the role of class in a world transformed by "market reforms" since the 1970s.[57] Davis charts the growth of urbanization without industrialization, indeed in a context of deindustrialization in many countries, coupled with falling agricultural productivity in rural areas. The political consequence is that, in the absence of a formally constituted proletariat, class struggle is replaced by "myriad acts of resistance" that emerge from a chaotic plurality of "charismatic churches and prophetic cults to ethnic militias, street gangs, neo-liberal NGOs and revolutionary social movements."[58] Davis is right about the culprits of the recent underdevelopment on the continent, but wrong about the working class. His argument presumes an earlier homogenous and self-conscious Western working class that, in the real slums of nine-teenth-century Manchester or 1930s Chicago, was in practice al-ways riven by divisions: respectable artisans versus the unskilled, men versus women, the employed versus the unemployed, white versus black. It is tempting to ask when, even at great moments of working-class action, there has ever been a "monolithic subject." Indeed, our concept of the social movement in general refutes any notion of a single monolithic agency having existed in the past or arising in the future.[59]

Actual class reconfiguration, and how it has manifested itself in the "myriad acts of resistance" in the global south, does not, however, suggest a working class entirely dislodged from its his-torical agency. It is undoubtedly true that that a combination of rural and urban in the formation of the working class character-ized the process of "proletarianization" in most parts of Africa in the nineteenth and twentieth centuries—from migrant labor in the mines of southern Africa in the 1900s to oil extraction and processing workers in the Niger Delta since the 1970s. Similarly, recent research on Soweto, a large South African township now incorporated into Johannesburg, suggests a community not of slums and shack dwellers, but rather of integrated communities of the formally employed, semi-employed, informally employed, and unemployed, commonly within the same household or neighborhood.[60] As a consequence, household members may be simultaneously engaged in and supportive of conventional indus-trial action organized by trade unions and community-based ser-vice delivery protests initiated by social movements. There is, therefore, no division between labor-based struggles and "myriad acts of resistance"—they are in practice mutually reinforcing. In-deed, in South Africa, both types of actions have reached un-precedented levels in recent years (see chapter 4). There is, of course, the danger that, without progressive political leadership, working-class anger can become focused on the wrong enemy: for example, in the outburst of xenophobic violence in South

Africa in 2008. Nevertheless, the potential cross-fertilization of these struggles—community and workplace—does not live only in the minds of activists, but expresses the real household, and wider community, political economy of contemporary urban South Africa.

As this volume makes clear, South Africa is in many respects different from much of the rest of the continent. Although we cannot easily generalize from the experience of Soweto, our own research suggests that a mix of formally and informally employed households in diverse urban spaces can also be found in cities and towns in much of the rest of the continent (though perhaps in different proportions). The picture of "complex coherence" resembles the shantytown (*bidonville*) evoked by Fanon, who saw such emerging areas as precisely the likely sources of radical social action. How should such contexts be understood?

Conclusion: The state of the African working class

An accurate characterization of Africa's labor force must capture what has happened during the neoliberal period. During the last twenty years, capital has made great strides in labor productivity, both through introducing technology and through applying pressure on workers to speed up, work harder, and work more.

At the same time, African states have withdrawn support from small-scale agriculture and promoted cash crops that require concentrated capital and centralized landholdings. As a result, processes of primitive accumulation have either resumed or accelerated—far beyond the pace evident in the period of state capitalism. The immediate postcolonial state reforms in support of farmers (such as assistance with irrigation, credits and subsidies for seed and fertilizer, or direct tariff protection) constituted a political intervention that stemmed the flow of migration to the cities. The withdrawal of such support is a political intervention that goes beyond everyday economic processes. As a result,

Africa has finally begun to experience the reduction of the active agricultural workforce that was central to the capitalist revolution in western Europe. The vast reserve army of urban migrants thus created, like its European predecessor, has not been easily absorbed into the urban workforce, but rather been "turned *en masse* into beggars, robbers, vagabonds, partly from inclination, in most cases from stress of circumstances."[61]

In this respect, Mike Davis's thesis in *Planet of Slums* is correct. Many of the urban unemployed created over the past thirty years cannot be counted as members of a reserve army, because they have never had a wage job and cannot expect ever to have one. On the other hand, this group is mixed together in the cities with the employed segment of the working class. The political consequences of this are vital for radical social movements. They may follow a lead from the working class, but in this the proletariat faces competition from other forces: from sectarian and communal organizations, from religious movements, and from the intelligentsia, among others.[62]

A further impediment to working-class leadership in Africa is that class power has been diluted. This has taken place not just because workers have lost their jobs, but also because of a flood of destitute urban residents whose presence in the cities and *bidonvilles* is a product of renewed primitive accumulation and neoliberal stagnation.

Analyzing the particular role of social movements in African society requires an understanding of the very real effectiveness of such movements in bringing about progressive change on the continent *and* their limitations in sustaining and deepening those changes. The authors believe that social movements in general and working-class-influenced movements in particular have a vital role to play in bringing about the sorts of changes that would improve the lives of the vast majority of Africans and even enable them to wield significant power over societies whose trajectory has, for the most part, been determined by elites, both international and indigenous. However, it is therefore necessary to explain historically how social movements have influenced social change and why this influence has rarely translated into more effective and lasting transformations in African society. It is to this history that the book now turns.

CHAPTER 3

AN EPOCH OF UPRISINGS: SOCIAL MOVEMENTS IN POSTCOLONIAL AFRICA, 1945–1998

Introduction

This chapter considers the historical development of social movements across Africa from 1945 to 1998, divided into three distinct periods. The first period, between 1945 and 1970, is commonly understood as that of "classic nationalism" and development. During this period, nationalist organizations successfully mounted campaigns to oust colonial powers from their newly emerging nation-states and gradually took over governance of these nations, acquiring the responsibilities and dilemmas of the late-colonial and postcolonial developmental state. The intellectual leadership of these nationalist movements played a particularly crucial role in this period of national liberation, which is explored in this chapter. In addition, nationalist movements received the varied support of sections of society organized in forms we would recognize today as civil society or social movements. Some of the most important of these were trade unions, women's movements or organizations, religious and/or church-based groups, and rural and/or localized social movements. These interacted with self-consciously nationalist organizations, usually led by educated elites, and commonly mobilized the support of their constituencies for nationalist movements in return for the perceived benefits for their members that they hoped or expected would follow the achievement of national independence. Each of these movements developed with and related to the processes of decolonization and then the independence settlement. These movements were not, however, simply "pressure groups"; on the contrary, labor and other popular organizations played a central role in shaping these processes of political change. Though the struggle for independence was often organized within nationalist parties, these party structures were frequently transformed by a general radicalization—even if the extent of radicalization varied greatly across the continent. As the colonial edifice crumbled, symbols of authority broke down, workers refused to tolerate old conditions, trade union federations demanded a general increase in salaries, missionaries were driven out, and soldiers mutinied. Working-class involvement was the tipping point in these movements, but as a coalescing influence on the multiplicity of social forces that we describe in this chapter.

Following national independence, nationalist leaders, now in government, faced significant difficulties in managing these expectations. The common responses of newly governing parties, utilizing the institutions of the state now under their control, were repression, incorporation, or a combination of the two. This chapter sets out some specific examples of how this process unfolded in particular postcolonial polities. While it could be argued that the new ruling elites, in control of the levers of state power and patronage, were in a position of relative strength toward social movements, this did not mean that such movements were permanently prevented from representing their constituents' interests, nor that incorporation held no benefits for such movements. Rather, the specific relationships between the new ruling parties and the states they controlled, and the variety of social movements they related to, were not pre-determined and developed in a range of ways during this period.

With the onset of international recession in the late 1960s, coupled with what Ruth First described in 1970 as the "bargaining process with co-operative elites . . . and . . . the careerist heirs to independence," a second period of social movement activism emerged.[1] This phase lasted from 1970 until approximately 1990 and saw both social movements and an entirely new expression of resistance to the imposition of the first structural adjustment programs on the continent. The 1977 revolt in Egypt against the government's decision to raise food and gasoline prices under the auspices of the IMF was a trigger for the first wave of anti–structural adjustment protests that represented the major popular response to the onset of the continent's profound and enduring economic crisis, and a rejection of attempts by national governments and the international financial institutions to make the urban poor pay the price of a crisis entirely outside their control. But this period also marked the renewal of what can be called "non-traditional nationalism," which was brought about by what Basil Davidson described at the time as "the African encounter with the 'curse of independence' and the struggle against Portuguese colonialism."[2] This was the completion of nationalist liberation in the Portuguese colonies of Angola, Guinea-Bissau, and Mozambique by a leadership that was more critical of the flag independence of the 1960s.

In the 1990s, the quickening pace of structural reforms to African economies led to what has been described as the second wave of revolts against IMF and World Bank–imposed reforms, the third period under analysis in this chapter.[3] The social movements in question were organized around a set of democratic demands, sparking the pro-democracy movements that spread across Africa from 1990 onwards. Africa exploded in a convulsion of pro-democracy revolts that saw eighty-six major protest movements across thirty countries in 1991 alone.[4] Even without critical attention, this figure was an eloquent riposte to those at the time who preached Afropessimism.[5] However, like nationalist movements before them, the unity displayed by pro-democracy movements in ousting dictatorial regimes commonly masked profound divisions regarding the outcomes they wished to see from this process of democratization. Coinciding as it did with the collapse of Soviet communism and the emergence of a unipolar US-dominated world, political liberalization coincided with the dominance of market-based economic liberalization as the singular solution to the economic problems of the world in general and of Africa in particular.

The period saw an extraordinary return of trade unionism. Trade union and labor militants frequently organized protests, became the backbone of new political organizations, and co-ordinated and led the disparate social groups (with disparate demands) that had begun to emerge. We describe in this chapter a convergence of forces between impoverished students, civil servants from obliterated public services, the urban poor, and the working class. These new protest coalitions indicated an African political economy transformed by the hammer blows of structural adjustment. These social movements succeeded in gaining political influence, but against retreating states that had simultaneously experienced declining state provision of social and welfare services and the effects of soaring unemployment and poverty. The response of African social movements to the challenges posed by neoliberal globalization in the late 1990s and the early twenty-first century are addressed in the larger part of the overall study.

Nationalism and its discontents, 1945–1970

The movements for national independence which accelerated in postwar Africa and which (in most cases) achieved their aim in the early 1960s were, in many respects, uneasy coalitions of the discontent. Their declared unity in ridding their territories of colonial rule masked the extent of disagreement regarding their respective visions of the postcolonial state. Mass support for national independence had been mobilized around the promises made by nationalist leaders, not simply to achieve flag independence, but rather to overcome poverty and inequality and, implicitly at least, establish a new social and economic order. National trade union federations frequently demanded increases in salaries and new workplace practices, but in focusing exclusively on independence, nationalist parties failed to satisfactorily develop programs of social reform. Even in the midst of the nationalist struggle, with its emphasis on African unity against the colonial powers, cracks appeared as particular sections of an uneasy nationalist coalition began to question the representation of their concerns after independence. Women activists, who had carried out substantial protests against colonial rule in a number of West African countries, were virtually invisible in the leadership of nationalist movements, except in the form of segregated Women's Leagues. In some cases, trade unions in particular sought to retain their autonomy from nationalist organizations—not because they did not support them, but because they realized that handing all political and economic power to a nationalist leadership could lead to a new form of African dictatorship which would not further their aims.

Why did a wider politics beyond "independence" not emerge? Though the reasons are complex, many of them relate to the dominance of nationalist and Stalinist ideas. The emergent African working class engaging in anti-colonial struggles was relatively small, without a developed, independent, and clearly articulated ideological position. It emerged into a political context dominated both by nationalism and by a Stalinist form of communism that saw political progress in distinct stages, with the question of "socialism" entirely postponed until the transition to "democracy" was complete. A few communist parties in Africa (for example, Egypt and South Africa) adopted this position, but it was also influential on the nationalist intelligentsia across the continent. This intelligentsia expounded an elitist politics of top-down transition that saw itself as the custodian of the new state, presiding over a model of independence in which development would be achieved according to models and plans derived in significant part from the rapid industrialization of the Soviet Union in the late 1920s and 1930s. The language of development after independence may have been peppered with socialist terms (with references to "comrades" and "class struggles"), but the substance of the transformational model was state-dominated capitalism of a type approved of at the time by international organizations such as the World Bank. The new nation-states were engaged in a global race to "catch up" with the West and compete with each other. Even among those nations not aligned to the Eastern Bloc, Joseph Stalin's philosophy resonated among the new African leaders: "To slacken the pace would be to lag behind; and those who lag behind are beaten. . . . We are fifty or a hundred years behind the advanced countries. We must make good this lag in ten years. Either we do this or they crush us."[6] In these circumstances, it proved difficult for a genuinely emancipatory politics based on working-class organization from below to develop.

Trade unions and the working class

The working class did play a leading role in the struggle for independence in many African countries. The 1940s witnessed a major outbreak of industrial action in much of Africa. In 1945 the first general strike in Nigerian history paralyzed the colonial machine for six weeks and led to a period of "labor nationalism" that lasted throughout the late 1940s. This mass struggle also encouraged the founders of the left-wing Zikist Movement, who called for strikes and boycotts and attacked Nigerians who collaborated with the colonial state. In Senegal, the extraordinary railway strike of 1947 was a major factor in the birth of the nationalist movement. The 1946 Rhodesian railway strike heralded the development of modern nationalism in the urban locations of Bulawayo, while the growth of the Northern Rhodesian mineworkers' union in the Copperbelt region was a key initial base for mass nationalism.[7]

The evident effectiveness of the new postwar unions highlighted their potential for providing support for emergent mass nationalist organizations. Colonial officials, having sought to create "non-political" unions, worked hard to ensure they remained separate from the new organizations. On the other hand, new nationalist parties, although led by elites, identified the power of the new unions and sought to persuade them to take industrial action for nationalist purposes. A number of important actions took place. For example, a 1952 general strike in French West Africa for a new Labor Code was a huge success, supported by the communist-aligned African trade unions and by the vast majority of nationalist politicians. During general strikes in some territories, for example in Nairobi in 1950, union leaders and political leaders were united by their arrest by colonial police.[8]

There was, however, periodic and significant resistance by new union leaders to fully fledged alliances with nationalist organizations, partly because of their moderation, but also because they feared the manipulation of their organizations by nationalist leaders whose interests were not the same as their members. Union members were among the most active participants in nationalist activity, but this did not translate into organizational support from the new unions. Again, the Northern Rhodesian story provides an instructive example. In 1953, the African Mineworkers' Union refused to endorse a two-day protest by the nationalist African National Congress against the settler-inspired Central African Federation. This created discontent and suspicion between nationalists and unionists that continued well after independence in 1964. These tensions raised questions regarding the dual identities of Africans as members of a new organized working class and as potential subjects of independent nations.[9]

Generally, however, such concerns were initially masked by collaboration between nationalists and unions in most countries. Certainly, individual union leaders emerged as prominent nationalist figures: for example, Sekou Toure in Guinea, Tom Mboya of Kenya, and Joshua Nkomo in Southern Rhodesia/Zimbabwe. In the run-up to independence, more evidently radical nationalist parties were able to form alliances, official or tacit, with union leaders. By the late 1950s, some of these nationalist leaders found themselves in lower levels of self-government. As independence approached, nationalist alliances with labor movements were focused not on industrial action to win political change, but on preventing strikes to smooth the path to independence. Now in the position of managing fledgling states with highly peripheral capitalist economies, they now discouraged industrial action in the interests of "national development." In 1957 in Dahomey/Benin, the Minister of Labor, himself a former trade unionist, found himself dissuading his former members from taking strike action that would disrupt the economy. While union leaders often resisted such appeals, there was, as Femi Aborisade identifies, the "lack of a visionary and strategic labor leadership."[10]

In many countries, the autonomy of labor movements was rapidly eroded after independence. This was not a question of right-wing politics against left-leaning union movements. Indeed, some of the most radical nationalists practiced new versions of corporatism that presented the incorporation of labor movements as a progressive step that would enable the representation of workers' grievances within the political system. This was symbolically represented by the appointment of many former labor leaders into government. In French West Africa, eight of the nine new Ministers of Labor were former trade unionists.

The Tanganyika African National Union (TANU) government of Julius Nyerere, for example, created the National Union of Tanganyika as the sole legal representative of workers and banned independent unions and all strikes. Former trade union leader Sekou Toure told the unions to be patient in their demands, insisting there was no "plurality" of (class) interests in African society. Such ideas were replicated by many new African leaders, who argued that the developmental concerns of the rural poor had to come before those of relatively privileged urban workers. In some respects, new African rulers replicated colonial anxiety regarding uncontrolled urban citizens; they had witnessed the significant impact that relatively small numbers of organized workers could have on a colonial economy highly dependent on a few industries that generated most of their income. New African states, and the political parties that controlled them, positioned themselves as the sole agency responsible for the redistribution of wealth, a position rejected by many trade unionists.

As noted above, in many new states, versions of African socialism became the state-sponsored ideology. Some postcolonial African leaders suggested that precolonial African societies had been communistic in nature, with a lack of class divisions,[11] and that class antagonism was a Western imposition on the essential harmony of postcolonial society; in this context, African socialism emerged as a justification for state-led development. If there were no class divisions in society, none could be officially recognized (or allowed to emerge). Dissent had to be proscribed, and when it occurred it was blamed on foreign or neocolonial influence.[12]

While some labor leaders found themselves the well-paid leaders of official incorporated trade unions, many workers who had played an important part in furthering nationalist struggles still sought to express their grievances through industrial action. In countries with relatively powerful and well-organized labor movements, such as Zambia and Nigeria, there was significant resistance to attempts at incorporating trade unions.[13] In many other countries, however, this incorporation was largely successful, and there was a substantial downturn in industrial action. Post-independence African governments were more successful in preventing industrial action than their colonial predecessors. This was commonly presented as a form of corporatism or tripartism, collective decision-making that prevented the development of pronounced class conflict and ensured that workers' aspirations were addressed within recognized state structures. In some places, this was furthered by nationalizing some strategic industries. Many workers experienced state intervention into the economy, presented as a progressive step towards a form of socialism, as an increased level of repression; the income earned by their industries, supposedly to be used for national development, was believed by many to be misused for the enrichment of the ruling elite. In these more industrialized countries, industrial action continued, albeit at a lower level than before. Nationally incorporated union leaderships, written off by their members as hopelessly incorporated state officials, were consequently unable to play the role that was expected of them by those states by acting to prevent strikes and disputes. In this context, workers called local strikes and other forms of protest, utilizing some of the methods used by colonial-era workers before the legalization of trade unions.

This failure to develop an independent working-class politics spoke of the suffocation of liberation movements by the twin domination of nationalism and Stalinism. But it also pointed to the immaturity and weaknesses of the trade union movement itself. Where there was no organization and politics of working-class self-emancipation, another social group filled the vacuum. This group, as we shall see, was the intelligentsia. Made up of students, graduates, and junior members of the colonial bureaucracy, the intelligentsia saw themselves as the class that would liberate the new nation on behalf of the poor. In their view the poor would play at most a subservient role in the movements for independence. Once in power, this group transformed itself into what Frantz Fanon described as a "voracious class" happy to accept dividends from the former colonial power.[14] Though trade union leaders were often part of the student-intelligentsia, working-class action after independence burst through the asphyxiating embrace of African socialism and began to develop its own interests and identity. We now turn to other movements that were active before and after independence.

Religious movements and the struggle for independence

African church-based movements played a significant role in the expression of anti-colonial discontent from the start of the twentieth century. While missionaries promoted literacy to enable conversion, this, ironically, became key to the development of independent African Christianity. Africans who could read the Bible, rather than relying on missionary interpretations, could reach their own conclusions regarding the word of God. African preachers could find no theological basis for segregation, forced labor, or the annexation by settlers of their land. In various forms, Africans began to establish their own versions of Anglican and Catholic churches. A further source of independence came with the arrival of important new religious ideas from the United States, particularly the African Methodist Episcopal Church (AMEC). AMEC was increasingly popular among Black Americans, and it provided clear evidence that Christianity did not have to be white-led. AMEC preachers were evangelicals whose fire-and-brimstone message suggested the possibility of radical "millennial" change.[15]

John Chilembwe's revolt against colonial rule in Nyasaland (today's Malawi) in 1915 was another unexpectedly radical result of mission education. Chilembwe criticized the labor practices of settler farms, but found that appeals to his Christian colonial masters went unanswered. In 1915, Chilembwe led an armed revolt against the local white population, killing three of them. The revolt ended quickly and Chilembwe was killed as he fled.[16] Willing as they were to die for their cause and expressing millenarian ideas, the influence of religious martyrdom on the rebels was clear. Chilembwe's rebellion succeeded in shattering the myth of happy natives in which many whites sincerely believed. The colonial masters began monitoring independent churches closely, scrutinizing their teachings for signs of such dangerous ideas, even if few had any direct political intent.

Elliott Kamwana in Nyasaland, a member of the Watchtower Society of Jehovah's Witnesses, freely adapted the Watchtower message of an impending end of the world in which Christ would come and select the chosen few for salvation. Kamwana predicted the end of the world in October 1914: only the baptized would be saved, the whites would leave, and taxes would end. Zionist churches were more responsive to the urgently felt needs of Africans. The tumultuous changes of colonization and the insecurities of existence reinforced a belief in witchcraft and a genuine fear of hell and damnation, which required a form of Christianity able to protect against such dangers. Whereas missionary churches imposed lengthy initiation processes before allowing new members to be baptized, Kamwana, like the Zionists, offered immediate salvation through unconditional baptism.[17] At times of economic distress, such radical teachings could provide the basis for potentially dangerous mass belief in the end of days and the inversion of the existing social order. In Kenya, the anti-colonial Mau Mau movement saw mission-educated Christians as pro-government loyalists and therefore its enemy, and framed conflict within African society in significant part in terms of theology and church membership; it had close links with independent churches such as the Friends of the Holy Spirit.[18]

There are numerous other examples—among them the prophet Simon Kimbangu in the Belgian Congo, the Aladura church in Nigeria, and Cheikh Ahmadou Bamba in French West Africa.[19] Prophets like Kimbangu and Kamwana were persecuted by the colonial authorities. While few of these churches had any real political content, colonial officials and social scientists alike suspected they might contain the seeds of nationalism: that they might become a form of politics by other means. Independent churches provided a popular and accessible explanation for the turmoil and change affecting African lives. In particular, they provided women with an opportunity for a form of advancement; they became leaders of many independent churches at a time when women had no leadership role in the established churches.

An example is the Lumpa Church of Alice Lenshina in Northern Rhodesia (Zambia). Lenshina experienced a spiritual awakening in 1953; she died and was sent back to Earth with a mission. She linked the teachings of her own missionary education with anti-witchcraft movements as well as criticizing aspects of settler rule. Thousands deserted the Catholic Church to join the Lumpas. In 1958, the Lumpa "cathedral," the largest church in the district, was completed. As elsewhere, colonial officials saw Lumpa as a manifestation of dangerous anti-colonialism. In fact, Lenshina's retreat from worldliness put her on a course toward confrontation with organized African nationalism, which grew in the late 1950s. Lenshina's converts withdrew from wider society into Lumpa communities; Lenshina forbade them to join the new nationalist parties. On the eve of independence in 1964, confrontation between the Lumpas and Kenneth Kaunda's United National Independence Party escalated when police were sent in to break up the Lumpa villages forcibly; seven hundred people died in these confrontations.[20] As elsewhere, secular nationalists struggled to manage relations with churches that saw God as their only authority. After independence, the Jehovah's Witnesses, who refused to sing the national anthem or to send their children to government schools, were oppressed in different ways by a number of new African governments.

Although the established churches played little part in the anticolonial struggles, they quickly realized the need to change their ways as independence approached. In the late 1950s and 1960s, new African bishops and priests were hastily ordained. Nationalist leaders had been highly critical of missionaries' involvement in the colonial project, but they needed the schools and clinics the missions provided and, in most cases, continued to encourage the presence of churches, so long as they kept out of politics.

Despite the belated and limited nature of Christian support for African independence, relations between the new states and the official churches were reasonably good. The Catholic and mainline Protestant churches worked hard to build their relationships with the new ruling forces. The new African governments, struggling to meet the expectations of their populations, were grateful for the churches' continued provision of education and welfare services. The legacy of the failure of the established churches to condemn colonialism meant that established religions were generally unwilling to directly criticize government policy—certainly not publicly.[21] As they had during the colonial era, senior bishops sought direct links with government leaders to represent their concerns. At times they collaborated significantly with the ruling structures of political parties, reinforced by the church's paternalistic view that social change was better led from above by unifying political parties. Official churches were as worried as these parties by the prospect of ethnic and social conflict.

Tanzania's Arusha Declaration of 1967—a statement of commitment to African socialism and self-reliance issued by the ruling party in Tanzania that was influenced by the radical Catholic education of President Julius Nyerere—was endorsed by a subsequent pastoral letter in which the country's Catholic bishops proclaimed: "We can see very well how closely it agrees with the true spirit of Christ and the Church."[22] In the 1970s, most established churches had little or nothing to say about emergent dictatorships and one-party states. Zaire's bishops were the recipients of mansions and Mercedes-Benzes, while in Rwanda, the Catholic Bishop of Kigali accepted a position in the Central Committee of the ruling Mouvement Républicain National pour la Démocratie et le Développement (National Republican Movement for Democracy and Development).[23]

Independent churches did survive the transition to national independence. Indeed, for many churches with a long-term vision of religious transformation, there was little difference between a colonial and an African government. In some respects, attempts to impose a sense of national belonging on the members of such churches created more social conflict than before. In the Democratic Republic of Congo, the Kitawala church expressed dissatisfaction with the slow pace of economic and social change just two years after independence, utilizing a combination of radical nationalism and millenarian explosion: "Before independence we dreamed that it would bring us masses of marvellous things. All of that was to descend from the sky. . . . Deliverance and Salvation . . .

But here it is, more than two years we have been waiting, and nothing has come. On the contrary our life is more difficult, we are more poor than before."[24] The Kitawala movement led to an uprising led by Pastor Alphonse Kingis that briefly seized Kisangani in 1964; Kitawala youth gangs massacred intellectuals before the movement was itself violently suppressed. Particularly under authoritarian one-party states, the slightest refusal to participate in state-initiated programs was sufficient to warrant public hostility or even repression. The violent suppression of Jehovah's Witness churches in Malawi and Zambia was justified on the basis that their members refused to accept the membership cards of ruling parties, to salute the national flag, and to sing the national anthem.

Women and the nationalist movements

The elite nature of many male-dominated nationalist leaderships meant that grassroots organizations of women often played a vital role in connecting such elites to an important base of mass support and mobilization. Nationalist leaders such as Nkrumah and Toure supported the mobilization of women, realizing this would widen the base of their support and accelerate the process of decolonization. Organizations of women, particularly of market merchants and traders, played an important part in widening anti-colonial movements in the post–World War II period in, for example, Nigeria, Tanganyika (today's Tanzania), Guinea, and Sierra Leone. In so doing, they challenged not only colonial assumptions regarding gender and sexuality, but also patriarchal authority within African society.

In Nigeria, the Lagos Market Women's Association played an important role in challenging colonial authority over women's economic activities, using tactics such as petitions, marches, and blocking roads to oppose taxes.[25] Prominent individual women were elected to positions within various political parties such as the Nigerian Union of Young Democrats; the separate Nigerian Women's Party sought to elect women to the Lagos city council in

1950. Women protestors challenged the requisition of their produce during World War II, and from 1946 on, the Abekouta Women's Union, led by Western-educated Fummilayo Anikulapo-Kuti, used the slogan "no taxation without representation," directing their protests against the chiefs who collected colonial taxes.[26] Kuti and other women were jailed for their part in organizing protests of ten thousand women in 1947, and Kuti traveled to London in 1947 with a delegation of the National Council of Nigeria and the Cameroons (NCNC), where she met with British trade unionists. The Abekouta Women's Union evolved into the Nigerian Women's Union, and many of its members went on to join emergent nationalist parties such as the NCNC. However, despite seeking to mobilize the support of such women, Nigeria's nationalist parties refused to adopt women as candidates in elections; in contrast, Nkrumah's Convention People's Party reserved 10 percent of Ghana's parliamentary seats for women.[27]

Generally, however, women who played an important part in the nationalist struggle did not attain leadership positions, except in women's leagues or unions. The members of the TANU Women's Section, led by Bibi Titi Mohammed, were semi-literate, married, middle-aged Muslim women; such women played a vital agitational and organizational role in turning TANU into a party with genuine popular support.[28] In so doing, they sought to ensure that the political equality that TANU was demanding was not simply equality between Europeans and Africans to govern themselves, but also equality between men and women. Many men were unhappy about this: Mohammed's husband divorced her because he refused to accept her political activity. In French West Africa, women such as Aoua Keita and Aissata Sow (the leader of a teachers' union) played a similarly important role in mobilizing women's support for the nationalist Rassemblement Démocratique Africain (African Democratic Rally) in the 1950s.[29]

Although postcolonial governments expressed rhetorical commitments both to gender equality and to overcoming the poverty of women, they generally perpetuated maternal and feminine stereotypes, suppressing independent women's organizations in favor of official Women's Leagues of ruling parties. Few women MPs were elected, and female ministerial representation was generally limited to tokenistic areas such as Social Welfare. Soon after Tanganyikan/Tanzanian independence in 1963, President Nyerere banned all independent women's organizations, establishing a single national women's organization, Umoja wa Wanawake wa Tanganyika (Women's Unity of Tanganyika, UWT). Although Mohammed was initially the leader of UWT, she was marginalized in favor of younger, more educated women with the capacity to manage administrative and financial organization—something that happened to many grassroots local leaders after independence. Whereas the Women's Section was an organization that sought to mobilize women politically, the UWT emphasized improving women's lives from above; their participation was not necessary.[30] The vast majority of women remained poor, often stuck in rural areas, and with little effective political representation; for many, the achievement of independence made little difference in their lives.

Rural Africans and nationalism

For many Africans, the 1940s were a watershed in relations with their respective colonial states. Hitherto, indirect rule (particularly in British colonies) and the sheer poverty of most administrations had meant that the colonial state was a distant master, with effective local authority in the hands of (often appointed) chiefs. From the late 1940s, however, the developmental orientation of what has been called the "second colonial occupation" of Africa meant that millions of rural Africans were for the first time confronted with new colonial officials offering developmental assistance, but also enforcing new rules and regulations that were thought to be necessary to improve agricultural efficiency and reduce environmental destruction.[31] Measures such as cattle-dipping to prevent the spread of diseases, contour ridging to preserve soil quality, and bans on cutting down trees to preserve the environment were now enforced. Peasants perceived these as a direct threat to their way of life, often evading them and in some cases directly opposing them by political organization. Rural Africans recognized that many of these measures were designed to benefit European settler farmers or to encourage the growth of a small class of commercial African farmers, so as to bring capitalist relations to the African countryside.

John Iliffe describes the impact of such initiatives in Tanganyika in the late 1940s through the example of the disastrous groundnut scheme colonial authorities implemented in conjunction with the multinational Unilever without consulting the local population.[32] The plan was thought up by the postwar British Labour administration to cultivate groundnut production in areas of what is now Tanzania. In conjunction with a subsidiary of Unilever, farmers (former Tanganyikan servicemen) planted large tracts of drought-prone land with groundnuts to produce vegetable oil for UK consumers. The project was an utter failure that collapsed with massive losses in 1949, ruining the land and throwing thousands out of work. While the postwar boom in cash crops benefited some rural farmers, the majority did not see any benefit from the significant increases in government spending in rural areas. Eastern-province politicians in Tanganyika declared in 1955: "We are faced with a serious invasion, more serious, in fact, than the first world war. . . . We are a poor people . . . and yet we are made poorer by the demands of taxes and working for projects which make us no better."[33] In response, many local African improvement associations and cooperative farming bodies were established to represent the common farming voice, often in opposition to chiefs. These became a vital link between nationalist politicians and rural communities. In Meru, the Tanganyikan African Association, the forerunner of TANU, actively resisted the eviction of Africans to make way for European settlers. As one local leader put it in 1953: "The eviction woke our Meru people up to the indignity of being ruled without our consent by foreigners. Now we nationalists are going to wake up all Tanganyika."[34]

Similar events unfolded elsewhere. Henrietta Moore and Megan Vaughan describe how food shortages in Northern Rhodesia's Northern Province, partly caused by labor migration, were blamed by colonial officials on Bemba peoples, who were portrayed as lazy. Some "progressive" farmers were identified and supported by colonial development initiatives, but government schemes required obedience to a series of restrictions on agricultural practice and proved of interest only to older men who were unable to pay off government loans. Such schemes were viewed suspiciously by the rural majority, who continued to practice a mobile form of agriculture the colonial authorities strongly opposed. As in Tanganyika, such improvement measures fed the growth of nationalist militancy—in Chinsali in Northern Province in 1961, five hundred houses and huts were burned in a protest held by the United National Independence Party against so-called hygiene regulations and laws against migratory farming practices.[35]

Such protests were a vital part of mobilizing rural support for nationalist movements. In the late 1950s and early 1960s, nationalists sought to recruit large numbers of rural Africans to the movements. This was a vital element in challenging the colonial stereotype that nationalist parties spoke only for the educated elites. In order to establish themselves in rural areas, they faced the challenge of finding issues on which they could mobilize peasant support. This created a dilemma that only really resolved itself after independence—nationalist leaders made promises to rural dwellers that such interference in their agricultural practice would be abolished after they came to power.

In the later national liberation movements of Africa—Mozambique, Angola, Zimbabwe, South Africa—the peasantry provided a vital base of support for guerrilla fighters seeking to overthrow colonial regimes. Following a model of guerrilla warfare influenced by Chinese Maoism, the Cuban revolution, and the war in Vietnam, it was argued that the peasantry, rather than the organized working class, were the real revolutionary force in mainly rural societies. Rural people not only joined the liberation movements in their exile bases, they hid soldiers in their communities, provided them with food and other supplies, and provided information on the activities of enemy forces. In Zimbabwe in particular, such support arose from discontent at land dispossession by white settlers—here, there was a strong expectation that national independence in 1980 would bring immediate change, leading to a locally organized, spontaneous movement of grassroots land occupation that the new Zimbabwean government first tacitly encouraged and then rejected.[36] However, this was a highly ambiguous relationship, based not only on shared goals but also on exploitative relations. Rural support was often extracted at the barrel of a gun by revolutionary movements that treated the peasantry as a resource to be exploited.[37]

Newly independent states inherited the developmental framework of late colonialism, but were equally unsure how best to achieve agricultural growth. Certainly, the new states developed and promoted a wide range of rural development schemes. Many of these were grandiose initiatives conceived by urban civil servants and development advisors from Western universities and agencies of the United Nations, with little or no real participation from the populations concerned. This was coupled with a tendency to exclude local rural leaders from any significant role in postcolonial governance. Although practice varied, there was a general distrust of chiefs, who, at least in British-ruled Africa, had played an important part in local government and were regarded as compromised by most new nationalist rulers. However, they were also unwilling to accept any significant decentralization to more modern forms of local government; many local councils established in the wake of decolonization lost their powers, particularly to raise funds. Tax collection and expenditure were heavily controlled by the central administrations. Many new states appointed a reinvented form of district officer, accountable to the president, who presided over his rural area with a level of unaccountable authority similar to his colonial predecessor. For these and other reasons, seen from the perspective of a rural village, the new African government in a capital city far away could appear as remote and unaccountable as the imperial administration had been before it.

Where agricultural development did take place, it was usually in spite of the new independent states, not because of them. The agricultural prosperity of the cash-crop farmers of West Africa continued, at least when the price of cocoa or coffee was high. However, such production remained dependent on the vagaries of the global economy—such goods continued to be sold as raw materials, rather than as processed products that might have added value and been controlled by Africans themselves. In many territories, the price paid to farmers for their produce was tightly controlled, as new states sought to generate income for themselves or to provide cheap subsidized food for growing urban populations. Marketing boards did provide some support to small farmers, but also monopolized the distribution and sale of particular crops at controlled prices. Some farmers rebelled against this by smuggling their produce abroad, to avoid such controls and sell at market prices elsewhere. Moore and Vaughan, describing Zambia, note that "by the 1970s, government interventions in the area, which had previously been justified as encouraging 'grass roots' political participation as well as raising rural incomes, looked more like strategies for the containment and control of peasant political activity."[38]

More generally, there was a lack of coherence in agricultural and economic development policy among independent governments. While most sought to make rural areas grow economically, they were worried about increasing inequality as a result. Encouraging the growth of a small, elite group of progressive farmers created the danger that a larger number of peasants would lose their land and (possibly) migrate to town or become a discontented landless proletariat. Many radical regimes sought to produce some form of collective or state farm structure: this would in theory provide a form of rural equality and improve access to services. In practice, however, it was usually disastrous and led to all sorts of human rights abuses. There was distrust, not solidarity, between party officials and peasants. Village collectivization in Tanzania—perhaps well-meaning, but authoritarian—displaced people from the land they knew. James Scott starkly describes the disastrous impact of Ujamaa villagization in the late 1970s, as state officials imposed collective villagization informed by top-down modernization models of development with as much authoritarianism as their colonial predecessors.[39] Bowen's work on Mozambique persuasively demonstrates how peasants, despite playing an important role in the struggle against Portuguese colonialism in the early 1970s, were later treated in ways that completely undermined their support for the nationalist party, the Liberation Front of Mozambique, FRELIMO, whose "agricultural strategy completely negated what independence meant to the peasantry."[40]

Peasants were not passive in the face of such problems, but their resistance was often individualized and hidden. Peasants simply refused to obey instructions supposedly designed to improve their agricultural practice, as they had done under colonialism. They deserted collective farms and returned to their own areas.[41] They did not generally organize identifiable social movements to directly resist such policies. Nevertheless, many rural communities were able to successfully challenge aspects of post-independence agricultural and economic policies with which they disagreed.

The role of students and intellectuals

The legacy of colonialism meant that Africa, like most of the Third World, lacked a national bourgeoisie. The coherence of a group of intellectuals fighting for independence was in direct proportion to the lack of organization and cohesion of other social groups in colonial Africa. In this vacuum they saw themselves as the liberators of Africa, representing the emergent nation. As Tony Cliff wrote about the intelligentsia: "They are great believers in efficiency. . . . They hope for reform from above and would dearly love to hand the new world over to a grateful people, rather than see the liberating struggle of a self-conscious and freely associated people result in a new world themselves."[42] The role played by African students in these movements was crucial. They believed that they embodied the aspirations of national liberation and saw themselves as the liberators of Africa, representing the emergent nation. Mahmood Mamdani writes that this liberation was undertaken by the "petit-bourgeois" intelligentsia through the levers of the colonial state:

> Intellectuals . . . saw the state and not the class struggle as the motive force of development . . . socialism was turned into a strategy for economic development, and no more. Development, in turn, was seen as a technical, supra-political and supra-social exercise. It was assumed that this objective historical process would erase the backwardness of the African people, rather than being itself the by-product of the struggle of that same people for social transformation.[43]

From this perspective, it was difficult even to glimpse the possibility of popular classes in Africa becoming a creative force capable of making history. Rather, history was seen as something to be made outside this force, in lieu of it, and ultimately to be imposed on it.

In contrast to the presence of an African capitalist class, the colonial state in colonial Francophone, Lusophone, and Anglophone Africa promoted an important layer of functionaries and bureaucrats to operate the state machinery, local administration, and services. By the 1940s this group was made up of civil servants, teachers, graduates, nurses and clerks. In part this reflected a desire by the state to "civilize" a layer of bureaucrats, though as decolonization approached, the *évolués*— literally meaning "evolved" in French—became mediators between the popular desire for radical change and the colonial state. By the 1950s, this group, though numerically small, had started to develop a coherent political and social identity. Peaceful and negotiated independent settlements were secured in alliance with the intelligentsia. Still, the colonial machine could not always control these processes, so occasionally the young natives they became unruly subjects leading militant nationalist movements (in the Congo, but also, for example, in Guinea).

Importantly, this social group frequently grew out of a student milieu. So trade union bureaucrats and colonial staff had been, and sometimes still were, university students educated abroad on scholarships. Often these students became imbued in the left-wing and communist milieu at American, British, and French universities in the 1930s and 1940s. Early on, students from African colonies built their own organizations. The West African Student Union was founded in London in 1925 and became a "training ground for Nigerian nationalists."[44] A similar structure for African students in Paris was the Fédération des Étudiants d'Afrique Noire en France (Federation of Black African Students in France, FEANF). One ex-member described brilliantly how FEANF worked as a cadre school for nationalist politics: "One learnt to live, to think and to act together, FEANF was a school where we took our first political lessons. It was within FEANF that African students formed a concept of African nationalism. . . ."[45] A large number of African nationalists who led their countries to independence hailed from what we can term the student-intelligentsia: among them were Amílcar Cabral, who studied in Portugal, Leopold Senghor (in France), and Kwame Nkrumah (in the United States and Britain). Nkrumah, Ghana's first leader, became inspired by socialist ideas and the presence of Black Marxists in the west. Nkrumah boasted that during his stay in London in the 1940s, he habitually read the paper of the British Communist Party on the London Underground.[46]

For politically organized and militant student-intellectuals, therefore, the Soviet Union was an inspiration. It represented for them, as it did for millions, a state that seemed to offer the possibility of real existing communism, enabling equality, solidarity, and struggle. Not implicated in the plunder of the colonies, and offering bellicose denunciations of imperialism, the Soviet Union and the Communist Parties that were its international representatives also seemed to pose a genuine political alternative to Western capitalism. Perhaps even more important was Moscow's tantalizing model of development. Here, after all, was a country which only a few decades before had shared some of the features of the colonial world. At the turn of the twentieth century Russia was still semi-capitalist, with a large peasantry and a small proletariat limited to certain industrial centers. Massive industrialization after 1929 propelled the Soviet Union into the major leagues. By the 1950s the Soviet Union was a superpower, surpassed only by the United States.

This remarkable transformation was secured through mass industrialization and rural collectivization. The devastation and mass violence involved in this process are well known, but for the African student-intelligentsia the lessons were clear. Nkrumah, in the vanguard of such thinking, was extravagant in his praise for the Soviet Union. Developmental advances, Nkrumah and other leaders agreed, would be achieved via the structures of the new postcolonial states. Colonialism had in most cases severely hampered the growth of an indigenous bourgeoisie. As one study of the Congo puts it, the "profitable sectors of the economy were already cornered by foreign . . . corporations. Therefore all that [aspiring African elites] could sell was their political power and influence in the state machinery."[47]

The continental student-intelligentsia had a high degree of organizational coherence, political identity, and, in the Soviet Union, a coherent project for national independence. Independent movements propelled the student-intelligentsia into the existing state machinery. When they assumed control over states, Nkrumah, Senghor, and Nyerere, for example, saw socialism as the state ideology. As we have seen, "African socialism" was presented as an authentic African ideology that justified early attempts at state capitalist development. African socialism raised the state above class antagonism while declaring class to be a European phenomenon unknown or foreign to African societies.[48]

The first wave: Economic crisis and structural adjustment, 1970–1990

The first generation of postcolonial African analysts gradually came to see independence as a charade that barely disguised the imperialism of former colonial powers (as analyzed in chapter 2). The experience of Ghana, also illustrative of the period, had revealed two things: the difficulty of industrial development in a world dominated by Western imperialism; and the façade of African socialism. The centerpiece of Ghana's attempts to industrialize was the Akosombo Dam on the Volta River. It was hoped that the dam would provide energy to allow the local supplies of bauxite to be turned into aluminum. Instead the American company Kaiser, which ran the aluminum works, imported semi-processed bauxite from Jamaica, claiming that it did not make economic sense to use local sources of bauxite a hundred miles away when they it could import it from an island 2,500 miles away! As Robert Biel has put it, "the four big companies which dominated the world aluminium industry were brought together through the personal intervention of US leaders Nixon and Kennedy, to ensure that Ghana did not establish a basis for independence."[49]

The second lesson of the Ghanaian experience concerned the very socialism on which the state claimed to be based. Ghana had experienced a period of mass mobilization between 1949 and 1951 that led to limited self-government. But after independence, the movement that had been built and mobilized was forgotten, and increasingly what counted "was the exercise of power rather than the mobilization of the masses."[50] Nkrumah was isolated in the political administration and centralized state he had inherited from colonialism. By the time of the coup that toppled him in 1966, support had disappeared and opposition had grown. For regimes like

Ghana, Mali, Mauritania, and Guinea, which were regarded at the time as radical, social change was instigated by a state machine that bore a close resemblance to the colonial state with which they claimed to have broken.

In the 1970s, new movements began to develop as a consequence of the first structural adjustment programs implemented across the continent. Although the economic crisis of the late 1970s was international in its reach, the pain of the consequent adjustment was carried by the Third World, and particularly by states that relied heavily on importing oil and buying heavy machinery on credit from the West. For many states on the continent, the results were catastrophic. For example, by the mid-1970s, coffee and cotton made up two-thirds of exports from Ghana and Chad, respectively, while falling copper prices in 1977 meant that Zambia, a country dependent on copper for half of its GDP, garnered no income from its most important resource.[51] As the global crisis spread, loans turned into debts, and national adjustment and restructuring became requirements for further loans from the IMF and World Bank. More and more African states saw their macroeconomic policies shaped by the conditions imposed by IMF and World Bank technocrats. New voices now called for "belt tightening" and austerity.

The result was a period of increased social unrest that began in Egypt in 1977. The government's decision to raise food and gasoline prices as part of a program of financial stringency under the auspices of the IMF provoked fierce rioting in major cities across the country. The first wave of popular protest also involved four out of the five countries of the Arab Maghreb Union—Morocco, Mauritania, Algeria, and Tunisia—drawing in virtually all of north Africa. Throughout the same period, a wave of popular protest against similar austerity measures swept across the subcontinent.

The removal of consumer subsidies led to substantial cost-of-living increases for the urban population in the early and mid-1980s. This came in a context of rising popular discontent with the failures of the postcolonial state to address the expectations raised during the transition to independence. However, there were limited possible avenues for the expression of legitimate public discontent. As we have seen, most independent civil society organizations and social movements had either been suppressed or incorporated into the state structures, a position from which they were no longer free to criticize state policies. In these circumstances, some incorporated civil society leaders began to express limited criticisms of specific government policies while expressing their overall loyalty to the one-party state. Meanwhile, although many nationalist parties had initially been vibrant organizations throughout many parts of their countries, local structures of the parties had rapidly deteriorated, removing another possible avenue for the expression of discontent.

In this context, the lack of formal official leadership meant that discontent was instead expressed in a number of countries as riots and social disturbances of a level that had not occurred in most countries since independence. In Tunisia, for example, the abolition of food subsidies in December 1983 by the ruling Destour party led to a doubling of bread prices and substantial riots. Destour, like ruling parties elsewhere, had incorporated trade unions, youth and student bodies, and women's groups into its structures. Tunisian trade unions had specific representation in parliament, and eight trade union MPs voted against the removal of food subsidies; however, the official trade union body did not endorse any public demonstration of discontent. Abdelkader Zghal illustrates how riots were organized on a local level by the unemployed and by young women, while the ruling party lacked any significant structures on the ground. What was noteworthy was that President Bourguiba reversed his decision on food subsidies, angering donors but assuaging public opinion. African ruling parties, apparently all-powerful and in control of society and the economy, had their weaknesses revealed both by their inability to control unrest and by their reversal of policy.[52]

Similar events unfolded elsewhere. In Zambia, the early 1980s saw a series of conflicts between the United National Independence Party (UNIP), its international donors, and the Zambian public. As the economic situation worsened, the IMF and World Bank took increasing control over day-to-day economic policy. Bates characterizes urban Zambians as pro-UNIP, but it was more the case that urban Zambians' discontent with many aspects of UNIP policy proved to be the straw that broke the camel's back. UNIP had sought to position itself as a popular party that spoke for the poor; its supremacy over all aspects of public life was crucial to maintaining its power. It could therefore not be seen to be forced to implement policies simply because donors told it to. President Kaunda therefore endorsed the removal of food subsidies in December 1986. When food prices rose, riots followed; crucially, these were not directed primarily against the IMF, but against the ruling party. On the Copperbelt, workers and the unemployed fought with riot police, attacking UNIP offices. As in Tunisia, the government was forced to reintroduce the subsidies. Donors responded by reducing financial support, making the auction system unworkable. Workers then declared major strikes, demanding pay increases to compensate for inflation. Kaunda claimed that "the initiators of the strikes were politically motivated." His forces had major clashes with the trade union movement, which heavily criticized the removal of food subsidies.[53]

The prime minister, Kebby Musokotwane—who served under President Kaunda as prime minister for four years starting in 1985—claimed that the government still had the capacity to direct economic policy. Such a statement had potentially dangerous consequences. If UNIP was the powerful and effective force it claimed to be, it had to take responsibility for unpopular policies; if responsibility lay with external agencies, the weakness of the one-party state was exposed. Ultimately, popular discontent proved more influential than the IMF. On May Day 1987, Kaunda froze the price of essential goods and introduced new controls over the economy.

The World Bank concluded that "the early demise . . . of the adjustment package imposed by the IMF resulted from an unrealistic . . . assumption that the majority of middle and lower income urban Zambians would tolerate pauperisation."[54]

Although UNIP sought to retain state controls over the economy for a while longer, its dependency on international donors meant that this could not be sustained. More crucially, structural adjustment, while unpopular with many ordinary people, had an unintentionally positive impact for social movements. By exposing the ruling party's weakness in preventing popular unrest, and in particular demonstrating the potential for such unrest to achieve the removal of unpopular policies, it encouraged dissidents of various kinds to more openly criticize the one-party states.

The strength and effectiveness of this first wave of struggle in post-independence Africa was based on wide coalitions of the popular classes, though the working class in a narrow sense was usually centrally involved through the trade union movement. The impact of unrest depended on the participation of the wider "African crowd," including the lumpenproletariat of the shantytowns, unemployed youth, elements of the new petit bourgeoisie, and university students.[55] Generally spontaneous and directed predominantly towards current economic reforms and austerity measures, these struggles also contained elements of a critique of regimes' legitimacy and deployed notions of social justice.[56] Given their limited degree of political organization, these movements generally had a restricted effect, but in some cases, they took on the character of a political opposition, challenging policies and changing the prevailing political configuration. In most cases they served to redefine the terrain of struggle and to provide the basis for the emergence at a later stage of political movements aimed at changing governments rather than just policies.

The targets of these protests included the international financial agencies (particularly the IMF), the governments that adopted the austerity policies, and the representatives of the big corporations (foreign and national) that benefited from "liberalization." In Nigeria, for example, it was students who spearheaded the fight against the government's homegrown structural adjustment program in the 1980s. But student activists in the National Association of Nigerian Students were no longer simply a political vanguard. The collapse of the conditions of study across the country's universities saw student status converge with a general societal meltdown. Fuel price increases demanded by the World Bank in 1988 led students to initiate nationwide protests against structural adjustment programs (SAPs). Jeremiah Dibua explains: "Students viewed the increase in prices . . . would visit untold economic hardship on the majority of Nigerians while making it difficult for impoverished parents to finance students' education."[57] While the "demand for economic liberalization" may have weakened formal democratic structures, in some cases it created an extraordinarily explosive and vibrant cocktail of social forces.

One early factor in the first wave of protests was the role of university students, previously regarded as a privileged social group. Structural adjustment completely refigured educational priorities. Under the auspices of SAPs, universities suffered major funding shortfalls, and students frequently organized the first protests. One commentator maintained that in the escalation of student protest since the introduction of SAPs in Africa in the early 1980s there has emerged a new "pan-African student movement, continuous in its political aspirations with the student activism that developed in the context of the anti-colonial struggle, and yet more radical in its challenges to the established political power."[58] The effects of SAPs proletarianized the African student body, breaking them from their postcolonial past as members of the elite and, in the 1980s, forcing them to instigate some of the first anti-government protests that fed into the nascent pro-democracy movements of the end of that decade.

The second wave: Pro-democracy movements and choiceless democracies, 1990–1998[59]

The wave of pro-democracy movements which swept across Africa in the early 1990s is often portrayed as a singular and unexpected event with little connection to what had gone before. While the influence of Eastern Europe's anti-communist revolutions was considerable, particularly on the timing of Africa's pro-democracy movements, they were the spark that turned the dry tinder of popular social and economic discontent into a raging bonfire. The fire was fanned by the impact of the structural adjustment policies that were, by the late 1980s, being implemented by governments of all political persuasions. Although the eventual outcome of these movements was the wholesale implementation of economic liberalization programs by most of the new democratic governments (ironically reflecting the dearth of alternative ideological approaches in the wake of the collapse of communism), this fact should not deflect attention from the material basis of many pro-democracy campaigns. These were in significant part popular movements witnessing a resurgence of social forces that appeared to have been suppressed or incorporated in the late 1960s and 1970s, but that had already begun to reassert themselves in the anti–structural adjustment initiatives of the 1980s.

Indeed, the protests that marked the start of the 1990s were eloquent testimony to the devastation that structural adjustment and the free market had already brought to the continent. A second wave of popular protest, now more explicitly political and more ambitious, spread across the continent like a hurricane. From 1989 on, political protests rose massively across sub-Saharan Africa. In the 1980s there had been approximately twenty recorded incidents of political unrest per year; in 1991 alone, eighty-six major protests took place across thirty countries. By 1992, many African governments had been forced to introduce reforms, and in 1993, fourteen countries held democratic elections. Over a four-year period from the start of the protests in 1990, a total of thirty-five regimes were swept away by protest movements and strikes. Many held elections for the first time in a generation. The speed with which these changes took place left observers breathless: "Compared with the recent experiences of Poland and Brazil . . . African regime transitions seemed frantically hurried," one commentator noted.[60] The effects of the IMF and neoliberalism in the region at the end of this period had one entirely unforeseen benefit: they brought workers, peasants, and the urban poor together on an unprecedented scale to fight with extraordinary militancy and courage against food and fuel price hikes and political oppression—and often for wholesale political transformation.

For more than ten years, the IMF and the World Bank had been forcing many African states to implement "reforms." They insisted on cuts in the public sector, including to subsidies and health and education budgets, as a condition of new loans. Zaire's government, for example, was forced to reduce expenditure on health, education, and research.[61] One student described the conditions of life at the University of Lubumbashi, one of the country's largest universities, in 1989: "Us, students and tomorrow's elite of Zaire, the youth of the [Jeneusse du] Mouvement Populaire de la Révolution [Youth of the Popular Movement of the Revolution, JMPR] were compelled to go to the toilet in the bush, like animals. We went there every day, in the hot and rainy season. The night like the day . . . even the 'largest library in central Africa' was not saved, and was used as a WC. The outside world must know the extent that Mobutu had humiliated us."[62]

However important the role of mismanagement and corruption, the deterioration in economic conditions as a result of austerity policies in a context of global recession was ultimately to blame. Despite its great mineral riches, by 1988 the Congo was ranked the eighth poorest country in the world. The World Bank reported that it had a per-capita income of $160 a year, while real incomes had fallen to just 10 percent of their pre-independence level. Between

1973 and 1985, the average income fell by 3.9 percent a year. The agricultural picture was no better. By the late 1980s Zaire had gone from being a net food exporter to paying out more than 20 percent of its foreign exchange on food imports. Twenty-eight years after independence, the country was saddled with a seven-billion-dollar foreign debt.[63] On April 24, 1990, Mobutu declared Zaire's "Third Republic" and announced that a multi-party system, initially comprised of three parties, including the JMPR, would be introduced within a year. The move stunned the country; during a televised address, Mobutu himself cried. There followed a four-year period of popular participation and political debate that had not been experienced in the Congo since the assassination of Lumumba thirty years before. This was described in one recent account as Congo's "second revolution."[64]

Sudan provided an early example of the political power of orchestrated popular protest with the 1985 overthrow of President Nimeiri and the establishment of a multi-party system that lasted until 1989, when a military coup d'état brought President al-Bashir to power. In Algeria that same year the Front de Libération Nationale (National Liberation Front, FLN) regime, which had brutally repressed mass protests the previous year, undertook a dramatic political liberalization. This allowed many new parties to form, including Islamist groupings like the Front Islamique du Salut (Islamic Salvation Front, FIS), and municipal and national elections took place over the subsequent two years. Mass demonstrations at the time of the Gulf crisis and the first US-led intervention in Iraq (in 1990–91) involved huge support for the Islamists, who called not only for solidarity with their Iraqi brethren but also for the establishment of an Islamic state in Algeria. In 1990, the FIS dominated the municipal elections and toward the end of 1991 appeared poised to gain electoral success in the national elections on the basis of a massive growth of popular support. The FLN government, unprepared to accept the popular will, imposed a state of emergency and banned the FIS.

In 1989, the full-scale pro-democracy movement started in Benin. Students demonstrated against the government in January, demanding overdue grants and a guarantee of public sector employment after graduation. The government, crippled by financial scandals, capital flight, and falling tax revenue, thought it could respond as it always had: by suppressing the protest. But the movement grew to incorporate trade unions and the urban poor. In an attempt to preempt the movement, the president, Mathieu Kérékou, declared that his party, the People's Revolutionary Party of Benin, had jettisoned "Marxism-Leninism" and agreed that multi-party elections could be held in the future. In a pattern followed by other countries, he set up a commission that eventually created a national reconciliation conference that included the opposition movement, trade unions, students, and religious associations.

Emboldened by events, trade unionists, led by postal workers and teachers, left the government-controlled National Federation of Workers' Unions of Benin. By the end of the year the capital, Cotonou, was convulsed by mass demonstrations. When Kérékou attempted to befriend demonstrators during one of these protests he was jeered, threatened, and forced to flee. In February 1990 the National Conference of Active Forces declared itself sovereign and dissolved Kérékou's national assembly. Obstinately, he still insisted, "I will not resign, I will have to be removed." After his defeat in the 1991 presidential elections, he asked humbly for forgiveness and asserted his "deep, sincere and irreversible desire to change."[65]

Meanwhile, mass demonstrations and general strikes forced the pace of democratic change on the continent. Unions together with a variety of popular forces fought regimes hanging on to power in Burkina Faso, Burundi, Cameroon, the Central African Republic, Chad, Comoros, Congo, Côte d'Ivoire, Gabon, Ghana, Guinea, Kenya, Lesotho, Madagascar, Mali, Mauritania, Nigeria, Swaziland, and Zaire. Even where elections were not held and heads of state clung to power, the pattern was the same: trade unions "sought not simply to protect the work-place interests of their members but have endeavoured to bring about a restructuring of the political system."[66] The African trade union movement demonstrated greater independence and militancy than at any time in its history. In other countries, alternative social movements came to the fore: for example, in Kenya, where Christian church leaders played an increasingly important role in criticizing the autocratic rule of the Kenya African National Union (KANU). In a situation where most other groups lost their capacity for autonomous expression, churches were able to resist such pressures and resist KANU hegemony. Bishop Muge criticized vote rigging in one-party state elections in 1983 and 1988, arguing that the church should protest "when God-given rights and liberties are violated."[67] He highlighted corruption charges and, in 1989, called on the Moi government to release all detainees; the same year, Bishop Okello, drawing an explicit comparison between Africa and change in Eastern Europe, foretold that all African dictators would fall within five years. After KANU launched a "debate" on multi-party democracy in 1990, President Daniel arap Moi claimed that the Catholic Church was attempting to undermine the government and Bishop Muge died in a car crash in mysterious circumstances, unleashing widespread popular anger and causing a decisive rift in church-state relations.[68]

In Zimbabwe, students spearheaded resistance to the Zimbabwe African National Union–Patriotic Front's (ZANU-PF) simultaneous plans to liberalize the economy and introduce a one-party state. In 1989 a student leaflet denounced ZANU-PF's Investment Code as "a further entrenchment of capitalism in Zimbabwe . . . an acquiescence to the IMF and World Bank sponsored programs . . . and incompatible with the doctrine of socialism."[69] The Students' Union condemned the suppression of a doctors' strike: "The use of force which was exercised on Doctors while they were airing their clear, legitimate grievances is really an authoritarian and neo-fascist tendency and hence it has to be condemned." The university was closed in October 1989, following the arrest of Student Union leaders.

Morgan Tsvangirai, general secretary of the Zimbabwe Congress of Trade Unions (ZCTU), denounced the closure in strong terms and was detained for more than four weeks.[70] In 1991, when the ZCTU organized a May Day event under the theme "Liberalization or Liberation," workers paraded with banners denouncing the SAP: "Employers liberated, workers sacrificed." "Are we going to make 1991 the Year of the World Bank Storm?" Meanwhile, the Ministry of Labor distributed its own leaflets telling workers to "suffer now and benefit later."[71] Arthur Mutambara argues that students were the first group to stand up against Mugabe—even before the trade unions—but that students and workers combined in popular protest: "The labor movement was progressive, but they took longer to give up on Robert Mugabe. In fact the labor unions continued to endorse the party in elections."[72] By the mid-1990s the pace of pro-democracy resistance picked up and at the end of the decade a coalition of trade unionists, students, and middle-class intellectuals founded the opposition Movement for Democratic Change (MDC).

The pro-democracy movements were in many respects similar to the previous generation of nationalist movements that came together to achieve independence from the colonial powers. These movements came together quickly from a range of social forces; sought unity around a single common goal; rapidly evolved from single-issue movements into political parties in many cases; and having agreed only on what they were *against,* were in some cases thrust into power with little time to consider what they were *for.* In new multi-party movements, trade unionists who had fought against structural adjustment found common cause with business people who hoped multi-partyism would further open the economy. But the trade unionists and militants who opposed these alliances with business lacked the organizational and political clout to resist the influence of these forces and the growth of these cross-class coalitions in the emerging movements. The coalitions blamed all of the country's problems on the existing ruling party, offered slogans with simple solutions, and promised that political change would overcome all problems. As with nationalist movements, this temporary unity undoubtedly smoothed the path to new multi-party democracies; but as with nationalism, it created unforeseen difficulties regarding the direction of these states after their achievement.

Take two examples. In the Congo in 1990, student support galvanized the main opposition party—the Union pour la Démocratie et le Progrès Social (Union for Democracy and Social Progress, UDPS), led by Étienne Tshisekedi—during the country's second revolution and triggered a wave of strikes and trade union militancy. But these processes took place in what the Congolese intellectual Loka Ne Kongo described in 1995 as the failure of the opposition to "organize itself to install across the country a parallel administration, police force and justice system."[73] There simply was no independent politics and organization based on the working class that could have expressed the popular desire for the immediate departure of Mobutu's dictatorship and an end to foreign domination. In those countries where the working class *did* lead the "transitions," it was unable to impose a project of radical political change on these movements. Likewise, when the working class dominated the mass movements against Zimbabwe's Mugabe for a brief moment between 1998 and 2000, the voices and activism of the middle class were softened. But with the failure of the working-class movement to maintain (and aggressively assert) political hegemony in Zimbabwe, the influence of the "middle classes and NGOs" soon dominated the MDC.

The period of democratic struggle, or "transition," as it was described in academic literature, was fraught with contradictions. By the early 1990s, the collapse of state-socialist regimes in Eastern Europe and the Soviet Union was being heralded as the "end of history" and the final victory for liberal capitalist democracy. This left many trade unionists, students, and activists without their ideological moorings. So even though the pro-democracy movements had been galvanized by resistance against structural adjustment, when new multi-party governments came to power, they invariably pursued the same policies of structural reform. There were no clear political alternatives to the Washington consensus. Movements rallied around slogans of "change" with little ideological content.

This wave of political movements took diverse forms and attracted diverse social elements, often giving rise to serious misgivings about the extent of their progressiveness among leftist commentators, particularly in areas where the populists used the religious ideologies of Islam or Christianity to mobilize support. While some of these political movements remained closely linked to working-class struggles, others, particularly those rooted in the rural areas, took on the dimensions of ethnic, tribal, and religious struggles. For example, the "great turn" toward militant Islam in the 1990s constituted a major development in northern Africa, as the popular classes discovered an "authentic" voice in which to express their profound disillusionment with capitalist development and with the corrupt and authoritarian regimes that presided over it. The possibility that these Islamist movements were also themselves corrupted by populist authoritarianism and might aim to establish even more oppressive and sectarian regimes greatly preoccupied the left. Outside observers, mesmerized by the terrorist violence of the most extreme militant Islamists, have all too often missed the very considerable variation between the different Islamist and Islamic groups and movements and the extent of popular support for the broader-based, more moderate groups—and underestimated the possibility of accommodation, complementarity, and even fusion of popular working-class movements and Islamic revolutionary traditions.[74]

One of the major results of the "dual transition" of the early 1990s was the further acceleration of economic liberalization by the new governments the pro-democracy movements had helped put in place. Opening up hitherto relatively closed economies to market forces led in most countries to local, uncompetitive companies closing, with a consequent fall in formal employment. Removing subsidies on basic goods led to a rise in the cost of living which particularly affected the poor. Introducing charges for social services such as health, education, water, and sanitation led to declines in the standard of living, literacy, and life expectancy and increases in infant mortality. The partial demolition of state-provided health services coincided with the dramatic rise of HIV/AIDS in Africa. Agricultural producers were supposed to be the main beneficiaries of liberalization; however, while some countries saw modest increases in cash-crop production, this widened the gap between the most prosperous farmers and the vast majority of poorer peasants. It also left them dependent on world market prices and placed further power in the hands of Western buyers. Although the removal of state controls on agricultural prices was widely welcomed, dismantling government agricultural support was generally damaging to farm production—the market did not step in to replace state support for, to name a few examples, fertilizer, seeds, and tools. In some countries, farm and wider business lobbies argued for re-establishing state agricultural support.

The negative effects of structural adjustment policies on many, if not most, poor Africans was evident by the late 1990s. However, it became clear that despite the achievement of formal multi-party democracy at the start of the 1990s, many elected governments were implementing economic policies that were apparently against the interests of their people. How could this apparent paradox be explained? Certainly, part of the explanation was that the democratic transition of the early 1990s was less than complete. Many countries tacked multi-party democracy onto otherwise highly authoritarian political systems that still limited effective free speech, kept parliamentary scrutiny weak, and, most importantly, left a huge amount of power in the hands of newly elected presidents. The goodwill that surrounded the pro-democracy movements allowed new leaders great leeway in decision-making and limited effective scrutiny over their power.

In this context, the agreements signed between the new African governments and the IFIs were usually secretive, not debated in

parliament, and imposed without proper democratic debate in society. As Graham Harrison put it: "Democratization in the era of
structural adjustment means that the key macroeconomic policies
which a state undertakes are not open for democratic discussion
within a country."[75] The paradox of multi-party democracy, then,
was that in many countries there was now a wide choice of political
parties, but no obvious formal political expression of alternative
economic policies. Politics became in large part about implementation, corruption, regionalism, and patronage rather than genuine
policy differences.

Conclusion: Democratic transition to what?

During the 1990s profound changes took place in most parts of
Africa, as long-standing repressive regimes were effectively challenged and overthrown or replaced. The outcome did not always
strengthen the formal structures of democracy, but the changes
generally broadened and deepened popular involvement in the political process. While John Saul and Colin Leys write despairingly
of "the tragedy of Africa," they nevertheless recognize that, in addition to the "thousands of activist groups" that constitute a vibrant
civil society in Africa today, "there are also resistances directed
more broadly and self-consciously against the kind of parasitic
governments that attempt to ride the African crisis to their own
advantage."[76] As the following chapters will show, the second part
of the decade saw a deepening and widening of democracy, if not
within the formal institutions of party politics then in the informal
arenas of urban politics, in the slums and shantytowns, in the
workplace, in the schools and colleges, and in the public spaces and
streets of the major cities.[77]

Saul became less skeptical about these waves of popular
protest and political opposition, but he continues to highlight
some of the undoubted weaknesses of these movements.[78] While
accepting that waves of protest opened up space for civil society to

operate, he argues that the results benefited the middle classes—and the neoliberal agenda—rather than popular interests; they achieve liberal democracy rather than genuine popular democracy. He was disparaging of the democratic transition, suggesting that, in most cases, it has done "little more than . . . stabilise property-threatening situations by a momentary re-circulation of elites."[79] We would, however, distinguish between those sections of the middle classes who joined and played a role in the leadership of these popular movements and the property-owning classes and political elites. It is necessary to examine the particular nature of social movement mobilization in particular circumstances, something which this book aims to do.

These changes have left African states with reduced capacity to dominate social movements as well as to respond to their demands and aspirations. Democratization, while limited or curtailed in some countries, has opened up the space available for the expression of social movements' aspirations, while not generally translating into effective influence on governmental policy-making. Globalization has reduced the extent of autonomous national sovereign decision-making, but also opened up the potential for cross-border communication and cooperation between social movements to present alternatives to neoliberal globalization. The responses of social movements in Africa to the complex and contradictory changes of the last decade is the subject of the following chapters.

CHAPTER 4

CRACKS IN THE MONOLITH:
SOCIAL MOVEMENTS IN POST-APARTHEID
SOUTH AFRICA

The mass movement against apartheid in South Africa was one of the last great liberation movements of the twentieth century and the ending of apartheid one of the century's most momentous achievements. In the country's first democratic elections in April 1994, the millions involved in the liberation movement swept the African National Congress (ANC) into government with more than 62 percent of the vote in a near-100-percent voter turnout. It is not hyperbole to say that the election of Nelson Mandela as the first Black president of South Africa was the high point of this struggle, signaling a fundamental shift in the course of South African political history. It inspired hope not only in South Africa but across the world as the global media heralded the "rainbow nation," the "miracle nation," and the "new South Africa." The early years of the transition to a non-racial liberal democracy captivated the world and were championed in a plethora of bestselling books, such as *Tomorrow is Another Country* by Alistair Sparks.[1]

Eighteen years on, a raft of political and social changes have taken place. Many of the rights long won and taken for granted in much of the world—such as the right to strike and to form political parties—are now enshrined in South African law. Beyond institutionalizing regular free and fair elections based on one person, one vote, the new Constitution of the Republic of South Africa (1996) and the Bill of Rights enacted a range of progressive changes that commit the state to combating all forms of discrimination. Built on the cornerstone of progressive liberalism, these founding documents went much further and enshrined a number of socioeconomic rights that were self-evident for much of the Black population: the right to have access to adequate housing, sufficient food and water, health care, social security, and no arbitrary evictions.[2] It imposed obligations on the new government so that "the state must take reasonable legislative and other measures, within its available resources, to achieve the progressive realization of each of these rights."[3] Crucially for the mass organizations that made up the liberation movement (trade unions, civics, women's, youth, and faith-based groups, among others), these could be enforced through law, giving citizens the right to challenge the government and hold it accountable above and beyond elections.

Since 1995, the ANC government has also presided over the biggest economic expansion in contemporary South African history, as real gross domestic product (GDP) has risen on average 3.5 percent per year and access to housing, water, and electricity increased for millions of Black people. From 1993 to 2004, the percentage of households with access to piped water and electricity for lighting rose from 59.3 to 67.8 percent and 51.9 to 80.2 percent, respectively.[4] Through social assistance, the government has distributed billions of rands to the poorest. Through child support, disability grants, and the old-age pension, the number of people receiving social grants between 1990 and 2006 rose from 2.6 to 12 million, reducing poverty among the poorest households.[5]

Yet, despite this progress, South Africa today faces a social crisis precipitated by widespread poverty and inequality, mass unemployment, and the world's largest HIV/AIDS epidemic. The fallout from this process has resulted in a state of near-permanent political infighting inside the governing Tripartite Alliance as different factions maneuver for influence.[6] Since the start of the global economic crisis in 2007, unemployment has risen to more than 31.2 percent as nearly a million jobs have been lost.[7] In the years immediately preceding the recession, approximately 5.5 million people were infected with HIV, many of them unemployed.[8] In 2009 South Africa overtook Brazil as the country with the widest gap between rich and poor, with a Gini coefficient index for income inequality of 0.679.[9] A report by the Organisation for Economic Co-operation and Development in January 2010 notes, "In sum, there is something of a consensus around the direction of post-Apartheid inequality and poverty trends even if there are disagreements about the precise levels at any point in time."[10] Using the most conservative estimate, by 2004 there were some 15.4 million people living below the R250 per capita per month poverty line.[11] Although income poverty has fallen slightly, the gap between rich and poor has grown wider as the income of the richest ten percent rose from 54 to 58 percent of total income between 1993 and 2008. Inequality within each of South Africa's four major racial groups and between groups also widened. That is, just over twenty years after Nelson Mandela's release from prison, the gap between rich and poor Africans (intra-African inequality) is bigger than the gap between white and African people.[12]

Consequently, life in post-apartheid South Africa is characterized by extremely uneven social and economic development, the result of which has been "a staggering collapse in the sense of social justice, ethics and moral values," where "the dream of a caring and compassionate society, which many fought for during the liberation struggle, has turned into a nightmare" as millions are mired in poverty.[13] Given what has been documented elsewhere in this book, it would not be unreasonable to find that those organizations and people who make up social movements have been bought off and subsumed under the political wing and largesse of the post-independence ruling party.

While the ANC acts as a monolithic bloc in the electoral arena and has attempted to use civil society to close down and crush dissent, this has not prevented factures and tensions from developing in and around the ruling Tripartite Alliance and the emergence of new, if small, constellations of social forces critical of the government. To understand how and why this has happened and to assess the political prospects of social movements, it is important to consider the interdependent processes that constitute the totality of lived experience. For example, just twelve weeks after the 2009 general election in which 65.9 percent of voters re-elected the ANC for the fourth consecutive time, the country was scandalized by a spate of riotous, violent township protests involving tens of thousands of people. While the protests caught many pundits by surprise, the complexity of South African political life and the stubborn nature of social movement protest were captured by one analyst who noted that in South Africa, "they don't just vote, they throw bricks as well."[14]

From the outset we want to make it clear that, while at a general level the breadth and depth of social movement activism is not at the levels it was in the mid-1980s at the height of the liberation movement,[15] it has, we would argue, made significant contributions to democratic life since 1994: simultaneously nurturing, cementing, and challenging the boundaries of a South African body politic by making claims and demands and by claiming ownership of and winning important social and political gains. To do so in an environment riven by the "twin virus" epidemics of mass structural unemployment and HIV/AIDS is all the more remarkable and demands our attention in much the way that the history of rebellion against apartheid did.

This brief overview, then, provides the broad contours upon which any understanding of social movements and the South African social and political landscape can be mapped and followed. To understand the role of social movements in South Africa, we need to interrogate the nature of those contours and map their genesis in the liberation movement. We begin this chapter by looking at the history and role of social movements in ending apartheid and constituting democracy up until the advent of majority rule in 1994. We then show how the liberation movement struggled to adapt to the new conditions of legality during the initial phase of the transition to democracy under the presidency of Nelson Mandela until 1999.[16] As the euphoria of the Mandela years faded, we look at how the "sharp jostle of experience" under the presidency of Thabo Mbeki gave rise to a range of new township-based organizations that clashed, collaborated, and vied with the pre-existing movements, adding to the chorus of demands for "a better life for all."[17] We then look at the period from 2007 onward, when amid a rising tide of strikes and "service delivery" protests, former Deputy President Jacob Zuma replaced Thabo Mbeki as president of the ANC and was subsequently elected as national president in April 2008, rocking South African politics. The backdrop to this was a new wave of sustained social movement activity that made South Africa one of the protest capitals of the world, showing once again that social movement activism is woven into the very fabric of South African life.

Social movements and the rise and fall of the apartheid state: 1948–1994

When the Dutch East India Company built a settlement at the Cape of Good Hope in 1652, it set in motion a distinctive capitalist mode of production, a process that resulted in the development of rural wage labor and subsequently, as "white" capital moved into mining and industry, a Black working class. Effectively forced into wage labor in farming, mining, and, increasingly, industry, the Black working class began to develop in both rural and urban areas. From the unification of South Africa in 1910 until democracy in 1994, the Black population was denied political rights based on racial status. The ruling class created social and economic structures to foster the efficient and profitable exploitation of labor, underpinned by a system of state-administered labor controls (referred to as the "pass laws" or "migrant labor system") that strictly controlled the movement of Black workers and reinforced the "color bar" that legally reserved skilled jobs for white workers. Wage labor increased as people were separated from the land by the Native Land Act of 1913; African farmers were increasingly proletarianized, resulting in an influx of landless people into urban areas.

Before the election of the National Party (NP) in 1948, growth accelerated through the expansion of industry during a period of import substitution industrialization.[18] Setting up parastatals (partially state-owned companies) like the Iron and Steel Corporation established a manufacturing base that dominated economic growth strategies up until the late 1970s and helped lay the basis for capitalist development. What was distinctive about the process of industrialization in the 1930s and 1940s was the way the government was able to help provide a cheap and strictly controlled Black working class. As import substitution industrialization continued during the 1940s, economic expansion was accompanied by an increase in the size of the workforce and demand for labor so that by 1946, the number of African people living in urban areas had risen by 36 percent from the previous decade.[19]

Historically, the rise of labor movements can be traced to times of rapid industrialization that created an urban working class of unskilled and skilled workers denied access to labor rights and social provisions. In South Africa, the ability of the white ruling class to render the majority of the Black population a permanent migrant labor force without citizenship rights depended on the successful repression of Black political and industrial organization. This in turn required both violence and a monopoly on the executive and legislative apparatus. Upon its election in 1948, the NP generalized the migrant labor system to cover the whole of the African population through a series of laws, resulting in the system of repression and control that became known as apartheid ("separate development"). Black people were denied political rights to stop them from becoming an integrated urban working class with their own trade union and political organizations, as the working classes of Western Europe and the United States had. In spite of this, and because of growing urbanization and the expansion of industry, new forms of resistance emerged and Black political and trade union organizations grew.

The contours of the liberation movement

South Africa boomed during the postwar "Golden Age" of capitalism (1950–73) and grew rapidly into a medium-sized industrial power. Between 1946 and 1975, growth averaged more than 7 percent, with employment (mainly African) in manufacturing growing faster than any other sector at 4 percent annually, from 855,000 workers in 1951 to 1.6 million in 1976.[20] The economy diversified to include a growing manufacturing industry, summoning more African skilled labor into the growing cities. South Africa's development into a technocratic state with a complex bureaucracy, managing a growing economy that provided for most white people, appeared economically sound and politically impenetrable.

However, the intensification of apartheid did trigger the development of popular organizations and protests. In the early 1950s, trade unions demanded better wages and conditions. In 1954, women in the Communist Party and the ANC founded the Federation of South African Women to campaign against the imposition of pass laws on women. The Defiance Campaign against Unjust Laws, a multi-racial civil disobedience campaign set up in 1952, sought the removal of six apartheid laws; it reached its peak with the Sharpeville massacre in 1960.[21] On June 25 and 26, 1955, three thousand activists convened a Congress of the People in Kliptown, outside Johannesburg, and adopted the Freedom Charter, a statement of the movement's central principles and demands, before being dispersed by police.[22] The same year, fourteen government-registered unions left the Trade Union Council of South Africa because it would not admit African unions and formed the South African Congress of Trade Unions (SACTU), which became closely linked to the ANC. Notwithstanding this, general repression and harsh laws governing protest and trade union organization resulted in little overt challenge to apartheid in the late 1950s and early 1960s, with strikes virtually unheard of. A period of political and industrial stability ensued. Rapid industrial development had altered the size, racial composition, and skill levels of the growing labor force. The Black population was diverse and stratified by class and gender. Drawn into urban areas, these people—migrants, the lumpenproletariat (township and rural unemployed), and an industrial working class, together with sections of the petit bourgeoisie and students—came to form the mass base of the liberation movement. This process had a political effect on the ability of people to organize; industrial expansion, technological change (one consequence of which was continuing high levels of both rural and urban unemployment), and "better" education facilitated agitating and organizing opportunities. The denial of basic human rights to the vast majority, along with increased racism, segregation, and oppression of Black people, generated profound social repercussions. This gave rise to an independent labor movement and other civic and township-based organizations that were to form the backbone of a liberation movement that could now articulate popular mass-based demands.

A wave of mass strikes between 1973 and 1976, creating a climate of revolt that spread across the country as student activists began to forge links with workers through discussions about wage levels, legal advice, and organizing. The context was the impact of the global recession of the mid-1970s that reverberated and developed into the deepest and longest recession in South African history. In response to the onset of crisis, the nationalist stage of state-led development gave way to a monetarist phase—and to a growing and more militant opposition.[23] This crisis displacement fueled protests, particularly by the growing and increasingly organized Black working class after the years of repression in the 1950s and 1960s.[24] Newly formed organizations pulled together trade unionists, previously unorganized workers, intellectuals, and students. They emphasized rank-and-file factory organization, with a view to building strong factory-based unions and stressing wider political concerns in the longer term. This laid the basis for a new generation of trade unions and a period of industrial militancy that profoundly destabilized the apartheid economy.

The workplace was not the only area where conflict and protest developed. Education was segregated and unequal before apartheid; the increase in Black education was intended to provide the country with a bigger skilled workforce linked to the changing nature of the economy and the labor process.[25] The recession hit the poorest hardest. Unemployment climbed to a record two million; in 1975 the cost of living for a family of five in Soweto increased by 10 to 12 percent.[26] The police shooting of Soweto schoolchildren on June 16, 1976 marked the beginning of eighteen months of national revolt.[27] Anger and frustration dovetailed with the political work of Black consciousness groups like the South African Students Organization, led by Steve Biko, giving expression to the anger at the heart of a generation of young African people in Soweto. The riots served to bring a section of the working-class community together by fusing disparate individuals into a collective. The Soweto Uprising radicalized many students; some went on to become union activists in the workplace, where demands could be backed up by direct action in the form of strikes.[28]

Politically, the late 1970s and early 1980s marked a rise in the dominance of ANC (often simply called Congress) politics within the growing liberation movement, but also the growing role of new trade unions such as the Federation of South African Trade Unions (FOSATU). Formed in 1979, FOSATU represented a new development on the left. It was politically independent of the ANC and the South African Communist Party (SACP) and their now-exiled trade union wing SACTU. FOSATU emphasized working-class politics and the strategic importance of an organized working class to force change; its activists, working in unions like the National

Union of Textile Workers and the National Union of Metal Workers South Africa, were often accused of being "workerist" or "economistic." Congress activists characterized this as a form of class politics that reduced the democratic aspect of the struggle against apartheid to a working-class struggle against "capital," thus reducing class struggle to economic struggle. They saw trade unions such as FOSATU as idealizing the essential form of socialist organization, with scant regard for other forms of political and community organization.

However, other "community unions" were indeed influenced by SACTU; they used mass mobilizations to build strikes, forge links with local communities, and display an overtly political profile that promoted the ANC. This period was a major turning point in the struggle against apartheid: it demonstrated the willingness, courage, and confidence of African people to physically confront the army and police and it shattered the relative social and political stability that had characterized South African politics since the Sharpeville massacre of 1960. Linking the militancy of the youth in the townships with independent working-class organizations created the embryo of a mass social movement that would challenge the regime in the 1980s.

Reform, repression, and revolt: The 1980s

The 1980s gave birth to the third major period of large-scale popular unrest since the early 1970s, culminating in two states of emergency and the founding of the Congress of South African Trade Unions (COSATU), the biggest trade union in African history. The decade began with a boycott by twenty-five thousand students in Cape Town that spread across the country. Black workers' organizations launched countrywide strike actions on a scale not seen since 1973. Another recession began in 1982, and the ruling class began imposing monetarist policies such as tax cuts for the wealthy, cuts in food subsidies for the poor, and a 7 percent sales tax on basic goods that penalized the Black working class. That working class was growing: the number of African workers employed in production was now more than two million.[29] The growth of the independent unions and the wider liberation movement was aided by the founding of the National Union of Mineworkers, with forty thousand members.

In the townships, housing provision had not kept pace with industrial expansion since the 1960s, municipal infrastructure was poor, and there was little electrification and social provision.[30] Government fiscal problems—worsened by economic recession and guided by a monetarist diktat in response to the ongoing structural economic crisis—kept social spending to a minimum in order to reduce state expenditure. The regime attempted to sow divisions among Africans by extending property rights to stimulate the growth of a Black middle class, but this strategy failed because building funds for housing had to be raised through a Black Local Authority (BLA). Rejected by the liberation movement as a substitute for proper representation, BLAs were an attempt by the apartheid regime to establish "autonomy" through local government structures for African residents of urban areas. Yet, as government economic policy was now informed by monetarism, BLAs received less government funding and sought to generate revenue through rent increases and service charges that worsened with the economy.

Like the independent unions, township-based civic organizations—known as "civics"—took advantage of government reforms and mobilized around local issues such as rent increases, evictions, and problems with water, electricity, roads, and street lighting. In a further attempt to use political reform to stave off more revolt, President P. W. Botha set up a new constitution and a tricameral parliament that included Indians and Coloureds for the first time, a measure calculated to divide the opposition. Again, this allowed the liberation movement to mobilize and politicize against a reform, thus revitalizing previously dormant organizations such as the Indian Congress. This mobilization eventually led to the formation of the United Democratic Front (UDF) in August 1983.[31]

The aim of the UDF was to link civics and other organizations both nationally and regionally and to provide leadership in broader political campaigns in order "to unite a broadest possible spectrum of people across class and color lines."[32] A popular alliance that drew on ANC traditions of non-racialism and Christianity, its formation was part of the ANC leadership's attempt to influence the growing liberation movement. As UDF co-president Albertina Sisulu explained, "The UDF formation was pushed by the leaders when the leaders saw the people getting out of hand."[33] Linking with trade unions, they built solidarity and consumer boycotts and became a prominent force in the campaign to boycott local government elections. This also reflected the ANC-led Congress Alliance tactic of linking township, social justice, and workers' rights organizations in popular and multi-class alliances.

The history of building multi-class popular alliances goes back to the African nationalist leadership of the ANC under Nelson Mandela, Walter Sisulu, and Oliver Tambo in the 1950s. Recognizing that industrialization and urbanization were changing the social composition of African society, they sought to build alliances with trade unions and working-class township communities. This strategy dovetailed with that of the Communist Party, which, under orders from Moscow, pursued a "people's front" that brought together differing social groups to strengthen national liberation. This meant dropping its earlier radical criticisms of nationalism. After 1950, the Communist Party, working inside the ANC, began to push its arguments for "revolutionary nationalism" as a prelude to socialism, linking this justification to its theory of "colonialism of a special type." Briefly, this theory argued that Black South Africa was a colony of white oppressors, so its first objective had to be national liberation—linked to which was a two-stage approach to socialism. The first stage, national liberation, would be led by the ANC, and the second, socialism, by the SACP.[34] This theory gave priority to the struggle for a "national democratic revolution"—one person, one vote, in a unitary state. The growing alliance between the two organizations gave the ANC political access to a bigger and broader social group of poorer Africans and workers. This early marriage of socialist and African nationalist ideas set the political tone for the direction of the African labor movement until the rise of the independent trade unions like FOSATU in the early 1970s.

So, despite the mass action of the mid-1980s and the ANC's association with the SACP, which gave its politics a socialist gloss, the ANC leadership-in-exile played little part in mobilizations. ANC activists and supporters were nevertheless involved in all manner of struggles, and the leadership-in-exile made renewed efforts to relate to the unions and others through key positions in COSATU. Primarily, the ANC's long relationship with the SACP helped it connect with growing demands for "socialism" in the trade union movement. The ANC also related to its mass base by setting up popular fronts such as the UDF, through which it could internally popularize itself and the national democratic revolution. In the mid- and late 1980s, "the dominant position within the ANC remained one that emphasises alliance building and contesting the so-called middle ground, through nation building and reconciliation—implying a nationalist alliance with differing social groups."[35] This suggests that trade union and other struggles, partially directed from exile, were aimed, at best, at "servicing broad class coalitions" (popular fronts—strategic alliances with other classes, especially business) that sought to focus social and economic demands into demands for national elections.[36]

However, "workerists" in and around FOSATU argued that popular fronts would mean that workers' interests would come second to those of the "liberal" or more "progressive" sections of business. In the factories, mines, and offices, they argued, workers can begin to develop the collective power to end exploitation, whereas political struggles that coalesced around community politics did not have the same social weight as workers at the point of production—and so were often crushed. This was no academic debate. The differences raised important questions about what strategies and tactics could best be used to articulate the concerns of the Black majority. Congress (or populist) politics eventually more or less won the day, especially with the formation of COSATU in late 1985, and began to dominate the liberation movement.

The exiled leadership of the ANC, who had fled the country for fear of persecution, attempted to turn the campaign by Umkhonto we Sizwe (Spear of the Nation or MK, the ANC's armed wing) into a "people's war" and called for Black people to make the country "ungovernable" by creating "liberated zones" in the townships. Creating expectations of imminent and armed insurrection, the ANC national executive proclaimed 1986 the "Year of Umkhonto we Sizwe." Ideologically, the ANC, now the unofficial leading organization of the liberation movement, seemed more uncompromising and clear that a political system under its leadership would be "people's democracy" and that in accordance with the tenets of the Freedom Charter, it would seize the "commanding heights of the economy" and nationalize them. Despite such revolutionary rhetoric and renewed efforts to connect with mass action, however, at another level the ANC advocated negotiations.[37]

The ongoing social conditions for major confrontation—rent increases and workers' and students' grievances—gave rise to strikes, protests, and violence across the country between 1984 and 1986.[38] In October 1984, up to two hundred thousand students around Johannesburg (the area known today as Gauteng) boycotted school. The unions and civics organized a stay-away (a form of protest similar to a general strike) around worker, civic, and student issues in which eight hundred thousand people participated, with more than 90 percent of workers in unionized plants taking action and as many as four hundred thousand students boycotting school.[39] A two-day stay-away in November 1984 signified a new phase in the history of protest against apartheid as opposition organizations jointly coordinated action. Economic grievances came together with community and student unrest, with unions playing a leading role. This was "a milestone in the history of resistance as it was the first time since the 1950s a regional stay-away had been organized by a formal alliance of industrial unions and political organization."[40] The regime declared a state of emergency in July 1985, detaining eight thousand people and charging twenty-two thousand with protest-related offenses in the first eight months of the emergency.[41] The formation of the UDF, the SACP, and the formal alliance in exile of the ANC (whose prestige grew massively in this period) represented the slow crystallization of a mass social movement of opposition increasingly dominated by Congress politics. The movement was consolidated and strengthened when at the end of 1985 COSATU was formed, with thirty-five affiliates representing nearly half a million members beneath a banner proclaiming "Workers of the World Unite!"[42]

Striking back: The 1986 strike waves

The partial state of emergency lifted in March 1986 was reimposed in June and in the year that followed, twenty-six thousand people were detained. There were mass arrests, beatings, torture, and political assassinations.[43] The ruling class was under pressure to restore order and the basis for capital accumulation.[44] The police and army rounded up and imprisoned, without trial, a core group of one hundred trade union activists, underscoring the importance and power of COSATU. Yet the resilience of the liberation movement, particularly organized labor, was self-evident. Despite some of the harshest repression in South African history, by the end of 1986 there had been 793 strikes involving 424,340 strikers, an increase of approximately 43 percent compared to 1985.[45] Mass strikes and protests dominated social life; "By mid-1986 it seemed that . . . revolution was 'around the corner.'"[46]

Yet severe repression dealt a devastating blow to sections of the liberation movement, as street committees and UDF and civics' strongholds collapsed. In townships such as Alexandra (near Johannesburg) and Crossroads (near Cape Town), which were at the forefront of protests between 1984 and 1986, pro-regime groups regained control. Despite this, workers were still ready to fight. In 1987, half a million workers struck for more than six million working days, including the giant mineworkers' union, which carried out the largest strike in South African history up to that point.[47] Consequently, as civics and other community-based organizations were marginalized by repression, COSATU found itself carrying the mantle of the fight against the regime. It could fall back upon the locals and shop-floor structures—the core activist base developed in previous years.

As the end of the 1980s approached, structural economic faults continued to give rise to fiscal and general economic crisis and weakened the regime's ability and confidence to set the agenda. At times, townships such as Alexandra were in a state of near-permanent siege. In an attempt to regain the initiative and shore up votes for an upcoming general election, the regime attacked COSATU's offices. Police seized copies of its news magazine and even bombed COSATU House. COSATU set up a "living wage" campaign and together with the UDF used the election as an opportunity to signal their defiance. (COSATU and the UDF now routinely issued joint public statements, signifying the hegemony of the ANC.) The result was that 1.5 million workers and around a million students took part in demonstrations, underscoring the mass basis of the opposition to the regime and support for the (still-banned) ANC.

The regime responded with legislation banning sympathy strikes and, in February 1988, banned seventeen anti-apartheid organizations. The UDF and COSATU were prohibited from taking part in political activity. This did not prevent the biggest stay-away protest in South African history: three million people took part in a three-day protest in June. The general election to confirm F. W. De Klerk as president proved to be a turning point in National Party history: its 1987 majority of eighty in the House of Assembly was cut to twenty in September 1989. On September 6 and 7, 1989, as white South Africans went to the polls, two to three million workers took part in a stay-away. Hundreds of thousands of Coloured and Indian people boycotted the election, signaling the ongoing resilience of the liberation movement.[48] In particular, the confidence and organizational strength of the labor movement was reflected in the fact that more labor days were lost through work stoppages between 1986 and 1990 than in the previous seventy-five years.[49]

The country was politically unstable, and with the economy showing no signs of recovery, President De Klerk was under pressure from business to provide stable conditions for capital accumulation. Externally the regime had been stalled, in effect defeated in Angola by government and Cuban troops at the battle of Cuito Cuanavale in May 1988. This shifted the military balance of power in Southern Africa away from Pretoria, eventually forcing the apartheid regime to grant Namibia independence. As the international sanctions that began in 1985 continued, capital flight deprived business of much-needed investment, putting huge pressure on the regime to find a workable solution to the continuing political crisis of legitimacy, representation, and rule. South Africa's economic woes increasingly required a political solution. Events beyond Pretoria proved the tipping point as the Eastern bloc collapsed in 1989, removing the international communist threat of which the regime had perceived the liberation movement to be the local flag bearers. On October 15, 1989, De Klerk announced the release of eight high-ranking ANC and MK political prisoners.

The ongoing recession had reached its deepest nadir by 1988–89. In August, the ANC launched a new Defiance Campaign to demonstrate to the regime the depth of its popular support and so present itself as the force that represented the Black majority. The civics, too, revived, their numbers swelling to approximately two thousand by the end of 1989; that year there were forty-nine rent and bond boycotts in the Transvaal's eighty-two townships.[50] This was the political backdrop to the Conference for a Democratic Future, held in December 1989 by liberation groups. The tone of discussion papers at the conference suggested that the path ahead would be that of negotiation as they endorsed, despite fierce discussions, the Harare Declaration, a document that made explicit the ANC's desire for a negotiated settlement, thus presenting the ANC as the head of the liberation movement. The process of struggle against apartheid had reached a point where the *Financial Times* could write: "What once seemed impossible now appears likely: the release of Mr. Nelson Mandela in an atmosphere of relative calm; the beginning of negotiations which will lead to some form of franchise for blacks."[51]

From grassroots to government, 1990–1994

With many anti-apartheid organizations unbanned and key leaders such as Nelson Mandela released from prison, the ANC became the de facto political representative of the liberation movement. While representing the liberation movement in negotiations with the regime, the actions of the ANC leadership can be understood as those of a "government-in-waiting" wanting to achieve a political solution that ensured long-term stability for itself. We know from the preceding chapters that transitions from liberation movement to independence party were underpinned by policy changes made in light of the strategic context. For the ANC, the political landscape upon which the liberation struggle had been fought was being transformed.

Though the ANC leadership was not committed to socialism, like many African national liberation movements it viewed the Soviet Union as some sort of model or check on US imperialism. The collapse of Eastern-bloc "communism" deprived the ANC of material and ideological support, and the variants of capitalism to which it could look to for guidance were limited. Other Third World state-led capitalist governments were under increasing pressure to reform along the lines of the emerging neoliberal Washington consensus. The weakness of the independent left inside the liberation movement meant that an alternative guide to practice and policy was missing. Consequently, the ANC's strategy shifted so that "any compromise became tolerable if it did not block majority rule."[52] For the ANC leadership, this required concessions to avoid a political backlash and to convince the white bourgeoisie and international investors it could be trusted to govern. This also meant controlling its supporters, especially militant mass organizations like COSATU.

While the ANC, preoccupied with ending apartheid, had no substantial economic policy, its initial suggestions echoed work done by COSATU's Economic Trends Group captured in the notion of economic "growth through redistribution." This was in contradistinction to the "redistribution through growth" (trickle-down) ideas that reflected neoliberalism—many of which found their way into the ANC's 1990 "Discussion Document on Economic Policy" that formed the basis for controversial Growth Employment and Redistribution (GEAR) policy in 1996. Again, this was no academic debate. With a euphoric liberation movement—with COSATU at its heart—differences were not purely "technical realities" but constituted an element of the ongoing class struggle in ideological terms.

The process was not uncontested inside the Alliance. However, with SACP activists putting forward a "left version" of the two-stage theory of national democratic revolution (NDR)—liberal democracy first, "socialism" later—to justify tactical changes, what independent opposition existed was not able to mobilize others around its demands, and so critical voices were marginalized. Insofar as COSATU's leadership were predominantly SACP activists, they were committed to the NDR. In this way, the role of SACP activists inside COSATU was crucial. Without any fundamental or credible opposition to the left as an ideological and organizational counterweight, the shift was easier. The SACP's attempt to "de-Stalinize" the party in the process of democratically remaking itself suggests why so many independent ("workerist") activists, such as former FOSATU general secretary Joe Foster and former leaders of the National Union of Metalworkers of South Africa Moses Mayekiso and

Enoch Godongwana, joined the ANC and SACP. We can only speculate whether the failure of the independent left to build a political and organizational alternative in the workplaces and townships was one of the reasons behind its failure to counter the general direction of COSATU and the transition led by the ANC.[53]

Tensions remained. One hundred and twenty thousand people greeted Mandela at an unannounced rally at FNB stadium in Johannesburg on February 12, 1990, the day after his release, a striking symbol of the expectations for change. The significance of these dramatic days was not lost on those who took to the streets. This was not mere jubilation; it was political, as workers called for, among other things, a living wage and union recognition. As workers presented Mandela with a gift of a red car, symbolic of their aspirations, Moses Mayekiso stated, "We look to comrade Mandela to initiate a process of political settlement which will incorporate the needs and aspirations of workers."[54]

As the ANC leadership edged closer to elected office, they deemed their more militant strategies of the 1980s inappropriate as the organization underwent its own transition to a party geared to electoral politics and government. In his autobiography, Mandela recalls seeing at a protest rally of two hundred thousand in June 1992, after the murder of forty-six people in Boipatong by supporters of the Inkatha Freedom Party, banners that read, "Mandela give us guns" and "Victory through battle not talk," and thinking "it was time to cool things down." Some ANC leaders called for abandoning negotiations, but he argued that "there was no alternative to this process."[55] This revealed the dilemmas and tensions the ANC leadership faced, their general commitment to negotiations, and how they viewed mass action. This was expressed by ANC deputy president Walter Sisulu: "We've got to get it across to people that we cannot work miracles, that we cannot overnight provide a house and a job for everyone—yet somehow we must keep their trust that we will try our best to improve everyone's lives."[56] Nonetheless, the ANC used its leadership role to pressure the regime. A stay-away of four million workers in August 1992 was the largest political strike in South African history—demonstrating the willingness of the masses to take action.

Different sections of the liberation movement were also gearing up for the elections. COSATU held a special congress demonstrating its evolution to strategic unionism—a strategy through which the labor movement engages on an institutional level with the state and business to effect economic and political reforms. The ANC adopted the COSATU-inspired Reconstruction and Development Programme (RDP) as the centerpiece of its electoral platform. Keynesian in tone, the RDP was the program for a "new South Africa": a pledge to build one million low-cost homes, provide electricity to 2.5 million houses by the year 2000, and provide running water and sewage systems to one million households. The potential clearly existed for COSATU to forge a working relationship with the ANC and influence the policy-making process, and the RDP encouraged this: "The RDP is focused on our people's most immediate needs, and it relies, in turn, on their energies to drive the process of meeting these needs . . . the people of South Africa must together shape their own future. Development is not about the delivery of goods to a passive citizenry. It is about active involvement and growing empowerment."[57]

As the ANC made increasing references to the role of markets and failed to make specific commitments to nationalization, tensions persisted. Leading ANC activist Tokyo Sexwale (now Minister of Human Settlements) noted, "If you give them politics, a flag . . . and you think that's change, you are merely preparing for a second, more deadly revolution."[58] The pace of events quickened after the assassination of SACP leader Chris Hani on April 10, 1993. Two stay-aways and huge marches, organized in six days in response to Hani's murder, gained 90 percent support in the Pretoria-Witwatersrand-Vereeniging area (now Gauteng) and around 88 percent in Natal (now KwaZulu-Natal), demonstrating that the ANC was indeed a government-in-waiting. In June 1993, elections were set for April 27,

1994. The ANC commenced its elections campaign in February 1994 and tens of thousands of COSATU shop stewards and other activists from social movements became a major driving force; COSATU handed over all of its offices and full-time staff to ANC election teams. Finally, a strike by civil servants in Bophuthatswana homeland in February quickly turned into a full-scale uprising as students and sections of the police and army joined workers, and the "Bop" Uprising in March became the last turning point on the path to elections.

From liberation to liberalization: April 1994–June 1999

The political dimension of the crisis of apartheid rule was broadly solved in April when the ANC won 252 of the 400 seats in the National Assembly and an overall majority in all but two of the provincial elections. The elections were a victory for South African social movements, who expected President Mandela and the RDP to begin solving the economic and social legacies of apartheid and to draft a new Constitution that would repeal apartheid legislation and enshrine equality before the law. Yet as we have seen, the evolution of the ANC and its policies represented a shift to the political center. Its resemblance to a traditional social-democratic party was reinforced when Mandela retained the NP's finance minister, Derek Keys. In doing so, he "delighted investors, businessmen and white South Africans . . . the outside world . . . [with] his commitment to free-market economic and political moderation."[59]

The ANC government set about establishing a new relationship with the external world, structured by South Africa's location in the international division of labor and the post-1989 historical context. A process of political change was initiated in which the NDR was institutionalized, although, as we shall see, this was marked by political conflict and ideological disagreement within the Alliance and through the emergence of post-apartheid social movements, particularly from 1999 onwards. The "New South Africa" was re-classed as an "emerging market"; with the economy growing by 3.3 percent in 1995, poverty reduction became increasingly conditional upon a more orthodox economic strategy of "redistribution through growth." Business leaders pressured the government to make the economy more competitive, aware that this would "almost certainly require a showdown with the country's big trade unions."[60] This was signaled by a nurses' strike in October and November 1995 over poor pay and working conditions that gave an early glimpse of disillusionment with the new government and the belief that politicians were jumping aboard a "gravy train" to enrich themselves. Nurses proclaimed, "We refuse to subsidise the government and their fancy cars. Viva RDP. We want some gravy."[61]

In March 1996 the office overseeing the implementation of the RDP was closed and passed to the deputy state president, Thabo Mbeki. This was quickly followed in June by the release of a new macroeconomic strategy called GEAR, whose cornerstone was "fiscal discipline, tax concessions, moves towards scrapping exchange controls, sale of state assets and increasing flexibility in the labor market."[62] The fiscal policies in GEAR contradicted the ANC's aims for social equity proposals as set out in the RDP. Although GEAR was based upon creating 833,000 jobs through a growth rate of 6.1 percent over four years, this was dependent upon attracting foreign direct investment.[63] One element of this was to reduce trade tariffs and export subsidies, exposing South African companies to foreign competition, particularly Chinese, and world markets, in the process exacerbating tensions with labor.

Business leaders hailed GEAR as "investor friendly"; the *Economist* praised the ANC government for introducing a "conservative macroeconomic policy" and reassured investors that "for all the fears that resentful ANC socialists would confiscate wealth, the new breed shares the same capitalist aspirations as the old."[64] While the SACP leadership praised the ANC for resisting "free-market dogmatism" and keeping a key economic role for the public sector, COSATU reflected some of the unease workers had with the government, although complaints from the left centered on GEAR not being discussed first in Alliance structures. Other critics noted that GEAR "represented as much a form of self-imposed structural adjustment as anything else" and that this was not the start of the ANC's slide to neoliberalism, "but was the aggregate of drifts" since the party's un-banning in 1990.[65] A showdown between the COSATU and the ANC government seemed inevitable.

In 1997 the economy only grew by 1.7 percent, and 142,000 jobs were lost even as the labor force grew by 320,000.[66] In social policy, major pieces of legislation were enacted, principally the Housing Act of 1997, which repealed apartheid housing legislation. The government began working toward its goal of building a million houses within five years by providing a means-tested housing subsidy of up to fifteen thousand rands. This was enough to build a "starter dwelling," but people had to raise further finance through bank loans. Between April 1994 and December 1997 more than seven hundred thousand subsidies had been processed, but only 385,000 houses were built or under construction. The RDP target was effectively scrapped, as the Housing Department took to combining the number of houses built and the number under construction. Housing, one of the key planks of the RDP, began to cause much consternation in community and labor circles.

"Normalizing" labor relations

Like other post-liberation ruling parties discussed elsewhere in this book, the ANC government did not waste time in trying to co-opt organized labor so as to regularize the relationship between labor and business as part of an attempt to create political and economic stability. COSATU leaders from the liberation movement were made ANC members of parliament and given jobs in government departments. A raft of legislation relating to labor was passed. The first was the Labor Relations Act (1995)—which COSATU supported despite its concerns. This law regulated relations between employers and employees and introduced a new system for resolving disputes—the

Commission for Conciliation, Mediation, and Arbitration. The Basic Conditions of Employment Act (1997) entitled all employees to basic conditions such as a maximum forty-five-hour working week; the Employment Equity Act (1998) gave practical expression to affirmative action. Although these changes enshrined in the new Constitution the right of employers to hire "scab" labor, the sanctity of capitalist social relations, and private property, they were welcomed by COSATU and many workers.[67]

Incorporating the existing labor leadership into corporatist bargaining arrangements to avoid conflict was another aspect of the ANC's strategy. The introduction of the National Economic Development and Labour Council tied shop stewards into a bureaucratic process of negotiations that forestalled action and effectively pressured the COSATU leadership and shop stewards into "policing" their own members. This was part of a wider restructuring of industrial relations designed to coerce union officials into controlling the rank and file and to "normalize" industrial relations in ways similar to those found in Western Europe. COSATU called a national general strike on June 4, 1997, to protest government proposals on basic employment rights in the Basic Conditions of Employment Act (1997). At the first post-election COSATU Congress in September 1997, Mandela tried to get COSATU to give GEAR a chance "but was openly snubbed by angry delegates." The Congress unequivocally rejected GEAR.[68]

In December 1997, Thabo Mbeki took over from Nelson Mandela as leader of the ANC, effectively securing him as president after the June 1999 elections. Between 1996 and 1998, most of the targets set in GEAR were missed. Instead of economic growth, GDP fell from 3.2 percent in 1996 to 1.7 in 1997 and 0.1 in 1998. Instead of new jobs being created, job losses were 71,000, 126,000, and 186,000. Economic growth hinged on private sector investment, but shrank to minus 0.7 percent in 1998.[69] Trade liberalization meant that clothing, textile, and shoe manufacturers shed 22,000 workers (predominantly women) in 1998, and there was a net loss of 120,000 jobs between 1998 and 1999.[70] The rand crashed amid the Russian and East Asian financial crisis and in a further bid to attract foreign direct investment (now four times lower than in 1997) the corporation tax was cut from 35 to 30 percent (it was 48 percent in 1994). In November 1998, the government provoked further controversy that still haunts it today by announcing a thirty-billion-rand arms deal in which newly created Black empowerment companies would be boosted. Strikes increased, mainly around wages, putting further pressure on the government; the number of strike days, 3.8 million, was four times higher than 1997, although still not at the levels of the 1980s.[71] Some strikes, notably those by teachers, municipal workers, and state utility workers, had an anti-privatization—and therefore "political"—element to them. Other strikes turned violent, such as one in July 1998 over job cuts linked to privatization in which airport workers fought pitched battles on the tarmac at Johannesburg Airport. One week later, striking miners set fire to a utility headquarters.

In terms of social policy, the Treatment Action Campaign (TAC) launched on International Human Rights Day on December 10, 1998, to address the government's failure to provide medical and other support for the growing number of people living with HIV. While it went largely unnoticed at the time, TAC has gone on to become one of the most successful social movements. Building on the traditions of the anti-apartheid movement, it has built popular alliances with a range of forces like COSATU and the South African Council of Churches. Although not set up to challenge the government, it set about using allies in key places, including the state and the legal system, and took advantage of the new democratic freedoms to pressure the government. In the process, among other things, it forced the government to provide free antiretroviral medicines for people living with HIV.[72]

Although the ANC government missed many of the targets in the RDP and presided over the loss of half a million jobs in the first five years, voters demonstrated the extent of their loyalty in the 1999 general election by re-electing the ANC with 66.35 percent, thus surpassing April 1994.[73] Would there be any change in the direction of the ANC under the stewardship of President Thabo Mbeki?[74] Previous internal critics of the party, such as Winnie Madzikzela-Mandela, publicly said yes: Mbeki would be more radical.[75] However, doing away with the legacy of apartheid would necessitate an increase in expenditure on housing and other social provision. Yet, by sticking to the provisions in GEAR, the government was constrained within its own conservative spending limits. Soon after the release of the ANC 1999 election manifesto, ANC deputy president Jacob Zuma said, "Nothing was going to change in terms of government policy."[76] Additionally, "senior politicians, including Mbeki himself, have not given any indicators they will compromise and have instead promised financial markets accelerated implementation of GEAR." The corollary and contradiction is that, as *Business Day* noted, "although the ANC commits itself to increased social expenditure in the manifesto, the government has given no indication of reviewing its fiscal deficit upwards"—in other words, there were no plans to increase government spending.[77] Just six weeks after the general election, tensions spilled over onto the streets in August as one million public sector workers struck. They were angry because the government, as an employer and signatory to the International Labor Organization, was violating conventions by ignoring the collective bargaining process. At the center of differences over wages and plans to "restructure" the public sector was the government's GEAR policy.

Storm clouds gather over the Rainbow Nation

The advent of liberal democracy in South Africa took place under the leadership of an ANC government that accepted neoliberal policies as the best way to address the legacy of apartheid. It created corporatist institutions to restructure the relationships between state and society (including capital and labor) in an attempt to make South African capitalism more competitive. While formal rights and a liberal constitution represented progress, many problems and tensions remained. Uneven economic growth meant that racial inequalities persisted and were exacerbated by class, with the growth of a new Black middle class intensifying the inequality. Between 1991 and 1996, the proportion of Black households in the top 10 percent of all households increased from 9 to 22 percent; the richest 10 percent of Black people received an average 17-percent increase in income, while the poorest 40 percent of households experienced a decline of 20 percent. Much of this decline was concentrated in the period from 1994 to 1996.[78]

The re-election of the ANC in June 1999 could not simply be taken as a complete vindication of its work since 1994. The major cause of friction between the government and social movements, particularly labor, was GEAR. The credibility of GEAR (and by extension the government) depended on investors' belief that the policy could be maintained; this required disciplining labor, which created tensions. As the new millennium approached, economic policy was the area of greatest contestation. This gave rise to conflict inside the Alliance, particularly with COSATU, but it also created the conditions that framed the emergence of a number of post-apartheid social movements. In the next section, we will document how this also created a new structure of opportunity for agitation and mobilization in and around the Alliance, as the expectations generated during the liberation struggle and the initial transition phase of democracy fueled rights-based claims.

New millennium, new movements

Globally, the 1990s began with the collapse of "communism" and the rallying cry of "there is no alternative" to the free market. Yet, paradoxically, the decade ended with the November 1999 "Battle of Seattle," the coming-out party of the global anticapitalist movement, with its rallying cry "another world is possible." Similarly, commentators could be forgiven for being puzzled by the emergence of post-apartheid social movements under the ANC government.[79] However, when understood as a response to the local manifestation of neoliberalism expressed in GEAR, these movements' development begins to make sense. As we noted in chapter 2, they are a key component of the global and continental response to the impact of neoliberal capitalism on the lives of working-class people.[80]

Particularly after 1999, a range of locally based social movements emerged across the country. Community-based organizations such as the Anti-Privatization Forum (APF) and the Soweto Electricity Crisis Committee in Gauteng, the Concerned Citizens Forum in KwaZulu-Natal, and the Anti-Eviction Campaign (AEC) in the Western Cape were an attempt to coordinate working-class people's struggles against the ANC's relentless commodification and privatization of basic services. Early on, two key national events helped to put these organizations on the political map and broadly situated them in an adversarial relationship with both the ANC government and the Alliance. The first was a march of twenty thousand people outside the United Nations World Conference against Racism in Durban in August 2001; the second, a march of twenty-five thousand in September 2002 outside the World Summit on Sustainable Development.[81] The first, under the banner of the Durban Social Forum, was significant because it was the first large-scale, explicitly anti-government protest. The importance of the second, under the banner Social Movements United (led by the Social Movements Indaba Council), was that it was larger than an Alliance march at the same event and embarrassed the government in front of a global audience.[82] What these organizations and protests demonstrated to the world (and the growing global anticapitalist movement) was the turbulent and contested nature of life in the Rainbow Nation.

What fueled some of the anger was plain to see. Ten years after the first democratic elections, the Labour Research Services Bargaining Indicators noted that directors received on average annual increases of 29 percent while workers received 6.5 percent—barely keeping up with inflation. The percentage of national income going to capital rose, giving rise to popular claims that "the rich are getting richer and the poor are getting poorer."[83] In the context of executive directors receiving 111 times more than the minimum wage, Kevin Wakeford, managing director of Growth Africa, concluded that "economic policies have in fact been slanted in the favor of big business and at times they got away with murder." He argued that the working class and the unemployed, among others, "have patiently endured the hegemony of big business influence during the past decade."[84]

That the ANC strategy had not worked was implicitly recognized when, in the absence of private sector investment, President Mbeki announced in his 2004 state of the nation address that he would use state enterprises such as Telkom and Eskom to create enhanced conditions for doing business. The *Financial Mail* noted that "the mandate from Mbeki is unequivocal: make public corporations central to economic development and enable business to thrive through better service and cost-effective policies."[85] Effectively, this was a fine-tuning of GEAR, not a rejection of it. That rising inequality was a structural feature in the new South Africa was indicated by the Labor Research Services report and by a newspaper report that Patrice Motsepe (a Black mine owner) had, over ten years, amassed four billion rand in assets.[86]

No sooner had the stages been taken down after a series of government-choreographed events celebrating ten years of democracy than people were marching in the streets, as the country was engulfed in a number of violent strikes and protests. A number of events signified the growing scale of community-based protests and social movement actions. In September 2005, five thousand people, led by the recently formed Abahlali baseMjondolo (Shack Dwellers Movement, ABM), marched from the Kennedy Road informal settlement in Durban.[87] Targeting the ANC council, they called for the resignation of their local councilor due to a lack of housing and poor service delivery. ABM has since attempted to develop links with other rural-based peoples and unemployed movements across the country.[88] In February 2006 in Gauteng, people from Khutsong protested over their proposed transfer to the largely rural North West province municipality, fearful that this would decrease their chances of accessing municipal services such as water and electricity. After weeks of intensely violent community-wide protests, an incredible 99 percent of nearly thirty thousand local residents abstained from voting in the 2006 local government elections.

The fall of Mbeki and the breaking of the neoliberal consensus

By the end of 2006, there were on average approximately six thousand township and community protests a year, a greater rate than any other country in the world outside of China. That they were often, but not solely, organized by SACP and ANC militants is a strategic reminder to those who had written off the Alliance and many of the activists it comprises "as the mainstays of government policy" and for failing "to offer any meaningful responses to the changing conditions."[89] These protests, commonly referred to as "service delivery" protests, reflect a broader re-emergence of working-class action. A key turning point was the violent security guard strike of 2006. Although it was defeated practically, it reflected more than a fitful awakening. This was the start of an important convergence. While social movements and community revolts involved, in general, unemployed and informal workers, union militants were active in these movements, if not always leading the community-based struggles, as organized trade unionists.

The year 2006 signaled the revival of the organized working class, protesting in their communities and striking in the workplaces. Between 2003 and 2006, the number of days lost to strikes rose from half a million to 2.6 million, most of this in 2006.[90] A major strike by public sector workers took place in June 2007 and became the largest strike in South African history. It lasted four weeks, with eleven million strike days lost, and included more than seven hundred thousand workers on strike and another three hundred thousand for whom it was illegal to strike. Strike support groups were set up, militant pickets guarded workplaces, and political slogans critical of the ANC slowly emerged. Yet the leaders of the social movements and organizations such as the APF and AEC saw the fulcrum of the struggle exclusively in the social movements and failed to consistently respond to these new developments. COSATU's role in the Alliance led many activists on the left to discount the role of the working class—some even repeating the 1970s theory about the unionized representing a "labor aristocracy."[91] Consequently, the left made no consistent attempt to orient toward those strikes and protests in workplaces and unions. There were of course exceptions, but these were largely weak, inconsistent, and often limited to messages of solidarity or the occasional argument in the APF.[92]

We argue that as a consequence of these failures, the APF—as a symbolic and organizational example of the Social Movements Indaba (SMI) and the political uprisings against the commodification and failures since 2000—is in crisis. The failure to lead, organize, and develop a working-class base inside (or at least develop better links with) the main trade unions has been a major barrier towards the development of a radical left in South Africa. These are not historical arguments. Political transformations have followed from labor struggles. The re-emergence of more sustained strikes and township protests fed into the tensions and was reflected in the growing conflict and political maneuverings inside the Alliance. This resulted in open, growing criticism of Thabo Mbeki in the build-up to the ANC's national congress in Polokwane in December 2007. What had once seemed unthinkable now seemed possible: the replacement of Thabo Mbeki as leader of the ANC and consequently as the president of South Africa. The uprisings and strikes represented a revolt against Mbeki's neoliberalism.

Consequently, the militant strikes and the township protests over the last few years have had the cumulative effect of blowing apart the neoliberal consensus in the Alliance. Many, especially within COSATU and the SACP, hoped that the election of Jacob Zuma as president would usher in a new period of social stability and influence of the left inside the Alliance. The difference this time is that while previous protests have focused on issues such as lack of water and housing, today's protests are more generalized and violent. As protestor Mzonke Poni told reporters in 2010, "The only way the government notices us is when we express our anger and rage—then they understand how we feel." Zuma's election and the defeat of Mbeki was a major turning point.[93] As we have argued, the Alliance left, including elements of COSATU/SACP and millions who voted for the ANC, saw Zuma as a new broom. While we believe Zuma is a false messiah, this is not the point. He tantalized millions with the possibility of a new future for South Africa's poor. While we see the emergence of the social movements starting in the late 1990s as important, it was the SACP and COSATU leaders' articulation of anger and frustration with the government through Alliance structures that destroyed Mbeki. As we have seen, this has clearly had a significant effect on the Alliance. The emergence of the social movements, predominantly made up of poor, unemployed, and elderly people on welfare, and their creative and exciting forms of protest and struggle produced the first cracks in the ANC monolith. They have shown that you can challenge the ANC's craven commitment to neoliberalism and that there is a political life outside of the Alliance. But for us it was the power, the presence, and the social weight of the organized working class on the streets, in strikes, and on picket lines that finally snapped Mbeki's hold over South Africa.

However, given the scale of the uprisings that dominated the 1980s and the enduring strength of the trade union movement, notably COSATU, it is important to ask why the working class has not more directly challenged the direction of the ANC government. In part, both the leadership and the rank and file have pinned their hopes on elections as the best way to forge further change. Despite many militant protests, strikes, and fiery exchanges with the ANC (and at times SACP) leadership, COSATU's role (like its affiliates) is linked somewhat to its general function as a trade union. Its leadership and many of its members share, at a general level, a basic assumption with the ANC leadership that capitalism is immutable and so seek to effect "capitalism with a human face." In short, their preferred political option is to rearrange the pieces of the chess set rather than to throw away the game; hence, they turn strikes on and off like a tap to press for greater political leverage inside the Alliance.

However, this is not to reduce strikes as simply "procedural," as social movement activists such Oupa Lehulere and Dale McKinley of the APF do. Zuma triggered the convergence of opposition to Mbeki's politics. This—and the strikes and township protests—breathed new confidence into COSATU and SACP. The election created renewed opportunities to push back the neoliberal agenda. This shifting constellation of popular forces had the working class at its center. The way forward must be a unity between the organized working class, the township unemployed, and others who support the social movements. There is no Chinese wall or labor aristocracy that separates the two—the umbilical cord of inequality is what unites this working class. The disaster for the South African left has been a politics that has celebrated only the resistance of the poor while ignoring and denigrating the struggles of the organized employed. No united and cohesive movement has emerged from the recent protests, for such movements to develop the left must unite workers and unemployed. We make no claims that this will be an easy task or that the Alliance left has not been, at times, very hostile to other social movements. While COSATU and the SACP do not yet offer a counter-hegemonic alternative, such politics can emerge from this unity. Activists understand that movements do not emerge fully formed, but through a process of struggle and engagement. The xenophobic attacks on African immigrant workers in 2009 and the violence and domestic abuse widespread across South Africa express how people's frustrations are diverted.

Clearly, in the short term, it is unlikely that these struggles can be united. Although some social movement activists, such as Dale McKinley, make calls for unity in the working class, this conceals hostility to COSATU and the SACP. Such unity can only be achieved through engagement with the main organizations of the working class. One obvious step would be a united front of popular struggles seeking to unite township protests and the organized working class. COSATU and its immense social weight, based as it is around the point of production, will be central to this united front, organizing and forging links with the unemployed and the unorganized in the formal and informal sectors. McKinley and others assume that we can ignore the leadership of COSATU and the SACP and that unity is simply a game of leapfrog. For all their weaknesses in seeing change as coming largely through maneuverings in the Alliance, the leader of these organizations are respected by millions and cannot be ignored.

Instead, we argue that the struggles need a common platform of demands which can unite everyone irrespective of political allegiances and ideas. This politics speaks of years of united movements where people march and protest on what unites them, while debating what does not. This approach has been described in Latin American politics as "talking while walking." This future of common struggle is a challenge to the leadership of COSATU and the SACP, but also to the various independent organizations of the social movements: ABM, APF, TAC, and others. It offers the prospect of a unified struggle against neoliberalism in South Africa. If the global crisis has resounded with the death agony of neoliberal capitalism, the South African left has a responsibility to patiently craft unity against neoliberal capitalism which will inspire the continent north of the Limpopo to do the same.

Conclusion: A kaleidoscope of resistance and false prophets

As we argued at the start of this chapter, although social movement activity has not reached the dizzy heights of the mid-1980s, the country has been beset by a kaleidoscope of protests. The government has sought to defuse conflict with labor through corporatist bargaining relationships, but unlike many other post-independence African governments that were more successful in preventing industrial action than their colonial predecessors, the ANC government has, so far, been unable to prevent the development of class conflict or ensure that workers' demands were solely addressed through recognized state structures. Despite sometimes violently suppressing some sections of civil society while trying to court others, the government has failed to smother discontent; while it has also sought to reconfigure state and civil society relations, post-apartheid South Africa has been punctuated by a number of mass strikes and a range of social protests. In differing ways, the wave of near-uninterrupted township protests since May 2009 and the renewed efforts at reinvigorating Alliance relationships under President Jacob Zuma both testify to COSATU's continued use of direct action as leverage inside the Alliance.[94]

This climate of rebellion creates immense opportunities and challenges for radical activists to help organize the protests and unite the struggles of the unemployed township poor and the working poor into a political alternative that can begin to challenge the dominance of the ANC. At the birth of the new social movements in 2001, Ashwin Desai noted that activists "have raised, but not yet answered, the question of what organization/s will best serve the growing dissent."[95] Autonomist politics from the global anticapitalist movement have blown like leaves on the wind into South Africa, and many in the new social movements, understandably repelled by Stalinist and formalistic party politics, have long been reluctant to discuss or propose forms of collective organization that could begin to build this bridge and provide civil society activists with a practical, strategic, ideological, and educational form—that is, the notion of some type of party or other collective organization as a political home that is open to individuals to enter (rather than restricted, as today's social movement networking is, to representatives of groups). We would argue that such a vehicle is needed to further develop the cracks and fissures in the ANC monolith and to begin to constitute a political community that explicitly seeks to transcend particularistic identities while supporting and building on the struggles they generate among the working class.

CHAPTER 5

SOCIAL MOVEMENTS AFTER THE TRANSITION: CHOICELESS DEMOCRACIES?

Social movements played a central role in bringing about the transition to democracy that occurred (albeit to a limited degree) in much of sub-Saharan Africa in the early 1990s, as we saw in chapter 3. In the wake of these transitions, unprecedented political and academic attention was paid to the perceived role of "civil society" in strengthening and defending the new democratic systems being established.[1] Although this in part reflected the genuine role of social movements in enabling the transition to take place, as in Eastern Europe in the same period, it was as much a reflection of prevalent neoliberal normative thinking as it was based on any empirical analysis of the situation on the ground. Donors and Western intellectuals conceived of civil society as a positive alternative to the state-dominated model of development hitherto prominent in postcolonial Africa. Civil society could, by this way of thinking, not only hold government to account—it would also have a greatly expanded role in delivering services previously provided by the state and play an important part in reducing poverty and bringing about development.

From the start of the 1990s, the increased focus among Western donors and academics on the role of civil society was therefore shaped (and distorted) by the assumptions of those observers regarding the particular role that this sector of society was expected to play. Judgments regarding the effectiveness of civil society were commonly made in relation to these preconceptions rather than in relation to the aims and intentions of actually existing civil society activists. In addition (as we shall see), the objectives of the latter were themselves frequently distorted by their sudden popularity and the availability of donor funding in the 1990s. In a new form of "extroversion," many existing and (in particular) new civil society organizations defined themselves more toward the donor environment than toward those they claimed to represent.[2]

The particular role assigned to civil society by external observers also failed to take account of the decidedly limited and uneven transition to democracy that had taken place across much of Africa. While systems of multi-party elections had been (re-)introduced, many African states remained highly centralized and authoritarian. Newly elected governments, facing similar dilemmas as their predecessors, frequently reverted to the repressive tendencies of their immediate postcolonial and, indeed, colonial predecessors. Politicians seeking to defend themselves from popular criticism successfully utilized accusations of "neocolonialism" to undermine their non-state critics, claiming they were unrepresentative of popular opinion and following the agenda of their funders. By the late 1990s, the relative failure and/or unwillingness of this imaginary "civil society" to play the role ascribed to it, coupled with continued state repression of critical voices and the failure of neoliberalism to alleviate economic decline, resulted in a sense of disillusionment among earlier optimists. The flood of donor funding was reduced and many organizations were forced to end or severely curtail their activities.

However, this chapter will argue that it was precisely at this time when some independently minded civil society activists, seeking to break free of donor dependency and adopt a more critical attitude to the governments they had (in part) helped bring into power, recognized the need to engage more with the grassroots constituencies they claimed to represent. The late 1990s and early 2000s thus saw an increase in social movement–oriented activism in some of those countries that had made the transition to formal democracy a decade earlier. Just as in the pro-democracy movement, engagement with the global political context was influential. Now, however, normative neoliberal notions of a linked transition to political and economic liberalization were replaced by increasing criticism of neoliberal orthodoxy in general, and the rise of the anticapitalist movement in particular (see chapter 7), which provided inspiration and new models of analysis to many activists and organizations.

This chapter will explore the development of civil society and social movement orientation, activities, and analysis in Africa since 1990, in particular in those countries that made the transition to formal democratic political systems in the early 1990s. We will focus on Zambia and Malawi, but will also draw on experiences of social movement organizations and activists in Tanzania, which made parallel (but also distinct) transitions to democracy during this period.

Social movements and the transition to democracy

We need to challenge the myth that space for civil society to operate was only "granted" after 1991 by the new MMD [Movement for Multi-Party Democracy] government. In fact it was defended and fought for under the one-party state. This culminated in the creation of the MMD as a movement rather than a party.

—Father Joe Komakoma[3]

In Africa's one-party states of the 1980s, economic decline was coupled with a relative atrophy of the state's capacity to buy off opposition with patronage and to achieve effective repression. In this context, popular movements and more formally constituted civil society organizations played a significant role in opening up the space which enabled overt multi-party movements to establish themselves in the period between 1989 and 1992. However, it was equally true that (as noted elsewhere in this volume) the mass movements that emerged during this period had the potential to initiate a far more radical process of political and economic change than was manifested by these organizations, which tended towards more limited reformist goals, leading to the return of a very limited form of democracy coupled with a profoundly destructive process of economic liberalization. Harri Englund's seminal study of Malawi argues that the dominance of a liberal definition of rights, focused on civil-political individual rights rather than collective socioeconomic ones, hampered the capacity of these organizations to adequately represent the concerns of the country's poor.[4] As this chapter will illustrate, this distinction between mass-based activity and organizational reformism is crucial for understanding the ambiguous role played by many civil society organizations during this period.

In many cases, organizations of the types discussed in chapter 3—labor organizations and churches, for example—played a central role in enabling the transition to democracy or in establishing opposition parties. In Malawi, student demonstrations at Chancellor College in the late 1980s led some activists to go into political exile in Uganda and elsewhere.[5] From this position, they lobbied for a removal of donor funding to the Hastings Kamuzu Banda regime. This strategy began to achieve success in the post-1989 political environment, with the growing emphasis on "good governance"; Scandinavian governments reduced donor support to the Malawian government. In 1992, the country's Catholic bishops issued a pastoral letter criticizing aspects of Malawian society under the Malawi Congress Party. Their subsequent detention unleashed a campaign for multi-party democracy that achieved its goal in a referendum in June 1993. At this point, "pressure groups" transformed themselves into political parties. In 1994's elections, Bakili Muluzi and his United Democratic Front (UDF) party were elected into power. Muluzi was himself a former senior minister in

Banda's governments of the 1970s; after falling from favor, he had established himself as a prosperous businessman. The UDF achieved victory over the Alliance for Democracy, led by labor leader Chakufwa Chihana; both parties were, however, essentially neoliberal and drew support not via significant policy differences but from regional bases.[6]

In Zambia, mass urban mobilization was vital to the success of the Movement for Multi-Party Democracy (MMD), established in 1990, which held large rallies in support of an end to the one-party state of Kenneth Kaunda's United National Independence Party (UNIP). A substantial rise in industrial action provided an important impetus to rapid and largely peaceful change; strikes combined economic and political demands. Having endorsed the one-party state in the early 1970s, the organized churches played a significant role in calling for a return to multi-party democracy in the late 1980s, and in particular in aiding a peaceful transition to democratic rule in 1990 and 1991. The National Women's Lobby was formed with the specific task of ensuring women's participation in the new era of multi-party politics.[7]

These parties can be understood as, in part, the product of social movements that had offered limited and then more substantial criticisms of the UNIP-dominated state. This was symbolized in Zambia by the emergence of Frederick Chiluba, former chairman-general of the Zambia Congress of Trade Unions (ZCTU), as the first elected leader of the MMD in early 1991. Chiluba, unlike many of the former UNIP politicians who now joined the MMD, was seen as having "clean hands." However, once the MMD was established as a political party, the capacity of social movements to influence its policy and practice was severely limited. The MMD, celebrated as representative of a new wave of civil society influence over political change, was in fact dominated by many of the same elites that had controlled UNIP. A majority of Chiluba's first cabinet were former UNIP ministers or state officials and had a background in business; only one (except Chiluba himself) was a former trade unionist.[8]

More significantly, the limited development of civil society restricted its practical influence over government policy through the
party's embryonic structures. The labor movement, for example,
lacked both a coherent ideological position and institutionalized
representation to shape its relationship with the MMD.[9] This, as
elsewhere in sub-Saharan Africa, certainly had negative consequences for civil society once the MMD came to power in a land-
slide election victory in 1991.

The changing role of civil society in the 1990s

The return of multi-party democracy enabled new civil society organizations to flower because of three interrelated factors arising
from the transition to political and economic liberalism: the political space created with the collapse of the authoritarian state; the
general retreat from state provision of services, with civil society
rushing to fill the vacuum; and the sudden availability of international donor funding for civil society activities. There was an initial
proliferation of new NGOs, many with little or no organic presence in civil society.[10]

In Zambia, for example, the new women's organizations established to provide basic services tended to militate against the
more activist orientation of their national umbrella body, the
Non-Governmental Organizations Coordinating Committee
(NGOCC).[11] However, a number of organizations formed during
this period have stood the test of time, including NGOCC,
Women for Change, and the Foundation for Democratic Process
(FODEP). FODEP was initially established by church and student
groups as the ad hoc Zambia Election Monitoring and Coordination Committee in the run-up to the 1991 elections, and subsequently established itself as a leading body in civic and voter
education.[12] FODEP's capacity to generate self-sustaining local
initiatives in civil education is positively highlighted by Englund,
who contrasts it with the continued dependency of Malawian
democratic education on the agenda of central NGOs.[13]

Malawian civil society leaders acknowledge that a proliferation of organizations promoting liberal models of good governance and human rights took place in this period, shaped more by the availability of donor funding and priorities than the needs or aspirations of ordinary people.[14] Despite the country's overwhelmingly rural population, many organizations sprang up in towns and cities, where they had greater access to donor offices.[15] In a poor country, the growth of NGOs and their new access to external resources made the jobs and contracts they controlled an important commodity.[16] Donors directed funding to sectors they wished to promote, shaping the agenda of civil society and even stimulating the creation of particular organizations.[17] Similar tendencies were noted in Tanzania: established organizations felt it was incumbent to adopt programs addressing HIV because this was the donors' priority.[18] Civil society activities were competitive rather than coordinated, in many cases paying only lip service to consultation with their supposed clients or members. These tendencies reflect the tendency (noted elsewhere in this volume—see chapter 6 in particular) to the "commodification of resistance."

At the same time, a decline in trade union organization and resources led to their relative marginalization, particularly in Zambia, where they had been of great significance. Economic liberalization, including wholesale privatization and cuts to public expenditure, halved the number of formally employed Zambians. President Chiluba, despite his background in the labor movement, marginalized unions from economic decision-making as part of a retreat from UNIP's semi-corporatist model.[19] In the dying days of the one-party state, Kaunda had sought to weaken the oppositional labor movement by repealing legislation, allowing only one union in each industry. The MMD maintained this competitive labor environment, but liberalization was not matched by a more permissive approach to industrial action—as under UNIP, it remained virtually impossible to organize a legal strike. In 1996, the labor movement split in a dispute over its relationship with the ruling party and government, with the Federation of Free Trade Unions of Zambia (FFTUZ) surviving as an alternative labor confederation to the dominant ZCTU to this day. This did not, however, prevent the organization of highly effective waves of strike action in the public sector in particular in the late 1990s and early 2000s; during these actions, civil service unions found themselves on a collision course with the demands of the IFIs for reductions in the numbers and wages of public sector workers.[20]

In Malawi, by contrast, more permissive labor legislation (the Labour Relations Act of 1996 and the Employment Act of 1999) strengthened the country's union movement, which had been severely repressed under the one-party state. This enabled highly effective strike action by the civil services in 1993 and 1994, which paralyzed the country.[21] The Malawi Congress of Trade Unions (MCTU) was highly critical of the Muluzi government's economic policies. By the end of the decade, this comparative permissiveness had been rolled back; Englund reports that it became common for police to break up strikes with tear gas. In 2000, a splinter congress, the Congress of Malawi Trade Unions, was established with official backing, evidently as an attempt at divide and rule. It nevertheless remained difficult for individuals or groups of workers to utilize the law to advance their own material conditions, for example in relation to the unenforced minimum wage.[22]

Relations with post-transition governments

Despite the fact that most civil society activists saw themselves as central to the democratic transition, their relations with the post-transition governments they had helped bring to power were initially fractious and increasingly confrontational—there was no honeymoon period. Organizations that sought to deepen and sustain the hasty and interim transition to democracy frequently found that the new governments asserted direct control over the pace and degree of further democratic transition. In Malawi, calls for a South African–style "Truth and Reconciliation Commission" into human rights abuses under the Banda regime were rejected by the new UDF government. Civil society organizations initially accepted the institutionalization of reform, for example the Mwanakatwe Commission, established in Zambia in 1993 to review the constitution and propose a new one appropriate to democratic governance.

The report of the Mwanakatwe Commission in 1996 made recommendations in line with civil society's liberal aspirations: a reduction in presidential powers, stronger oversight powers for Parliament, and stronger rights to freedom of speech and assembly. The Chiluba administration, however, implemented specific aspects of the proposed reforms, altering the constitution to exclude former president Kaunda from the forthcoming presidential elections. FODEP assessed the resultant election as neither free nor fair and suffered "vicious" reprisals, in which charges of tax evasion were created in order to freeze its accounts.[23] Such actions, however, exposed the dependency of many civil society organizations (CSOs) on donor funds sent from abroad. By the mid-1990s, civil society criticism of the government led the state to repress its activists and organizations, which were accused of acting as fronts for opposition political parties and foreign interests. The 1997 election was followed by the harassment and detention of prominent opposition political leaders, including Kaunda, in 1997. Civil society activists were also threatened and detained, accused of aiding Zambia's enemies and being fronts for opposition parties. Prominent activists and journalists such as Lucy Sichone and Fred M'membe went into hiding.[24]

In Malawi, tensions with the Muluzi administration grew steadily during the 1990s. Government accepted (and welcomed) civil society organizations that provided services, but refused to engage with their advocacy initiatives.[25] Demonstrations by civil society on particular issues were frequently banned.[26] In some cases, donors pressured government to create space for civil society, reinforcing the notion that it was the former that was dictating the agenda of the latter.[27] The situation was complicated by the fact that opposition parties did seek to manipulate civil society organizations; this led some of the latter to avoid any issue which might be construed as "political."[28] In Tanzania, government officials were similarly reluctant to accept civil society organizations as legitimate representatives of the people—this was, they were told, the responsibility of MPs. This reluctance, however, decreased with time—partly because Tanzanian civil society organizations demonstrated their own local accountability, but also because donors forced government to engage with them.[29]

By the late 1990s, civil society in both Malawi and Zambia, increasingly critical of the centralization of power and the denial of free speech by the post-transition governments, came under more sustained attack. Politicians increasingly cited CSOs' dependence on external donors as evidence of their suspicious and unpatriotic nature. While civil society actively defended itself against such attacks, it was acknowledged that the proliferation of CSOs after democratization led to problems of coordination and accountability that made the accusation of outside manipulation difficult to disprove. In this context, CSOs increased their own coordination, as well as strengthening the links they had developed with the independent media, such as the *Post* in Zambia and the *Chronicle* in Malawi. In response to accusations by politicians that they were an unrepresentative, liberal metropolitan elite, CSOs worked to strengthen their grassroots linkages and consultation processes, particularly in rural areas.

By the late 1990s, the ranks of CSOs began to thin out, with some "briefcase" NGOs disappearing as the initial wave of donor enthusiasm and funding for civil society dwindled. Civil society was itself proactive in calling for regulation of the sector, aiming to replace a "period of 'charity' in which civil society was tolerated, but still lacked rights" with a legal framework in which their legitimacy was guaranteed.[30] In 1997, the Coalition of Non-Governmental Organisations of Malawi (CONGOMA) lobbied the government for legislation defining the legal position of CSOs. However, amid rising state–civil society antagonism in the late 1990s, the government presented a draft NGO Bill that not only required CSOs to register with CONGOMA, but also required the latter to act as a regulator of its own members on behalf of the state. The NGO Bill also included clauses threatening to de-register organizations engaged in "politicking."[31] Although the NGO Act was passed in 1999, it was not actually used to de-register critical CSOs. Nevertheless, the threat of its use hung over civil society and hampered the role of CONGOMA as an effective sector-wide representative body. At the same time, leading civil society figures were effectively silenced through appointments to senior state positions, for example as ambassadors.[32]

During Muluzi's second term in office (1999–2004), civil society clashed more often with the government, which sought to limit their access to donor funding. When the UK government's Department for International Development awarded the contract for its Transform program to the Malawi Human Rights and Rehabilitation Centre, the government blocked access to the funds.[33] This coincided with Muluzi's attempt to run for an unconstitutional third term in office in 2003, which was opposed by civil society in conjunction with churches and tribal chiefs.[34] International donors responded by withholding funding to the Muluzi government, which effectively deterred the alteration of the constitution to allow the third term, which did not go ahead. As had occurred in the last days of the Banda regime, much of civil society viewed this outside donor intervention positively, encouraging the deepening of democracy.[35] This transnational influence on NGO agendas and politics as a whole is, Englund notes, particularly pervasive in Malawi.[36]

Similar events occurred in Zambia toward the end of the 1990s: increasing clashes between civil society and the MMD government derailed attempts at voluntary regulation, with the latter proposing an NGO Bill that threatened to restrict the capacity of civil society to criticize policy,[37] and civil society strongly criticizing the Chiluba administration's evident corruption. Chiluba's bid for a (unconstitutional) third term in office focused civil society's efforts on what they saw as a threat to the peace of the nation.[38] A core group of advocacy-oriented organizations enabled the effective mobilization of civil society, coordinated by the Oasis Forum, which was established in 2000 by Zambia's three main church bodies, the NGOCC, and the Law Association of Zambia.[39] In some respects, the campaign against the third term replicated aspects of the pro-democracy movement of a decade earlier. Civil society's formal efforts were supported by displays of popular discontent, including the coordinated blasting of car horns in Lusaka every Friday evening; these were, however, relatively spontaneous initiatives of the "urban crowd" rather than coordinated actions by specific organizations with a popular membership. Despite state intimidation, the Oasis Forum and wider civil society led a coordinated and successful campaign (in which donors did not play a decisive role) that ultimately prevented Chiluba from running for a third term.

Neoliberalism and economic discontents

Across Africa, the new democratic governments that came to power in the early 1990s implemented, to a greater or lesser extent, programs of economic liberalization. This was despite the fact that protests against structural adjustment programs had played an important part in weakening the hegemony of their undemocratic predecessors (see chapter 3) and that some parts of civil society, from which some of the new democratic leaders had emerged, had been in the forefront of attacks on such policies. In Zambia, for example, the ZCTU under Frederick Chiluba had been a prominent critic of such programs in the 1980s. Now, however, his government implemented one of the most radical liberalization programs ever attempted in sub-Saharan Africa, removing all consumer subsidies, tariffs; and other barriers to imports; implementing a decade-long program to privatize 250 state-owned companies; substantially reducing state support to agricultural production;

and introducing user fees for health and education services. The result was a dramatic increase in poverty and little obvious improvement to the Zambian economy.[40]

From 1992 to 1998, Zambian GDP declined by an average of 0.2 percent per annum. Formal-sector employment fell from 544,200 in 1991 to 436,066 in 2004.[41] Social indicators drastically declined under the MMD. Education spending as a percentage of GNP fell from 4.5 percent in 1991 to 2.9 percent in 1994 (although it subsequently increased). In 2002, 33 percent of children were not attending primary school, while only 22 percent received secondary education.[42] Health expenditure fell in proportion with overall cuts in government spending at a time when the impact of HIV/AIDS was devastating. Infant and child mortality increased with the introduction of user fees; access to clean water and sanitation services declined. By 1997, Zambia had the distinction of being the only country in the world that had a lower Human Development Index score in 1997 than in 1975. The percentage of Zambians living in poverty rose from 70 percent in 1991 to 73 percent in 1998.[43]

In Malawi, there was a shift away from state-led agricultural development programs under Muluzi, who promoted "popular capitalism" and commerce as the keys to growth. There was an upsurge in donor-funded rural credit schemes, channeled through small traders' associations such as the National Association of Small Business Women and the Development of Malawi Traders' Trust. These funds dried up by the mid-1990s, having made little positive impact on rural livelihoods.[44] Toward the end of the decade, amid rising rural food insecurity, there were accusations that funds for agricultural development were being corruptly channeled to close associates of the president. Similarly, in Zambia, the privatization of strategic industries provided Chiluba and his ministers with opportunities for corruption.

For the first decade of democratic rule, the majority of civil society was relatively silent and acquiescent regarding the many negative effects of economic liberalization. Certainly, the global hegemony of capitalism in the wake of the collapse of communism undermined effective critiques of such policies from virtually all observers. It was accepted that debt-ridden, dependent states had little option but to implement the policies international donors demanded. In addition, there was widespread recognition that the state-dominated economic policies of the postcolonial era had led to inefficiency and corruption. Some civil society organizations initially gained from the redistribution of donor finance to the non-state sector and positioned themselves as alternative providers of welfare and development services. The few criticisms of such policies made in the 1990s limited their focus to specific issues of implementation and the need to alleviate their impact on the poorest sections of society.

By the turn of the century, however, it was increasingly recognized that neoliberalism had made Zambia's economic situation worse, not better. The long-delayed privatization of the strategic mining industry was shaped by Zambia's dependent relationship with the IFIs and international mining capital. The World Bank and IMF intervened in the process to shape the future ownership of Zambia's primary economic resource. Not coincidentally, mine privatization breached legal requirements for transparency in bidding processes and awards, consultation with stakeholders, and due regard for social and environmental impact. At this time, local civil society expressed strong criticisms of this particular sell-off.[45] While most observers acknowledge that some job losses and company closures were an inevitable byproduct of privatization, critics believe this was worsened by the influence of the IFIs. Joyce Nonde, president of the FFTUZ, argued:

> We are told IMF, World Bank, were pushing . . . over 200 plus institutions [into] private hands, and our expectation was that implementation was going to be done properly . . . but what did we see? Everything was done in a hurry. There was asset stripping, and there was selling of institutions at a very low price to dubious

people; and the workers who were laid off were not paid, they were just thrown into the streets. . . . What are you doing, you're creating poverty . . . the country has gone backwards, in terms of poverty, in terms of unemployment, and so on and so forth. And there's no person who's interested in saying, privatization has worked. . . . It's not the policy of privatization itself . . . it's the way it was done, and the way it's being done . . . we blame the IMF and World Bank for having put conditionalities and making the government rush into selling these things.[46]

In this context, the early 2000s saw some recovery in social movements' capacity to articulate widespread discontent with the results of neoliberalism and privatization. In 2002, trade unionists, CSOs, and opposition political parties demonstrated in Lusaka against the proposed sale of the Zambia National Commercial Bank (ZNCB) and two other state-owned companies. Initiated by the union representing ZNCB employees, the march led the National Assembly to vote against privatizing ZNCB, reversing government policy.[47] The sale of the bank was, however, a condition for the completion of Zambia's Poverty Reduction Strategy Program (PRSP) and the consequent relief of most of Zambia's international debt.[48] The IMF's action again highlighted the extent to which debt conditionality placed Zambian social movements in conflict not only with their own government, but also with the policies of the IFIs. The bank was eventually sold to Rabobank of the Netherlands in 2006; the new owners' commitment to retaining the ZNCB's network of rural branches and other social obligations imposed by the government reflected a partial success of the anti-privatization campaign.

The privatization of core state services was also highlighted in Malawi's PRSP, agreed upon in 2002. The privatization of Malawi's Water Boards was first announced by the Muluzi government in 2004. Initial opposition by civil society and an impending general election led to its postponement. The MCTU in general and the Water Employees' Trade Union of Malawi (WETUM) in particular initiated a campaign for popular control over water resources. They demanded greater transparency in the provision of basic services, focusing on the need for government departments to clear their own debts to the Water Boards so that their perilous financial position was addressed. WETUM proposed community and worker participation in the future management of the Water Boards. The World Bank noted that "over time, the levels of resistance to the program increased" but happily identified "high level political support" for privatization, and stressed the need for improved "communication" regarding the sale.[49]

In 2005, the government confirmed its plans to privatize the Water Boards. The following year WETUM lobbied Parliament, in which the government lacked a majority, to oppose the sell-off, now labeled as a "public-private partnership." WETUM, with the support of its allies in other public sector unions, its UK counterpart UNISON, and the Public Services International, drew on international experiences of such "partnerships" and their frequently negative impact on service provision. However, they were hampered by a lack of information regarding the factors driving the privatization process forward.[50] In 2007, the government initiated a new "communications campaign" ostensibly presented as consultation with stakeholders, but (as a leaked cabinet paper revealed) designed "to gain stakeholder support on the water sector reform."[51] Water privatization has, however, still not been completed to date. These types of campaigns, ostensibly focused on specific local issues, were successfully magnified by linking to global campaigns against the sell-off of state assets that were developing in the context of the emergent anticapitalist movement. For the union activists involved, those international linkages provided valuable comparative information and a multiplier effect, strengthening their local campaigns.[52]

Malawi experienced near-catastrophic food shortages in the early 2000s. While there were environmental reasons for this, the situation was severely exacerbated by the commercialization of the agricultural sector, with donors advising the reduction of expensive corn reserves and insisting on privatizing the Agricultural Development and Marketing Corporation (ADMARC) and introducing market pricing for the staple crop, corn. In the last few years, the government has recapitalized ADMARC and resisted donor demands for further commercialization, which has helped reverse food shortages and improve harvests. Similarly, the mid-2000s saw the Zambian government resist the further implementation of some liberalization policies, prompted in part by more active civil society resistance. Since 2004, rising international mineral prices have made Zambia's copper mining industry profitable for the first time in thirty years. This, coupled with the achievement of debt relief in 2005, has given the government some room to maneuver on issues on which there is popular discontent. In this context, civil society anger at the behavior of new foreign investors, for example in their employment and environmental practices, has translated into national politics. Growing anger at the health and safety standards of new mining investors was fueled by the deaths of fifty-one casual workers in a Chinese-owned explosives plant in Chambishi in 2005. Government ministers criticized the company and the Ministry of Mines froze the issuing of new mining licenses. A national day of mourning was declared to mark the burial of the deceased. At the funeral, police beat back protestors angry at the state's failure to regulate privatized companies properly. It is widely suspected that the new mine owners have evaded safety legislation by bribing low-paid government inspectors.

The frequency of wildcat strikes and violent incidents—both official violence and violent strike tactics—at Zambian mines increased significantly in the mid-2000s due to a combination of factors, including the fact that mineworkers found striking to be an effective tactic in the context of rising copper prices. Peaceful labor relations also continue to be severely hampered by labor laws, which remain essentially unchanged from the one-party state era. The trade unions that played such an important role in bringing the MMD to power expected the new government to liberalize these laws, but it has long delayed reform of labor legislation. Despite years of negotiation between government and the unions, amendments to the Industrial and Labour Relations Act promulgated in 2008 represented a major assault on the autonomy of the labor movement and did nothing to remove draconian controls on industrial action. The amendments, proposed to Parliament without discussion in the Tripartite Labour Consultative Council, include a reassertion of the labor commissioner's right to declare any industry an "essential service" in which strikes are entirely illegal. It also allows only one union to negotiate for workers in a particular sector, placing it in apparent conflict with both International Labour Organization conventions and with the existing Zambian constitution. The FFTUZ's Joyce Nonde believes this position was prompted by rising discontent among investors with Zambia's comparatively militant workforce.[53]

Popular anger over such issues helped shape the 2006 general election. The populist campaign of Michael Sata's Patriotic Front party, articulating discontent with foreign (particularly Chinese) investors, gained widespread support in urban areas and came close to unseating the MMD government.[54] In January 2007, an international report entitled *For Whom the Windfalls? Winners and Losers in the Privatization of Zambia's Copper Mines* was published in Zambia.[55] Funded by Christian Aid and published by the Civil Society Trade Network of Zambia and the Catholic Commission for Justice, Development and Peace (CCJDP), the report exposed the secret development agreements signed between the government and the new mining investors to public scrutiny. These agreements enabled the mining companies to pay internationally low levels of taxes on their activities. The *Windfalls* report received widespread media coverage and quickly generated popular anger. It was a very positive example of cooperation between local and international civil society.

In response, the government announced that it would enter into negotiations with the mining companies to revise the tax on mine royalties from 0.6 percent per year to the international norm of 3 percent. In January 2008, after discussions with the companies, the government announced it would unilaterally increase mining royalties and the wider tax regime, including a windfall tax on "excess" profits resulting from the historically high international copper price. While the mining companies protested and threatened to challenge the decision in court, civil society generally welcomed the decision—although trade unions were concerned with ensuring that the increased tax revenue would be spent on social development rather than lining the pockets of politicians. In May 2008, under the auspices of the Economic Association of Zambia, civil society representatives met with academics and government representatives in the Copperbelt city of Kitwe to discuss the potential distribution of the $415 million in tax revenue which it was estimated would be earned in the first year of the new tax regime. However, the new tax regime was subsequently reversed two years later, in the midst of the global economic crisis.

Like its counterpart in Malawi, the Zambian government has also benefited from breaking with IFI orthodoxy regarding the removal of agricultural subsidies, which proved disastrous when first introduced in the early 1990s. Since achieving debt relief, the Zambian government has provided significant increases in agricultural subsidies, particularly for fertilizer, which has generated significant electoral support for the party in rural areas and significantly contributed to the MMD's retention of power in the elections of 2006 and 2008.

The most recent wave of popular anger in Zambia against neoliberalism was, however, noteworthy for its limited level of civil society participation. Although trade unions were generally supportive of Sata's policies, much of civil society failed to give expression to the discontent evident across much of Zambia. Civil society leaders expressed to the authors their distaste at Sata's opportunist and occasionally racist rhetoric, but his political party was able to place itself at the head of popular discontent precisely because social movements singularly failed to do so. It appears that in many respects, liberal NGOs have incorporated donor ideas regarding economic orthodoxy and good governance into their praxis. This may in some respects reflect their increased participation in making and endorsing government policy since the introduction of PRSPs.

The politics of participation in the 2000s

While the 1990s were characterized by a general unwillingness among new democratic governments to engage with social movements, the first decade of the new century saw a significant change in relations between African states, civil society, and international donors. The new emphasis on participatory decision-making was a liberal response to decades of criticism that top-down economic liberalization, in the specific form of SAPs, had failed in large part because it did not enable popular ownership of and participation in creating such programs. The new mechanisms introduced, particularly the PRSPs, were linked to the Highly Indebted Poor Countries (HIPC) program. This meant that many sub-Saharan African countries were required to complete the conditions of a national PRSP before they qualified for the substantial debt relief promised by multilateral and bilateral donors in response to the Jubilee debt campaigns carried out in the run-up to the millennium. Tanzania signed its PRSP in 2001; Malawi and Zambia adopted theirs in 2002.[56]

The extent to which civil society is able to wield meaningful influence over PRSPs is pitiful. Many observers, including among more radical social movements, see them as a fig leaf for neoliberal programs which are local and participatory only in a tokenistic manner.[57] Most PRSPs contain requirements for further economic liberalization and, in particular, the privatization of remaining state assets. The emphasis in the new participatory model on locally owned and country-specific approaches to poverty reduction nevertheless made it incumbent on participating governments to engage more closely with civil society. This coincided, in both Zambia and Malawi, with the election of governments apparently committed to opening up such a dialogue. In Zambia, the election of Levy Mwanawasa as Chiluba's successor (following the successful campaign against the latter's third term) brought to power a new MMD president who was comparatively liberal in his approach. A lawyer by training, Mwanawasa unexpectedly initiated a process which led to his predecessor Chiluba having his immunity from prosecution removed and being charged with crimes of corruption. CSOs welcomed these measures, which vindicated their stance in the "third term" campaign. Similarly, Bingu wa Mutharika was elected as Malawian president in 2004; endorsed as the UDF candidate by Muluzi, Mutharika subsequently broke from the UDF to form his own Democratic Progressive Party (DPP). Mutharika, like Mwanawasa, was less directly confrontational in his dealings with civil society than his predecessor. Lacking a parliamentary majority, Mutharika's government sought to engage civil society officials in the decision-making process, though primarily to utilize their technical expertise rather than their political analysis. Mutharika, an economist by training, was initially strongly wedded to neoliberal economic orthodoxy, while emphasizing transparency in fiscal matters.[58] While some organizations, particularly those active in the global anticapitalist movement, advocated a boycott of any process involving the IFIs, the vast majority of CSOs in the countries under study saw participation in PRSPs as an opportunity, not a threat.[59]

A major limitation on effective participation was the complex, policy-oriented nature of the process. "Participation," for the donor bureaucracy, did not consist of popular gatherings designed to elucidate grassroots opinion, but rather meetings dominated by donor and government officials in which civil society representatives participated in a limited way, to the extent that they could engage in the policy-oriented discourse. New civil society networks were established to enable this participation, with others adapting their activist orientation to the new environment. In Zambia, the instructively named Civil Society for Poverty Reduction (CSPR) was established, while the Malawi Economic Justice Network (MEJN) was central to the Malawian process. There was civil society involvement in nineteen of the twenty-one working groups preparing the Malawian PRSP, but as in Zambia, they were excluded from those dealing with macroeconomic policy.[60] Four of the eighteen authors of the PRSP came from civil society, although only two were actually chosen by civil society organizations themselves.[61] Initially, the extent of civil society's participation in the PRSP was limited by the government's tardiness in providing information as well as its own limited capacity to engage with the process. However, participation seems to have become more meaningful as the process developed, particularly in periodic reviews of its implementation.[62]

Donor funding was provided to support such participatory engagement. This might suggest a circular process in which donor funding enables the creation of new networks with little grassroots ownership whose primary activity is to endorse and legitimize neoliberal policies with the stamp of civil society participation. Such an interpretation is, however, strongly rejected by organizations such as CSPR, which points to its accountability as a network of widely respected CSOs with a national reach—by 2006, CSPR had a physical presence in five of Zambia's nine provinces and was carrying out increasing levels of consultation and dissemination activities directly and via its partners in churches, trade unions, business associations, and other bodies.[63] Effective participation is nevertheless dependent on civil society's capacity to generate consensual positions—there is little space for diversity of views in PRSP-type negotiations.

CSPR points to the still-uneven acceptance of participation among government and donor officials, and there is a clear sense that the weakness of parliaments in many democratic states means that the executive continues to dominate decision-making. In Tanzania, which achieved initial debt relief as early as 2001, government acceptance of civil society participation was driven by donor pressure, but also by recognition that CSOs were often more efficient agents of service delivery to the poor than a broken-up and impoverished state.[64] While organizations like the Tanzania Association of Non-Governmental Organizations (TANGO) were initially critical of the lack of involvement of civil society at the start of the decade, civil society input was far stronger by the time the successor to the PRSP was being drawn up in 2005.[65]

The gap in understanding between experts like Mabvuto Bamusi of MEJN and wider civil society is nevertheless a real problem. MEJN produces educational materials in indigenous languages and uses visual representations to explain the relevance of the PRSP, but it is difficult to capture such policy complexity in a way that makes the positions adopted by specialist organizations fully accountable to those for whom they ostensibly speak. Notwithstanding such limitations, the successful completion of Zambia's PRSP and the consequent reduction in the country's debt burden from US$6.5 billion to $502 million in 2005 provided, for many in civil society, vindication for their decision to participate. In Malawi, $3.2 billion of international debt was canceled in 2006, leaving a debt stock of $850 million.

The increasingly participatory decision-making environment has also had a positive domino effect, increasing the potential for civil society engagement in other areas of policy-making. In Zambia, for example, the leading environmental organization, Citizens for a Better Environment, which in 2001 took the Anglo-American Corporation to court over pollution in mine areas, had by the end of the decade been engaged by the government to implement its Environmental Protection Fund.[66] Certainly, the successor to PRSP, Zambia's Fifth National Development Plan (launched in 2006), was drawn up with extensive civil society participation. Civil society "participation" is, however, acknowledged to be limited. In

Malawi, the new Malawi Growth and Development Strategy that has replaced the PRSP was drawn up with significant civil society involvement. However, it retained the neoliberal framework of the IMF's Poverty Reduction and Growth Facility, a study of which found that some of its conditions had increased poverty.[67] Jubilee Zambia suggests that 80 percent of the Fifth NDP was significantly influenced by civil society inputs. However, the remaining 20 percent that lies outside civil society purview contains a macroeconomic framework that continues to follow orthodox neoliberal lines. Zambian civil society is able to influence the ways in which government expenditure is allocated, but not the amount of money in the overall budget and where it comes from. Alert to this dilemma, Jubilee Zambia has sought to extend its influence into this still-protected area of policy-making, ensuring that all aspects of governmental activity are subject not to the strictures of the IFIs, but rather "conditionality from below."[68]

The new participatory culture also raised searching questions regarding the extent of participation of grassroots constituents in the organizations that claim to represent them. The establishment of the PRSP encouraged, in Malawi, the creation of new sectoral civil society networks in areas such as agriculture, health, and education; this coincided with a government policy of decentralizing decision-making to local levels. Such networks sought to demonstrate their links with grassroots opinion, but it is evident that in many cases they operate more as interlocutors, which are often closer to donors than to the grassroots. The Civil Society Agriculture Network (CSANet) is a case in point: established in 2001–2002 as an advocacy network with a membership of national and international NGOs, farmers' organizations, and others, it claims its beneficiaries to be the urban and rural poor. Yet its policy positions on, for example, ADMARC are clearly geared to a market-oriented agenda of commercial agricultural expansion involving a "leaner," commercialized ADMARC and subsidies targeted to the "productive poor."[69] CSANet, like many other civil society representatives, supported the appointment of (among other technocrats) minister of finance Goodall Gondwe (2004–2009), previously the Africa Director of the IMF, whom they praise for being less "political" in his approach.[70] It is questionable whether such organizations can be regarded as representative of the views of Malawi's vast rural poor, which appears to have supported, and benefited from, the recent expansion of ADMARC services. More generally, the extent to which the "top-down" decentralization and participation initiated in the last decade do anything to substantively increase "bottom-up" popular influence over the policies of states and donors warrants considerable skepticism.

Deepening democracy and constitution-making

The "opening up" of policy-making associated with the PRSP also provided a precedent for civil society participation in constitutional reform processes. Since the return of democracy, human rights and governance associations have continually stressed the need for a deepening of democratic law and practice in the still highly centralized and semi-authoritarian context of post-transition Africa. In Zambia a new Constitutional Review Commission, chaired by Wila Mung'omba, sat from 2003–2005, making recommendations similar to those adopted by the mid-1990s Mwanakatwe Commission (see above). It stimulated significant popular participation, receiving 12,647 submissions from ordinary Zambians across the country, including many from CSOs and local communities. The resultant draft Mung'omba Constitution sought, among other things, to strengthen parliamentary oversight powers (for example, requiring parliamentary approval for new international loans and ratification of a state of emergency), removed the president's power to set the date for elections, and provided for freedoms of speech and assembly in a new Bill of Rights. It also instituted a "50 percent plus one" hurdle for successful presidential candidates to clear (in 2001 Mwanawasa became president with only 29 percent of the vote in an election widely recognized as unfree and unfair).[71]

Civil society, now fully supportive of the process, initiated a major campaign to ensure that the new constitution would be adopted by a constituent assembly, thus avoiding the manipulation that occurred with the Mwanakatwe Commission and, indeed, has taken place throughout Zambia's history. Demonstrations and conferences throughout 2005 culminated that November with a "procession" of twelve thousand Zambians to Parliament. Attendees carried palm leaves and were led by church leaders in an attempt to avoid confrontation with the police. Simultaneous demonstrations took place across the country, including in small rural centers; some were organized by local members of organizations such as the CCJDP and the Citizens Forum, but others were apparently initiated by local activists with no organizational background. The demonstrations were partially successful: President Mwanawasa conceded the adoption of the new constitution by a constituent assembly; however, he refused to allow this before the 2006 elections, in which he was re-elected for the second and final time. Nevertheless, the endorsement and organization of mass demonstrations represented a change in the approach of civil society towards more social-movement-oriented approaches.

In 2007, following his re-election, Mwanawasa initiated the National Constitutional Conference (NCC), a constituent assembly–type process bringing together 550 political and civil society representatives in a year-long conference to finalize constitutional arrangements. The NCC, which met throughout 2008 and 2009, was increasingly viewed by many opposition politicians and civil society representatives as a delaying tactic; some boycotted the process. Many others, however, chose to participate in the NCC. Mwanawasa thereby successfully used the lure of "participation" to divide and confuse what had been a united civil society position. By early 2010, the NCC had still not submitted its overdue report to the new president, Rupiah Banda, who retains an effective veto over which aspects of constitutional reform will be put forward to Parliament.

In Malawi, the limited extent of democratic transition was tested in another form. Local elections scheduled for 2005, in the context of the decentralization proposals, were constantly delayed, revealing a practical unwillingness to reduce the centralization of power. A major constitutional review led by the Law Commission of Malawi took place in 2006, but the demands of civil society—to strengthen the Bill of Rights, include more checks and balances on political power, and strengthen anti-corruption laws—were not implemented. In 2007, a political confrontation between Mutharika and opposition leaders regarding the right of MPs to move from one political party to another created destabilizing political tension; the Supreme Court ruled that the Speaker of the National Assembly had the right to declare the seats of such MPs vacant, effectively undermining the ruling DPP's position in Parliament. A further controversy arose in 2009 over the right of former president Muluzi to stand for a third (non-consecutive) term in office. Three weeks before the election, Muluzi was charged with corruption while in office. Three days before the election, the constitutional court ruled him ineligible to stand again. Mutharika was subsequently re-elected with a decisive majority. While observers were relieved that these tensions did not lead to the type of post-election violence witnessed in Zimbabwe and Kenya in 2008, it demonstrated the still-incomplete nature of Malawi's transition to democracy. Civil society voices were notably reticent to address the political instability. The Catholic bishops whose statements had played such an important role in the early 1990s issued a statement declaring that Malawians had "sadly tolerated bad leadership and tendencies to take root such as self enriching leaders, mismanagement of economy, declining of education standards, immorality, the use of abusive language in public, careless privatization of government companies, irresponsible behavior in Parliament, corruption and bribery, injustice and savagery and murder. . . . This year's vote should be aimed at uprooting evil in our society."[72] Sections of civil society were critical of the neglect of the economy while these contests for political power took place, but otherwise there was little guidance regarding the election.

The position of civil society in the still-uncertain democratic spaces of Africa is exemplified by the recent passage of the long-threatened NGO Act in Zambia (see above). In 2005, an "NGO technical committee" was formed to liaise with government over the issue of regulation; a draft Code of Conduct was drawn up and circulated for consultation by the Zambia Council for Social Development, but was never implemented.[73] Under Mwanawasa, the immediate threat to NGO autonomy was substantially reduced, although it was still possible for the Minister for Home Affairs to unilaterally "ban" a CSO, the Southern Africa Centre for Constructive Resolution of Disputes, in 2004—a decision with no legal basis which was subsequently overturned by the courts.[74] However, following Mwanawasa's death in 2008 and the election of Rupiah Banda as president, a more authoritarian atmosphere returned. The autonomy and effectiveness of civil society, which had made considerable advances in recent years, was threatened after the passing of the NGO Act in August 2009: the Act imposed severe constraints on the registration of civil society organizations; among other measures, it threatened de-registration of NGOs whose activities were not in accordance with the national development plan. Attacks on the independent media, particularly the *Post,* increased. Whether civil society, with the election of Michael Sata as president in September 2011, has the capacity to resist the curtailment of its independence remains to be seen.

PRSPs: Co-opting social movements

Several general points need to be made about PRSPs. There were revolts against structural adjustment programs worldwide, increasingly tied together (at least in words) by the anticapitalist movement. The IFIs thus faced a worldwide crisis of legitimacy, and the PRSPs represented one strategy for legitimizing the continued insertion of these institutions into the policy-making of indebted states. The more or less explicit goal of this operation was to lure in and co-opt social forces that might otherwise be oppositional—in other words, to break the potential for political unity of the diverse social movements within each country. In the context of states that recently adopted electoral democracy, the PRSPs served to legitimize not just the IFIs but the state itself, by making a show of institutionalizing channels for peaceful reform.

On the side of the social movements, it is understandable that those who are struggling for reform would prefer there to be some channels for reform rather than none. Participation can thus be both a step toward democratization and a step toward co-optation. Ultimately, we see this as a process of institutionalizing a layer of intermediaries between the state and the grassroots. Civil society networks in Malawi, as we have stated, operated more as "interlocutors (which are in many cases closer to donors) than to the grassroots." By "interlocutors" we mean that CSOs became *intermediaries* between the state and ordinary people. This evolution of their role—to become bodies that mediate between the needs of the state and the needs of ordinary people (rather than bodies that represent or express these people's needs)—is, of course, what the state and the IFIs were aiming for.

Secondly, the criterion of success put forward by "participating" CSOs is the reduction of the debt burden, since PRSPs are linked to the HIPC program. Reduction of debt does relieve of the pressure on states to attack popular living standards, so CSOs can claim a victory on behalf of their "constituents." But as some of our CSO interviewees sharply assert, the actual demands from the grassroots—around which ordinary people can be expected to mobilize on their own behalf—have tended to be more concrete and specific than this. If that is the case, then CSO "participation" seems virtually bound *not* to be an expression of grassroots forces exerting their own influence over state policy.

Third, more radical voices in some countries have rejected official "participation" in shaping the PRSPs, as well as offering strategies and tactics for influencing the outcome of the process while maintaining their independence. But frequently, substantial radical alternatives have been absent—a case of several radical voices rather than forces.

Social movements and anticapitalism since 2000

Having set out the development of civil society and social movement activity in the countries under study, we now turn to their engagement with the anticapitalist movement since its emergence in the late 1990s. As we have seen, activists in these countries have sought to articulate an agenda of political rights and democratic governance and of social and economic justice; they have been in the forefront of political liberalization, but generally reject the implementation of economic liberalization which has been so dominant in Africa over the past two decades. It is evident from our research that the anticapitalist movement's articulation of some of these ideas on a global level not only provided inspiration to activists in these countries, but many also sought to engage with the movement or elements of it in a practical way. This does not mean, however, that they are uncritical of some of its assumptions and actions.

In Zambia, where social movement activists organized the first Southern African Social Forum in 2003 and the third African Social Forum in 2004 (see chapter 7), the devastating impact of economic liberalization in the 1990s and more recent battles over privatization provide local empirical context to wider struggles for fair and against "free" trade. More specifically, the growing presence in Zambia of Africa-based multinational corporations in retail (e.g., Shoprite, Spar) and the cellphone industry (CelTel) is cited by civil society representatives as evidence of globalization's influence.[75] Zambian civil society, boosted by its undoubted success in the "third term" campaign and its apparent increased influence in policy-making forums, recognizes the relevance of the anticapitalist agenda to its analysis. Leading CSOs such as Women for Change and CCJDP (now Caritas Zambia) are actively engaged in wider anticapitalist initiatives and are regular participants in World Social Forums (WSFs) and other social movement events. There is, however, skepticism that the structures of anticapitalism are always the best mode of mobilization. Two particular criticisms were expressed by Zambian interviewees who had attended Social Forums: first, that financial restrictions inevitably limited Zambian participation to one or two delegates, undermining the mass participation supposedly intrinsic to the model; and second, that the emphasis on Social Forums as a "space" limited their potential as a venue for specific mobilization.[76] At an organizational meeting of the Zambia Social Forum in 2006 attended by the authors, there was substantial confusion arising from the idea that the Forum lacked an agenda of its own. Some civil society leaders, themselves engaged with such processes, are skeptical of the movement's capacity to engage grassroots Zambians, whose need to alleviate their immediate poverty sometimes makes it difficult for them to focus on wider questions of global change.[77] But these issues are complicated. For example, activists fighting against certain privatizations were actually helped by the knowledge that such privatizations (and resistance to them) were happening across the world. There is clearly a difference between a more dispersed, atomized, and less-politicized poor population than those one finds in trade unions. In addition, many civil society activists have not found effective, concrete ways to link people's immediate needs with broader questions. These are African and global concerns—anticapitalist activists can be so abstract that their statements and arguments have little practical significance. There was, in addition, some skepticism that Social Forums provide an appropriate mode of mobilization. While many CSOs have sought to strengthen grassroots participation in their activities, this has not been demonstrably influenced by social movement discourse—rather, it results from both a sincere attempt to ensure greater mass involvement, and increasing recognition of the need to demonstrate popular legitimacy in the face of both state and donor skepticism.

The Social Forums held in Zambia have been characterized by the limited presence of grassroots activists, a particularly poor representation of mass-based organizations from the host country (for example, a lack of trade union delegates), and the dominance of international NGO agendas (see chapter 7). This reflects a perceived gap between what some term a civil society "elite" and a wider population that actively engages in demonstrations and protests like those in November 2005, but which struggles to relate to the complex issues often under discussion. Fr. Komakoma of the Justice and Peace Department of the Catholic Secretariat argues that civil society needs to overcome its elitism and relate more to this grassroots population, something that will require systematic initiatives in economic literacy.[78]

In Tanzania, the mass-based movement approach of the anticapitalist movement has proved influential and has been "borrowed" by local organizations, which have sought to initiate demonstrations on important issues. TANGO has sought to ensure that its representatives attending Social Forums include those from "up-country," that is, outside the urban center of Dar es Salaam.[79] However, although some national organizations have sought to raise awareness about events such as the World Social Forums, Deus Kibamba believes there has been insufficient consultation with and inadequate reporting back to grassroots constituents.[80]

Similar issues are raised by Malawian civil society organizations. As in much of the region, free trade has wiped out much of local industry, particularly in textiles.[81] The PRSP-linked sale of state-owned telecom, water, and electricity companies provided the framework for MEJN to work in collaboration with region-wide organizations such as the African Forum and Network on Debt and Development or the Southern African People's Solidarity Network, both based in Zimbabwe.[82] There is widespread criticism of South African–led domination of certain sectors of the economy, for example retail. The reversal of some government liberalizations, most importantly the supply of inputs to farmers (tools, seeds, fertilizers, etc.), has encouraged activists that the worst aspects of neoliberalism can be resisted. These campaigns are, however, rooted in research into local empirical experience—there has been a rejection of "emotional," sweeping appeals against neoliberal policies in the anticapitalist movement.[83] Many other organizations felt that the movement was something that existed outside and above their experience.[84]

We believe that we need to reject some of the hot air that passes for anticapitalist politics, but also resist a tendency by some activist groups to keep the generalizations to themselves and engage the "poor" at a patronizingly concrete level. Such practice does not involve overcoming the gap between CSOs and the grassroots but developing an unhealthy division of labor along the lines of Russian economism at the turn of the last century, where the middle class was supposed to engage in politics while the working masses engaged in "purely economic" struggle.

There is also strong awareness of, and resistance to, the tendency of northern/Western NGOs and social movements to impose their agenda and approach on their southern partners, whose dependence on their funding leads them to accept this agenda regardless of its local applicability, undermining the capacity of local movements to speak for their constituents and operate in a "bottom-up" manner.[85] Peter Chinoko of the local CCJDP emphasizes the need for more public education to enable effective mass participation in issues of economic justice.[86] It is the difficulty of bridging the chasm between the grassroots rural and urban poor they seek to represent and the international networks of both globalization and anticapitalist initiatives that represents the greatest challenge facing activists across Africa.

Conclusion: The limits of civil society organizations

This chapter has sought to establish a historical analysis of civil society and social movement ideas and activity in ostensibly democratic countries in Africa. It suggests that, notwithstanding the central role of some social movements in enabling the transition to democracy in the early 1990s, the new political systems were themselves characterized by authoritarianism and the centralization of power, thereby restricting the space available for "legitimate" activity by social movements. The "dual transition" of political and economic liberalization provided certain types of civil society organizations with new opportunities for service delivery activities, but the precipitate decline in the livelihoods of their constituents resulting from the unchecked imposition of neoliberal policies outweighed the limited positive effects of the retreat of the state. In addition, the increased (but temporary) provision of donor funding to CSOs accelerated a process of "extroversion," increasing the distance between such organizations and their constituents and distorting their policies and practices as well as leading to a proliferation of new NGOs with virtually no roots in society.

Although the situation varied considerably between different countries, it is suggested that by the late 1990s, the combination of increasingly repressive ruling parties and a reduction in donor support generated a stronger focus on accountability and coordination among more credible and politically oriented social movements. This led to a strategy of increased cooperation with each other and with new independent media as well as an increasingly critical approach to ruling parties and, to some extent, to the implementation of neoliberal policies (though this varied between countries and within sectors of civil society). In both Malawi and Zambia, a significant confrontation took place between civil society and the incumbent presidency—while this centered in both cases on the specific issue of the "third term," it reflected wider concerns regarding the nature of the democratic system and the legitimacy of public criticism of those in political power. While the campaign in Zambia generated considerable popular mobilization, in Malawi it was more dependent on coordination with discontented donors (reflecting these two countries' particular social composition and historical development).

The relative success of these campaigns increased the confidence of civil society actors and organizations. In a context of relatively increased space, enabled by both less directly repressive regimes and the new emphasis on "participation" in policy-making, CSOs were able to achieve increased influence over the development of some government and donor policies, though not to the degree that they were able to directly challenge the neoliberal basis of economic policy. The results of increased participation are mixed: civil society became more coordinated in the development and communication of its policies and more committed to consultation with its constituents, but the extent to which CSOs' positions reflected popular grievances and aspirations was limited by the "art of the possible" inherent in policy-making of this kind, and in the challenges of explaining complex policy positions to grassroots constituents in a way that enables effective accountability. Englund rightly concludes that in Malawi, most NGOs, while courageously opposing a return to authoritarianism and expanding liberal rights, have not proved to be useful vehicles for advancing the economic rights and aspirations of the majority of poor rural Malawians.[87] Although a similar division between liberal and socioeconomic rights is common among many of Zambia's NGOs, the country's comparatively urban composition and political identity has generated a more materialistic form of politics that has found expression among more progressive civil society figures, labor leaders, and political parties.

The relative decline of neoliberal hegemony has in recent years (culminating in the economic crisis of 2008–10) enabled limited adoption of policies that, in some respects, challenge free market orthodoxy—Zambia's short-lived new mining tax regime and both countries' agricultural subsidies are cases in point. This is in some cases a reflection of the successful translation of popular discontent into the political arena via social movements, particularly in Zambia. It is, however, noticeable that the relatively positive experience of participation has led some CSOs to internalize aspects of the neoliberal agenda. Many remain more aligned to the agenda of international/Western NGOs than to effectively expressing the wishes of the grassroots community they purport to represent. In addition, "participation" in PRSPs is done on the premise that CSOs are mediating between the state and the grassroots; this legitimizes and institutionalizes the influence of the state on CSO policy. This connection to the state is at least as strong a factor in producing the "CSOs/grassroots gap" as the CSOs' connection to the international NGOs.

It is evident that the capacity of social movements to operate legitimately in the semi-democratic environment of much of Africa remains precarious and subject to rollback by government, as demonstrated most recently in Zambia with the passing of the NGO Act. The failure to substantively deepen constitutional reform and effectively decentralize power means that organizations claiming to speak for the poor and marginalized in these societies need to deepen their efforts to ensure that the participation of these constituents is meaningful and not tokenistic.

We have to face realities, however. Many of these organizations are never going to deepen their efforts to allow their "constituencies" to truly participate and set the agenda. The reason for this is the "social niche" that has opened up for professional CSO staffers to pose as popular representatives—one that is heavily rewarded by salaries and the experience of "getting the ear of" state officials. A few of these organizations, in their role as mediators, will be susceptible both to pressures from above and from below. The trick (and challenge) is to find ways to build organizations that are independent enough to withstand pressure from above while being systematically and organically connected to pressure from below.

The experience of activists in these countries of the anticapitalist movement has enabled them to offer a more sustained critique of neoliberalism, and in some cases to mobilize mass movements to challenge the particular manifestation of such policies. However, many activists were also critical of the Social Forums' *modus operandi* and tendency to assume uniform solutions to problems that, because of uneven political, economic, and social development, find diverse expression internationally and in Africa in particular, a subject that will be further developed in chapter 7. In chapter 6, we turn to the experience of social movements in countries that did not successfully transition (even to a limited extent) to democracy.

CHAPTER 6

FRUSTRATED TRANSITIONS: SOCIAL MOVEMENTS, PROTEST, AND REPRESSION IN THE DEMOCRATIC REPUBLIC OF CONGO, ZIMBABWE, AND SWAZILAND

In contrast to the social movement experiences explored in the previous chapter, our study now turns to countries where movements to achieve democratic political systems and related social and economic gains in the 1990s were frustrated by dictatorial regimes, as well as by weaknesses and divisions within the ranks of the pro-democracy movements. As elsewhere, social movements were central to these efforts, but the particular interaction between the people, popular forces, and political elites did not bring about a meaningful democracy in the Democratic Republic of Congo (DRC), Zimbabwe, and Swaziland. In each of the cases explored in this chapter, some degree of formal democratic reform has been achieved or (in the case of Zimbabwe) was already in existence, and there is no hard and fast line between these and the sometimes-authoritarian democracies explored in chapter 5. Nevertheless, the experience of social movements in these three countries (and in many others on the continent) has been an ongoing campaign for democratic and social reform while also attempting to operate in a repressive and often physically threatening environment. This has raised particular challenges and questions regarding the role of social movements in such a setting that bears useful comparative analysis, particularly regarding the relationship between formal democratization and the realization of popular economic and social aspirations. However, the relatively disparate nature of these countries means that they are most usefully examined as discrete case studies.

In the early 1990s, the DRC experienced what has been described as a "second revolution," but the revolt was ultimately unable to unseat the country's notorious dictator Joseph Mobutu Sese Seko. This failure of internal social forces opened up space for a different, and largely external, political force to overthrow Mobutu in 1997. This transition by military means not only frustrated the impetus towards truly democratic governance, it also set off a devastating series of wars in the DRC. In Swaziland, pro-democracy movements challenged the monarchy's absolute power, forcing concessions and the first parliamentary elections in 1993. Despite further pro-democracy protests in the 2000s, and a new constitution in 2005, the old royal elite remained in charge. Swazi social movements remain torn between initiating popular action to achieve change from within and seeking to follow the twin paths of economic and political liberalization that have, we argue, so restricted the nature of democracy in much of the continent.

From the mid-1990s onwards, Zimbabwe's ruling party, the Zimbabwe African National Union–Patriotic Front (ZANU-PF), faced a profound challenge to its political hegemony, in which a formal democratic system masked a highly authoritarian reality. In the context of economic liberalization and declining living standards, protests and strikes drew tens of thousands into an ever-widening cycle of protest. By 1998 these pools of resistance developed into a direct political struggle that targeted the ruling party's hold on power. In 1999, a new party, the Movement for Democratic Change (MDC), was created by social movements in general and the trade union movement in particular. At the turn of the century, the MDC appeared to be on the brink of achieving its progressive model of democracy from the bottom up—but because of both the willingness of Zimbabwe's rulers to repress its opponents with violence and the MDC's retreat from social movement activism, the democratic movement was demobilized and defeated.

The case studies in this chapter therefore examine the frustration of these respective "transitions" and how these were frustrated by both the repression of incumbent ruling parties and the inability of opposition parties and coalitions to identify and pursue a political alternative that could overturn the old power. The consequences for the vibrant social movements that briefly brightened the skies over the continent were clear: many collapsed altogether, while others became dependent on foreign funds and were "commodified." A few, however, have survived and grown in a context of dictatorship, repression, and economic crisis. The hard lessons they have drawn regarding the complex relationship between national dictatorship, global economic context, and social movement activism are relevant for the wider struggles of social movements on the continent.

Democratic Republic of Congo: Crisis, resistance, and failed revolt

Beginning in 1990, a mass popular urban movement shook Zaire (as the country was then known) to its foundations. President Mobutu was almost dislodged by a combination of street protests and political opposition, but managed to survive in power. In 1997 Laurent Kabila, then a relatively unknown figure on the Congolese political landscape, came to power as the result of an externally supported military invasion. Mobutu fled, dying soon afterwards in exile. How could this little-known figure of the long and painful failure of Congolese guerrilla resistance succeed in ousting Mobutu when the popular movements of the early 1990s had failed to do so? We will argue here that the war, plunder, and catastrophe that gripped the Congo after 1997 emerged out of the defeat of the democratic movement of the early 1990s.

After rebellions in the countryside in the 1960s and 1970s made many abortive attempts to remove the Mobutu regime, the popular movement for democracy that came close to unseating him arose in urban centers.[1] However, the regime managed to manipulate a process of democratic "reforms" to divide and disorient opposition leaders who were prepared to compromise with Mobutu. The frustration of the "transition" revealed the absence of a serious opposition that was prepared to lead a popular movement for radical transformation. Loka Ne Kongo—Minister of Higher Education in the transition government of 1992–93—later characterized the opposition in the following terms: "The opposition suffered failure after failure, in large part because of their own impotence; all of the paths that could have led to the removal of the dictator, by non-violence, had more or less been exhausted."[2] These failures eventually demobilized and destroyed the popular movement that had made a transition possible.

In 1988 the Congo, despite its vast mineral wealth, was ranked the eighth-poorest country in the world. It had a per capita income of $160 a year, while real incomes fell to just 10 percent of their pre-independence level. Between 1973 and 1985—a period that, according to the regime, would see the country catch up with the West—per capita income had fallen by 3.9 percent a year (a decline exceeded only by war-torn Nicaragua). By the late 1980s Zaire had gone from being a net food exporter to spending more than 20 percent of its foreign exchange earnings on food imports. Twenty-eight years after independence, the country was saddled with a seven-billion-dollar foreign debt eagerly lent by international banks, Western governments (seeking to prop up the pro-Western Mobutu dictatorship), and financial agencies, much of Mobutu and his henchmen looted or spent on prestige projects.[3] With the end of the Cold War and the end of Mobutu's usefulness as a Cold War strongman, reform seemed both necessary and possible. Contemporary observers noted that, both in the wider context of African political change and in the specific context of Zaire, "even the most uncompromising dictatorships, such as those of Mobutu in Zaire and Banda in Malawi, are being forced to consider reforms that would previously have been inconceivable." [4]

As elsewhere on the continent, "structural adjustment," viewed as the solution to such problems, was a key factor that drove Congolese people onto the streets (see chapter 3). The Congolese government was "forced . . . to address budget deficits by reducing expenditures in 'non-productive' sectors such as health, education, research, and culture while increasing investments in trade and production. Mobutu respected only the first half of these conditions." [5] Following the rest of the continent, the government slashed funding to schools, health facilities, and public universities.

The transition

In the context of an unprecedented crisis and the continent-wide rise of democratic movements, Mobutu embarked in 1990 on an experiment to test popular opinion regarding Zaire's political situation and what should be done about it. When his failure to announce immediate reforms that April led to student rioting in Kinshasa, Mobutu took more decisive action, unilaterally initiating Zaire's Third Republic and declaring that a multi-party system would be introduced after a one-year "transitional period." This would be comprised of only two parties, including his own Mouvement Populaire de la Révolution (Popular Movement of the Revolution), which had ruled Zaire as a one-party state, and the then-illegal opposition Union pour la Démocratie et le Progrès Social (Union for Democracy and Social Progress, UDPS). In May, a "transitional government" was formed. Mobutu, seeking to manage the democratization process from above, announced that a special commission would draft a new constitution by April 1991 and that presidential elections would be held before December that year, with legislative elections to follow in 1992. He also announced the "depoliticization" of the armed forces, the police, the civil guard, the security services, and the administration in general.

It appeared, however, that the transition to multi-party democracy would not be so easy for Mobutu to control. Étienne Tshisekedi wa Mulumba, who led the UDPS, was released from house arrest to the jubilation of his followers. The security forces' attempts to repress the UDPS could not prevent a deluge of criticism and protests. In a Belgian television interview, Tshisekedi warned Mobutu that he was at risk of being removed by force unless he remained true to the promised "transition." Tshisekedi referred to Mobutu's close friend, the Romanian dictator Nicolae Ceaușescu, whose execution months earlier during a popular uprising had been shown in Zaire—prompting contemplation in Kinshasa of a similar fate for "Mobutu Sesesescu."

The democratic movement was bolstered by May demonstrations by students at the University of Kinshasa, who asserted that the reforms announced were "irrevocable." When their demonstration was violently suppressed, the students appealed for other universities and colleges to rise up in solidarity: "Do not cross your arms. Follow our example. The dictatorship is finished. We cannot go back. Take on the state. Demonstrate! March!"[6] Students at the University of Lubumbashi responded to this call, demonstrating daily in the city and at the university. On May 11, this student uprising was brought to a swift and violent end. Dozens of students who had led the strikes and demonstrations were killed by the security forces and their bodies disappeared. However, the massacre in Lubumbashi also exposed the reality of Mobutu's "reforms."[7] It prompted a wave of political protest and civil unrest across the country during the second half of 1990.

This wave of protest took place in the context of a rapidly worsening economic crisis. Hyperinflation destroyed the value of dramatic pay increases, and the prices of staple foods rose by the day. Civil servants struck for four months, demanding increases of up to 500 percent for the lowest paid; the strike ended when 100 percent pay raises were promised. The civil unrest was not only among public employees and salaried workers, but also among other wage

workers and the poor. There were "food riots" in Kinshasa, Lubumbashi, Bukavu, and Mbuji Mayi in December 1990.[8] However, these
strikes and riots, like those in other African countries at this time,
linked economic grievances to the need for political change; one of
the favorite slogans was "*Mobutu voleur!*" (Mobutu is a thief!)

As the process of political reform accelerated, constitutional reforms ended presidential control over the National Executive
Council and foreign policy and authorized independent trade
unions. Mobutu conceded that a full multi-party political system
would be established; the enabling legislation was adopted in November. There was now a proliferation of political parties. Prominent among these was the Union des Fédéralistes et Républicans
Indépendants (Union of Federalists and Independent Republicans),
led by Jean Nguza Karl-i-Bond, a former member of the ruling
party. By January 1991, nineteen new political parties had been formally registered, including the UDPS. The UDPS established a
coalition of opposition groups called the Union Sacrée de l'Opposition Radicale (Sacred Union of the Radical Opposition), which
eventually came to include 130 political parties. This reflected the
widespread nature and the diversity of opposition to Mobutu. As in
so many countries at this time, the floodgates of political reform,
once pushed ajar by cautious top-down reformers, were opened
more widely by popular pressure.

In February 1991, hundreds of thousands of workers, civil servants, and public service employees held a three-day general strike
to protest their working conditions, pay, and living standards and
to demand the government's resignation. Later the same month,
twenty thousand people attended an anti-government rally in Kinshasa organized by the UDPS. In March, a new enlarged transitional government was established, which the more influential
opposition parties and coalitions refused to join. They also refused
to participate in Mobutu's proposed National Constitutional Conference unless the president relinquished power. During widespread anti-government demonstrations, forty-two people were

killed and many injured when security forces opened fire on demonstrators in the town of Mbuji Mayi in April. Following this violence, Mobutu temporarily suspended the National Conference.

In July, in an attempt to divide the opposition, Mobutu offered the post of prime minister to Tshisekedi, whose grassroots supporters were shocked, but not passive. Congo expert George Nzongola-Ntalaja explains what happened next: "The politicised masses of Kinshasa . . . immediately after the announcement . . . descended on Tshisekedi's residence in Limete to force him to back down. For the masses, their 'saviour' should not cohabit with the 'devil.'"[9] Although he bowed to popular pressure, Tshisekedi made it clear that he was prepared to accept the post. While attempting to protect his democratic credentials, he damaged his reputation, perhaps irreparably.

The opposition, having previously opposed the National Conference, now believed it could use its strength to decisively shape the new constitution. Some 2,850 delegates, including nine hundred representatives of opposition parties, participated in the National Conference, which finally opened in August 1991. By September, however, the conference, from which representatives of the powerful Catholic Church had withdrawn, was overshadowed by the worsening political crisis. Further clashes took place between opposition supporters and the security forces, with heavy casualties. The demonstrations represented growing popular frustration with the slow pace of change at a time when the economy was in free-fall. Inflation had soared to around 10,000 percent a year, and salaried public sector workers (including soldiers) contemptuously rejected pay offers of 100 to 200 percent. Meanwhile, the state mining giant Gecamines, the only productive parastatal, stopped paying into the state treasury.

In October, Tshisekedi was named prime minister of a government in which Mobutu loyalists held the key posts of defense, foreign affairs, and planning. Only twelve days later, Tshisekedi's refusal to swear an oath of allegiance to Mobutu led to his removal and to the installation of a "Government of Crisis." This new government lacked the confidence of both the Western powers and the Zairian political elite. Meanwhile, there was a new wave of riots and impromptu demonstrations in many parts of the country against misery and hunger—but also against the "wealthy."[10] It is clear, however, that the opposition leadership regarded these mass mobilizations, riots, strikes, and demonstrations as a method to pressure the dictatorship to share power, rather than as a means by which genuine progressive change might be achieved.

Protest of hope: February 16, 1992

In early 1992, the political crisis came to a head. In January, troops briefly seized the national radio station, urging the removal of the government and the resumption of the suspended National Conference. Violence intensified as Christian churches attempted to mobilize against the suspension of the conference and the repression of sections of the opposition. More strikes broke out as civil servants and public sector workers demanded better wages and living conditions, as well as the restarting of the conference. Nzongola-Ntalaja, an eyewitness to these events, writes: "As in the past, ordinary people stepped in to change the situation."[11] The Catholic Church organized a "march of Christians" in the capital on February 16 to demand the National Conference. A million people took to the streets, exuberant and confident. In 110 parishes, local committees mobilized for the protests in which radical voices could be heard.[12] Other marches took place simultaneously in Kitwit, Kananga, Mbuji Mayi, Kisangani, Goma, and Bukavu. While in Goma and Bukavu there was little disruption, in Kisangani and Mbuji Mayi the demonstrations were brutally suppressed.

The organization of this demonstration—marking the high point of popular struggles—provides an insight into the dynamics and composition of social movements during the "transition."[13] The demonstration was called by the Comité Laïc de Co-ordination (Lay Coordinating Committee). This structure included many members of the National Conference, but also local militants with the capacity to mobilize their neighborhoods. The Catholic Church occupied a highly ambiguous space in the process of democratic transition. Church and parish groups were at the center of the protests during the "transition." They provided a base for neighborhood organization and brought together local militants from a range of political parties. The resultant parish groups organized local protests and lobbies and coordinated their action with counterparts in other areas. Radical intellectuals addressed parishioners, advocating the overthrow of the regime. They provided training in non-violent direct action and discussed Latin American liberation theology. They instructed participants on how to protect themselves against tear gas and how to behave when under attack by the police. They also organized solidarity during general strikes. Local churches in Kinshasa, and cities and towns across Zaire, were thus the headquarters of the popular movement.

Gustave Lobunda, a young priest from Kisangani, went on hunger strike in 1992 in protest at the closure of the National Conference. He describes how his actions—and those of thousands of others—were animated by a combination of ideas. The inspiration of the life of Jesus, he argued, "is to give your life for others . . . and each time that I hear at mass the phrase 'Do this in memory of me,' the desire to give my life as a gift for others becomes very strong." The inspiration for his hunger strike came from elsewhere:

> My hunger strike was also inspired by Gandhi and Martin Luther King, for whom I have always had a profound admiration. I have seen the film of Gandhi at least nine times. . . . I had time to get to know him in the book *This Night, Freedom*. And learnt about Martin Luther King through articles and by his biography written by Stephen B. Oates. . . . Gandhi and King have helped me to understand the value of human freedom, which is a gift from God . . . this consciousness of freedom is so strong that I cannot continue to live under a dictatorship.[14]

José Mpundu describes the demonstration: "On the day itself we only had one mass at 6 am . . . I must confess that I was a little scared. Scared that there wouldn't be a large enough turnout. But when I saw the number of people at the assembly point my fear disappeared." There were, he estimated, two hundred members of his parish and neighboring parishes. Shortly after they had set off they encountered an obstacle: "The army blocking the route . . . we sat down together according to our plans . . . the soldiers then tried to disperse us, by kicking us. . . . We left the avenue and reassembled in a parallel street where there were no soldiers."[15] Demonstrators marched holding crosses, Bibles, images of the Virgin Mary, and other religious objects. The crowds sang hymns and prayed. Another eyewitness explained what happened when the police started to fire: "We were scared by the firing and we advanced slowly towards the soldiers. Priest, nuns . . . Christians were on their knees praying and brandishing branches, bibles . . . as the soldiers fired into the air. The crowd were singing. . . . Thirty minutes later the soldiers had exhausted their ammunition and we continued singing religious songs, and we had crossed the first military barrier."[16]

Certain commentators associate the religious content of the demonstration with a lack of "politics." One academic account describes the "imaginary world" of the marchers, in which they were "motivated by the hope of a new Christian reign. . . . This Catholic crowd had the deliberation, calm and peacefulness of . . . a procession. Its strength was belief rather than politics."[17] This entirely misses the profound interconnection of belief and politics in this context. The aim of thousands of demonstrators was not the afterlife or a "new Christian reign" but the reopening of the National Conference. Churches were synonymous at this time with activism and protest, encouraging and mobilizing communities to become involved in the political changes sweeping the country.

The demonstration, notwithstanding its bloody suppression, both accelerated the political process and simultaneously revealed the unwillingness of opposition leaders to directly confront Mobutu.[18] In August 1992, Tshisekedi was elected transitional prime minister by the National Conference, replacing Karl-i-Bond. He was given a two-year mandate, pending the promulgation of a new constitution, which would supposedly curtail presidential powers. This was a period of great optimism: "Like Kinshasa, the whole country erupted in joyful dance from dawn to sunset on 15 August 1992."[19] Though the National Conference was celebrated, it was a space ultimately controlled by the president. Over the next two years, the Conference was intermittently suspended by Mobutu, as opposition figures were pulled into the regime's ever-shifting system of political patronage.

While Mobutu managed to disorient and buy off opposition figures, meaningful political debate had to a large extent shifted to the street. Far from being restricted to the forums of the National Conference, politics was discussed "on the sidewalks near newspaper stands," creating a "political organisation of young people calling themselves *parlementaires-debout* [street politicians] . . . organised in each municipality in Kinshasa and with a central organ for the city as a whole, these forums debated current issues, took decisions and sought ways of implementing them. Major actions involved publicly denouncing opposition politicians who were seen as faltering in their resolve for democratic change, and organising rallies and demonstrations in support of the various demands of the democracy movement."[20]

Frustrated transition

There were several moments in both 1990 and 1992 when Mobutu could have been removed by the popular movements described above. There was, however, a serious problem of leadership. Although many pro-democracy activists saw the UDPS as their desired vehicle of change, it failed to seize the opportunity to oust the regime when it was at its weakest. Commentators Gautheir de Villers and J. Omasombo Tshonda argued that "Tshisekedi's preoccupation with the premiership caused the opposition to lose sight of its real political objectives. Moreover, his confusing strategy disorientated supporters. 'Moses the saviour' was transformed into the 'Sphinx' without a clear political stance. His behaviour can best be explained as combat tactics between himself and Mobutu."[21] The UDPS, these authors argue, rather than seeking the overthrow of Mobutu, pursued a waiting game in which the situation would deteriorate so dramatically that Tshisekedi appeared to be the only realistic alternative.

The "transition" in the Congo was thus frustrated largely because of the failings of the opposition itself. Ludo Martins makes the case for a different type of movement that would have helped lead and coordinate the popular grassroots forces that emerged in the early 1990s. There was certainly an embryonic alternative in the parish committees, in neighborhood groups, and among trade union militants that, with more consistent leadership, could have created a movement that refused to compromise with the regime: "A revolutionary organisation could have expressed these needs: the immediate departure of Mobutu and all the dinosaurs; prosecution of all Mobutists responsible for repression and corruption; [and] the end to the foreign domination of the Congo."[22]

There were, however, many factors militating against such a movement. As elsewhere, the organized Congolese left was disoriented by the collapse of the Soviet Union. A generation of political leaders, militants, trade union activists, and intellectuals were loosed from their ideological moorings. The opposition kept deferring to the National Conference because it seemed to fill this ideological vacuum. While students and the urban poor (who were in no way nostalgic for Eastern Bloc communism) carried out effective direct action against the regime, the leaders they looked to, lacking as they did a transformative political project that might meet some of the grassroots demands, were consequently unable or unwilling to prize Mobutu's weakening grip from the levers of power.

In 1995, Loka Ne Kongo wrote that "the successive failure of the opposition, the betrayals of our leaders discourage and disarm . . . the population is hungry. One fears that tomorrow they will not listen anymore to the opposition." Six months later, Ne Kongo called for a program of "civil disobedience" involving popular refusal to cooperate with the state on any level. He was clear, though, that "this supposes that the opposition organises itself to install across the country a parallel administration, police force and justice system."[23] By this time, the tactics of the parliamentary opposition had collapsed; by September 1996 Ne Kongo concluded that "all the paths that could have led to the eradication of the dictator by non-violence are practically exhausted."[24] The failure of the opposition opened the field to Kabila's rebel army, which was then assembling in the east. By 1996 there was no effective anti-Mobutu force except the armed opposition led by Laurent Kabila and supported by foreign powers—specifically Rwanda.

The Congo since 2000

The decade following the frustration of Congo's popular movement against Mobutu's dictatorship saw three devastating military conflicts. The first war was fought with the remnants of Mobutu's national army in 1996–97, as Kabila's forces made their way westwards through the Congo to conquer the capital in May 1997. The second war, from 1998, saw Kabila's hastily assembled pan-African army pitted against his former supporters, Rwanda and Uganda. The third and final war was triggered by the conflict between Rwanda and Uganda in 1999. The old allies now fought against each other, frequently through proxy militias and rebel groups, for control over the Congo's extraordinary mineral wealth. Behind these countries were Western powers and multinationals that were happy to support Rwanda and Uganda and to profit from illegally exported wealth, "regardless of elements of unlawfulness."[25]

A deal signed in 2003 between the Kinshasa government, rebel groups, and the political opposition led to the formation of a transitional national government. Fighting, however, continued. Estimates show that approximately 3.8 million people died between 1998 and 2004. The "peace" agreement eventually led to

elections in 2006, which saw Joseph Kabila, the incumbent president and son of Laurent Kabila (assassinated in 2001), defeat his
main rival Jean-Pierre Bemba. For many people, these elections—
the first democratic elections held since the fall of the Congo's
first prime minister Patrice Lumumba in 1961—were a great step
forward. However, the ongoing war, and particularly the 2006
election, took place in a very different context from that of the
early 1990s, when popular movements created an atmosphere in
which ordinary Congolese people had the opportunity to influence national political change. Little has been done to encourage
the growth of independent social and political movements. Indeed, the elections seemed to confirm the country's dependence
on external patronage. The elections were run entirely with external funding and under UN supervision; there was little popular
mobilization and debate in the run-up to the polls, and little sense
that the main political parties contesting the elections offered substantive policy alternatives.[26] George Nzongola-Ntalaja correctly
depicted the elections not as an exercise in self-determination but
as a ritual justifying the country's political elite.[27] While the elections brought a semblance of stability to some parts of the country, war has continued largely unabated in the east. In a number of
provinces, especially in the east and northeast of the Congo, mas-
sacres and systematic rape by militia forces and rebel groups have
continued unabated. These groups are frequently supported by regional powers; their human rights abuses often take place under
the watch of the United Nations.[28]

What is the state of social movements in the Congo today?
Though various human rights NGOs have been active in the country since the election, they have faced escalating oppression. NGOs
have exposed harsh working conditions in companies, including ra-
diation poisoning from uranium mines, but in doing so have made
themselves unpopular with the state. For those human rights organizations and NGOs that have been operating in Kinshasa, the vehicle
of repression has been the Agence Nationale de Renseignements

(National Intelligence Agency). Robert Ilunga, president of the Amis de Nelson Mandela pour la Defénse des Droits de l'Homme (Friends of Nelson Mandela for the Defense of Human Rights), was arrested in Kinshasa in August 2009 for issuing a press release that denounced working conditions at a gravel-making company in the Bas-Congo province. The communiqué had referred to the involvement of Joseph Kabila's wife in the company. Ilunga was arrested and held without charge for nine days; the charges against him, leveled that September, were eventually overturned.

Harassment, intimidation, and violence against community-based NGOs are common. In 2010, Amnesty International detailed recent violations against eight significant human rights activists, and such violations intensified in the run-up to the presidential election in 2011.[29] Many of these organizations report on the flagrant abuse of workers and the environmental and working conditions in the DRC's mines, the primary source of government revenue. Golden Misabiko, Katanga branch president of the Association Africaine de Défense des Droits de l'Homme (African Association for the Defense of Human Rights), which drew attention to the state's involvement in the illegal extraction of minerals from Shinkolobwe mine, was arrested for propagating "false information" and sentenced in absentia to one year's imprisonment. He has been forced to flee the country.[30]

Much political uncertainty hung over the country in early 2012 as Tshisekedi declared himself president, claiming the elections had been rigged. The influential Catholic Church condemned the elections, citing the "climate of fear" in which they took place, and Willy Wabo, a civil society activist who condemned the election results, was murdered in North Kivu province. A report focusing on November and December 2011 by the American organization Human Rights Watch claims thirty-three people had been killed and at least 265 arrested and detained illegally, most of whom were linked to the opposition UDPS. Since the results of the elections were announced in February 2012, a number of government and opposition forces have been involved in riots and protests. In a worrying rerun of events after the 2006 election, President Kabila closed several media organizations in February. Congo remains far from a functioning democracy.

Zimbabwe: Struggle, dictatorship and social movements

Zimbabwe was once regarded as an exception in a continent of so-called failed states and bad governance. But since the late 1990s, the country has faced a crisis both political and economic. Popular opposition to economic decline fueled the growth of mass social movements, which then created an opposition political party, the MDC. As in Congo, there is a tendency to downplay the extent of popular unrest against the regime, with political conflict instead portrayed as between the country's two dominant parties. Yet, as this section will demonstrate, the MDC has its roots in the popular challenge to ZANU-PF in the late 1990s and the social movements on which it rested. That period saw what amounted to a mass popular revolt. Strikes by nurses, teachers, civil servants, and builders rippled across the country. In January 1998, housewives orchestrated a "bread riot" that expanded into an uprising of the urban poor. The protests, strikes, and campaigns were often explicitly against the government's Economic and Structural Adjustment Programs, ESAP and ESAP II, implemented since 1991, which closed factories, laid off workers, and slashed state funding to education. Discontent with the results of ESAP steadily increased throughout the 1990s and was increasingly expressed by the labor and student movements, together with a range of other civil society organizations.

Economic and political unrest: 1997–2000

One example of this period was the July 1997 clothing industry strike. Clothing manufacturing employed thirty thousand workers, but was undermined by cheap textile imports resulting from ESAP liberalization. The end of state support and tariff barriers led to a sharp decline for the industry.[31] Owners used a pay dispute as an opportunity to sack thousands of workers in a range of clothing outlets. Although the strike did not achieve its aims, it accelerated challenges to both the economic and political status quo. As the general secretary of the National Union of the Clothing Industry of Zimbabwe (NUCIZ), Joseph Tanyanyiwa, explained: "We would really control by means of workers' power."[32] Meanwhile, inspired by urban anti-ESAP unrest, the rural poor—particularly veterans of the war for independence—started to invade white-owned farms. Initially the regime evicted such "squatters" and arrested the movement's leaders.

Brian Kagoro, an important student leader in the period, described how demands converged: "The largest number of redundancies were created . . . so you now had students supporting their parents on their student stipends which were not enough because their parents had been laid off work. So in a sense as poverty increases you have a reconvergence of these forces. And the critique started off really being around issues of socio-economic justice. . . . Students started couching their demands around the right to livelihood."[33] This "convergence of forces" reflected the dynamics of protest in much of post–structural adjustment Africa. Previously distinct groups recognized that their interests—as unemployed graduates, students, and laid-off workers—were the same. These years of popular mobilization and political debate were described by one activist as a "sort of revolution."[34]

As the struggles against the government broadened to include new layers of society, so did the organizations that sought to give these groups a more coherent voice. In June 1999, women's organizations grouped under the National Constitutional Assembly (NCA) banner formed the Constitutional Women's Coalition, later the Women's Coalition. New faith-based organizations became active and older ones were reenergized. Since the mid-1990s, churches had encouraged and nurtured the rapid development of CSOs. The

Jesuit training center Silveira House hosted critical debates about the failures of ESAP and possible alternatives to adjustment. Other church groups strayed into the political arena, as the Zimbabwe Council of Churches (ZCC) trained election agents to monitor the 1995 election. Church groups were, in many respects, the seedbed for the development of CSOs. The meetings that led to the creation of the NCA were held at Africa Synod House, home to the ZCC. Similarly, the preparatory meetings of the MDC took place in the premises of the Zimbabwe Catholic Bishops' Conference.

The NCA, founded in 1997, sought to define a new relationship between political power and civil society by campaigning for a democratic and people-driven constitution. After the food riots of January 1998, a new coalition of human rights organizations was formed, initially to provide assistance to those who had suffered from government repression following the riots. This evolved into the Zimbabwe Human Rights NGO Forum. After the formation of the MDC in 2000 (see below), the ZCC organized meetings that led to the founding of the Zimbabwe Election Support Network (ZESN). The ZESN, a coalition of NGOs, would play an important role in training and monitoring the violently contested elections over the next decade. However, relationships between churches and civil society groups were fragile: for example, the ZCC, vital to the formation of the NCA, withdrew in 1999, accusing the NCA of being too political. Nor were all church groups opposed to the government; when ZANU-PF launched its own constitutional commission in opposition to the NCA, some church leaders decided to join.

In 1998, the University of Zimbabwe was closed for five months as students demanded that opposition forces be organized into a national political party—a workers' party. Students organized protests, marching with workers. Such demands ultimately led to the formation of the MDC in September 1999, with the Zimbabwe Congress of Trade Unions (ZCTU) playing a leading role. As Job Sikhala, a founding member, explained, "It was basically a party of the poor with a few middle class."[35] Morgan Tsvangirai, the

party's leader, stated in March 1999: "In our case, the main charac-
teristic is that we are driven by working-class interests, with the
poor having more space to play a role than they do now."[36] Many of
those who had been involved in the exuberant protests that had
rocked Zimbabwe expected the new party to bring about a radical—even socialist—transformation. However, "the foundation of
the MDC at the ZCTU's Convention . . . was, and still is, seen as an
opportune marriage between civil society and political interests."[37]
It was a marriage between genuinely popular political forces, sections of Zimbabwe's capitalist class, and political careerists. This
uneasy coalition meant that the MDC would remain jostled by
competing interests that sought to shape both the opposition's policies and its strategy in opposing ZANU-PF.[38]

ZANU-PF strikes back

The period from February 2000, when the government lost a vote
on a new constitution, and June 2000, when the MDC contested
parliamentary elections for the first time, was marked by the rapid
escalation of state-sponsored violence. Despite this, the MDC almost won the election, gaining fifty-seven seats against ZANU-
PF's sixty-two. This success threatened the very future of the
ZANU-PF regime, which rapidly accelerated the extent of its violence by to maintain its grip on power. It sponsored a new wave of
farm invasions in order to politicize the war veterans, and
launched the National Youth Service to indoctrinate and train
youths as a cadre to be mobilized against the opposition. In its first
five years, more than forty thousand youths completed training
programs.[39] Such forces were vital in maintaining ZANU-PF in
power despite the close result, amid widespread rigging, of the
2002 presidential election

ZANU-PF, having come close to losing power, gradually regained the upper hand by presenting itself as the sole voice of the
liberation movement. The MDC, by contrast, seemed cowed and
unable to mount a serious resistance, either politically or on the

streets. A decisive moment came in June 2003. The MDC's so-called "final push" was meant to undermine the regime with a week-long stay-away and a march on State House. However, it made no serious efforts to mobilize the available forces, leaving only students in Harare to organize a protest that was violently crushed. The government scored another victory against the opposition and emerged stronger.

In parliamentary elections in 2005, also widely believed to have been rigged, the MDC lost sixteen seats to ZANU-PF, which secured the necessary two-thirds majority needed to unilaterally change the constitution. Though the opposition had faced years of violent intimidation, the MDC was also by this stage hopelessly divided by a regime that had succeeded in outmaneuvering it. Munyaradzi Gwisai, a Zimbabwean socialist who was a member of the MDC until 2003, criticized the "hijacking of the party by the bourgeoisie, marginalisation of workers, adoption of neoliberal positions and cowardly failure to physically confront the Mugabe regime and bosses. It is . . . imperative that the party moves much more leftward . . . in order to realign to its base."[40] But it was not only socialists who criticized the opposition. In 2003 one loyal MP, Job Sikhala, explained how the party core had become "really fat and thick . . . it is almost a party of the rich. You cannot look at a person who was with you during the foundation of the MDC as the person who is there now." This disarray eventually led to the party splitting in 2005, with one faction now led by Arthur Mutambara, an important student activist in the late 1980s.

This disarray occurred in the context of almost total collapse of the economy. Between 2000 and 2005, the economy contracted by more than 40 percent. Today, Zimbabwe's GDP per capita is estimated to be the same as it was in 1953. Before the replacement of the Zimbabwe dollar with the US dollar and the South African rand in 2009, the country had the highest inflation rate in the world, reaching 165,000 percent. In 2007, the IMF calculated that 80 percent of the population lived below the poverty line. Schools collapsed, major hospitals suffered from basic shortages, and unemployment reached an estimated 80 percent, a situation which has not significantly improved following the establishment of the joint ZANU-PF/MDC government in 2009.[41]

While the economic crisis was triggered by the land seizures, it has been worsened by the implementation of direct and indirect sanctions by Western countries. The regime has swung wildly back and forth between price controls and market-based approaches. Land and business contracts were distributed to cronies while Mugabe mouthed platitudes about "foreign powers." Zimbabwe's reserve bank governor Gideon Gono pursued a haphazard program of cuts in subsidies, privatization, and debt repayment.[42] The regime's authoritarian neoliberalism continued unabated, albeit chaotically, for years.

Though land reform in Zimbabwe was celebrated across much of Africa as a historical blow against the legacy of colonial inequality, this was also a failure. In 2002, ZANU-PF stated that it intended to seize 8.5 million hectares (about twenty-one million acres) of land before the presidential elections that year, the majority of all land owned by white farmers in Zimbabwe. They succeeded in doing this by 2003, as the pace of land seizures and occupations came to an end.[43] Although the regime achieved high-profile land seizures, most of the large farms went not to the Zimbabwean poor, but to leading members of the ZANU-PF regime and their elite supporters. The regime did not have the resources or will to provide those Zimbabweans who were granted small parcels of the seized land with the training and equipment so that they could profitably cultivate their new smallholdings.

In this context, Zimbabwean social movements began to suffer from "donor syndrome," as Western-funded NGOs filled the political vacuum left by the failure of the opposition and the economic collapse. Zimbabwean-based organizations saw a massive inflow of funds. This distorted grassroots activism, leading to what has been described as the "commodification of resistance" as mobilization is increasingly paid for from NGO funds.[44] In the student movement, for example, the result was the "artificial" creation of the Zimbabwe Youth Democracy Trust in 2003 by ex-members of the executive of the Zimbabwe National Student Union, ZINASU. The Trust was funded by a Norwegian NGO, the Students and Academics' International Assistance Fund. Student activists were diverted into fighting over positions in the Trust and for control of the organization. Movements have also suffered from a "brain drain" as important members of a variety of organizations, many of whom were founding members of the MDC, have been forced to leave the country. But other elements were arguably more important. As a flood of donor money (and the agendas it bankrolled) distorted activists and campaigns, political demoralization arising from the failure to unseat the regime made many activists apathetic and disengaged.

Nevertheless, efforts to oppose the ruling party now came mainly from social movements rather than the MDC. Women of Zimbabwe Arise (WOZA) is an activist organization that led some of the most important protests, linking the issue of violence against women to wider themes of economic and social collapse from which women suffer disproportionately. The Zimbabwe Social Forum (ZSF), formed in 2002, became an alternative space for political discussion, bringing together those who sought to resist the regime. Both organizations managed—in the context of a decline in MDC-led action—to inspire and train a new layer of activists. Gender issues were an important theme for both movements. Tella Barangwe explained how she was politicized through her involvement in WOZA and the ZSF: "I think here in Zimbabwe they have got a different perspective towards women, when it comes to women exercising their rights sometimes men will use mocking words to discourage us from fighting. What we are fighting for as women. I was a WOZA member and I was then recruited into other organizations. From there I managed to become the Gender Coordinator in the ZSF and I was able to encourage women to join and become active."[45]

For much of the decade, Zimbabwean civil society activists were preoccupied with the question of their relationship with the regime. In 2006 the Zimbabwe Human Rights NGO Forum posed the dilemma starkly: "To engage or not engage the government of Zimbabwe." Some argued for engagement as the only way of securing concessions from the regime, while others rejected any cooperation. ZESN, for example, was clear in 2005 that "this was the most appropriate way of securing co-operation and concessions."[46] Yet WOZA made non-engagement their raison d'être: "Our mandate is to conduct peaceful protests in defiance of unjust law that sanction our fundamental and God-given freedoms of assembly, expression and association."[47] These divergent positions were challenged when an NGO Bill was almost signed into law in 2005. The proposed law would have made it illegal for CSOs to engage in questions of governance and democracy and prevented them from receiving funding unless permitted by the state. It was widely believed that this piece of legislation would entirely paralyze the involvement of NGOs.

A Zimbabwe Human Rights NGO Forum study in 2006 highlighted the "constructive involvement" of campaigners against the NGO Bill. Their interviewees identified the success of the campaign against the Bill which, though it passed through Parliament in 2005, was never signed into law. The study's conclusions about the real benefits of engaging the regime were cautious, to say the least: "In light of the government's preference to deny or ignore that human rights violations are an issue (let alone a problem), it is highly unlikely that the government would be prepared to engage civil society on these issues in a meaningful way."[48] ZANU-PF had developed a repressive legislative architecture that worked against the involvement and influence of CSOs in government decision-making.

The 2008 elections

The elections in March 2008 were nevertheless a major moment of attempted "engagement" in the political process by the MDC and CSOs. The elections illustrated many of the tensions in the MDC's relationship with allied social movements. The election tantalized Zimbabweans with the possibility of a defeat for ZANU-PF. According to the MDC's own calculations, Morgan Tsvangirai won 50.3 percent in the presidential poll, compared to Mugabe's 43.8 percent. For a week after voting had ended, Zimbabwe's normally ebullient ruling party was silent. However, once ZANU-PF had recovered from its surprise defeat, repression against the opposition intensified. More than seventy opposition supporters and members were killed. Thousands more were terrorized and driven from their homes. Many students who had worked closely with the MDC, acting as election agents and campaigners among rural activists, were chased and beaten by ZANU-PF thugs. Tinashe Chisaira was a law student at the University of Zimbabwe: "We would see those who were running away from ZANU-PF—women, children, those with broken limbs, people who had seen their homes burnt and children killed. It was a painful moment." However, instead of a coordinated and systematic defense of the results, the MDC characteristically vacillated as ZANU-PF unleashed its reign of terror. Chisaira remembers one moment: "One night when we were in Harvest House there was this message that some MDC activists had been attacked and then the word came through that able-bodied people must go and defend MDC supporters. But in the end they told us not to go."[49]

The MDC's inability to provide consistent leadership in the post-election period reflected the party's broader history of retreat from the popular mobilization that had created it. Chisaira argues that "the problem the MDC had was that it had distanced itself from those who would have fought in the trenches. We supported the MDC but they didn't support us. The workers, the populace, supported the MDC but the MDC no longer trusted in the people; no longer fully coordinated with the people. So when people were being beaten, Tsvangirai fled to Botswana."[50]

Zimbabwe since 2008

The MDC refused to contest the second round of the presidential election, an inevitable decision due to both the worsening election violence and the opposition's inability to lead a popular defense of the vote. Mugabe was victorious and his fraudulent election entrenched ZANU-PF's dictatorship. Protracted inter-party negotiations started soon after his inauguration. February 2009 saw the birth of an inclusive Government of National Unity (GNU), with leading members of the MDC assuming significant positions in the new government. Tsvangirai became prime minister. Tendai Biti, a longstanding member of the MDC, secured the important Finance Ministry portfolio. But other vital ministries—and real power—remained firmly in ZANU-PF hands.

For some social movement activists in the ZSF, ZINASU, and the NCA, the GNU signaled a defeat. However, within months of the GNU becoming operational, ZANU-PF did begin to reduce the repressive apparatus of the state. By 2010, activists could easily organize. Mike Sambo, national coordinator for the International Socialist Organisation (ISO) of Zimbabwe, sees the GNU as having delivered both limited economic successes and political failure: "The most significant change that has been brought by the GNU is the availability of basic commodities which had been scarce for five years. Right now you can go into any shop and get anything— of course only if you have dollars. So there has been a relative return to economic stabilization in terms of availability and also prices."[51] While activists celebrate the easing of repression and the economic crisis, there is simultaneously a sense of political defeat and disorientation among activists at the entry of the MDC into the GNU.

Meanwhile, the flood of donor funding that helped commodify some social movements in the 2000s has (as a result of the global recession and donor hostility to the GNU) slowed to a trickle, paralyzing the efforts of organizations dependent on external support.[52] The MDC is itself engaged in factional interference in social movement organizations—funding, for examples, some sections of the student movement and excluding others.[53]

Broken on the anvil of ZANU-PF repression and economic hardship, many social movement organizations have had short lives. While ZSF maintained an important presence for about eight years from 2002, mirroring the evolution and momentum of the global Social Forum process (see chapter 7), it has ceased to play an active role in civil society. However, many of the activists who animated the ZSF have shifted their focus to the official consultative process for a new constitution that began in 2010. Funded by the German Rosa Luxemburg Foundation, the Democratic United Front for a People-Driven Constitution (DUF) seeks to politicize the consultative process. DUF includes in its membership several unions, HIV support groups, and resident associations. Through active intervention in the process, DUF aims to radicalize the constitution to address issues such as gay rights, land and wealth redistribution, and political justice. One area of contention was the ZANU-PF's Indigenization Bill, conceptualized as a black empowerment initiative that insisted on 51 percent indigenous shareholding for foreign companies operating in Zimbabwe. The MDC opposed the legislation as hostile to foreign investment. Though liable to become a program of ZANU-PF patronage, the MDC's stance cast it to the political right. DUF activists aimed to radicalize the "indigenization" debate, arguing for wealth redistribution to workers and the poor.[54]

Since January 2011, there has been a disturbing intensification of violence against perceived enemies of ZANU-PF. Tsvanigirai's MDC parliamentarians were detained, including the party's prominent MP Douglas Mwonzora, joint chair of the Constitution Select Committee, who was arrested and held for "inciting public violence." But the worst repression has been reserved for social movement activists. The North African revolutions had a dramatic impact on activists. At the end of February, forty-five people were arrested for attending a meeting on the Arab Spring. Many were severely beaten and tortured. By early March most had been released, but six were held and charged with treason and detained for almost a month. These included prominent members of civil society and socialists in the ISO. After a prolonged trial on reduced charges of conspiring to overthrow the government, the six were found guilty in March 2012 and given suspended sentences and community service. They avoided lengthy prison sentences because of the impressive national and international campaign. However, the arrests and repression of activists signals the government's nervousness at the dissent stirred up by the impending elections that were expected in 2011, but delayed until later in 2012.

The MDC and social movements in perspective

The MDC has long been a paradox. Since its foundation, it has moved further and further away from the mass social movement base which gave rise to its establishment and toward Western states and neoliberal economic policies.[55] This has enabled ZANU-PF to portray it, cynically but not without an element of truth, as a party beholden to foreign interests and hostile to the real interests of the Zimbabwean masses. Despite this, as the 2008 election results proved, the party maintained, and has even increased, mass support among poor Zimbabweans in conditions of extreme hardship.

The MDC remains in part an expression of revolt against the disastrous economic policies implemented by ZANU-PF since the 1990s. It was formed by the labor movement and supported by students who appealed openly to the trade union bureaucracy for a party to confront ZANU-PF. The MDC's core support came from the urban working class in the main cities of Harare, Chitungwiza, and Bulawayo. But the MDC also attracted a range of social movement groups, as we have seen, that had helped it to form and could claim ownership over it. Middle classes representing local and international business interests also quickly gathered around the leadership of the party and achieved disproportionate control and influence. As early as the parliamentary elections in 2000, workers made up only 15 percent of the party's candidates.

As with many parties that arose from the pro-democracy movements of the 1990s, the MDC emerged out of mass popular unrest coordinated on the ground by social movements. These protests were themselves a product of the failures of independence and the more recent implementation of structural adjustment programs. But, during that decade, many leaders of trade unions and political parties came to accept that economic adjustment and good governance—the Washington consensus—were the best, perhaps the only, hope for Africa.

The answer also lies in the weakness of independent movements and voices that sought to resist the party's reorientation towards neoliberalism. Though the mass struggles between 1996 and 1998 showed the potential power of the working class, the protests, strikes, and movements often remained controlled by the trade union bureaucracy. Joseph Tanyanyiwa, general secretary of the NUCIZ, reflects the nostalgia for the late 1990s, when real political change from below appeared to be possible via the MDC: "It was a rising giant. People are still missing those days. . . . People are always saying, why can't we go back to those good old days where we would really control by means of workers' power. It is still a deep conviction that we can deliver workers from the bondage of oppression."[56]

Social movements have also been largely unable to influence the government. Indeed, ZANU-PF responded to the rise of social movement activism not only with repressive laws, but also by stimulating and creating reactionary social movements such as the state-sponsored war veterans' organization "from above." Brian Raftopoulos has observed how ZANU-PF's monopoly on nationalist history was not effectively countered by alternative visions of Zimbabwe in the period of democratization.[57] This points to the failure of opposition parties and social movements to develop their own "imagined communities" with successful organizing strategies.[58] ZANU-PF's authoritarian nationalism poses particular challenges to those who seek to imagine and construct an alternative future in Zimbabwe.

Swaziland

Like our other case studies in this chapter, the small southern African country of Swaziland also failed to experience a transition to democracy in the early 1990s. Swaziland did experience a brief postcolonial stint as a constitutional monarchy after independence from Britain in 1968. However, the Swazi royal establishment skillfully ensured that its Imbokodvo party won every seat in the first elections. Under the Tinkhundla royal system of government, the king reserved the right to make or veto all significant political decisions. (*Tinkhundla* translates literally to "council"; this electoral system is criticized by civil society for being undemocratic.) When in 1973 a more radical party, the Ngwane National Liberatory Congress, received 20 percent of the vote and three parliamentary seats, King Sobhuza II declared a state of emergency, suppressing opposition voices and banning political parties and trade unions. In 1979, a new parliament was established; its members were chosen partly by the king and partly by indirect elections.

Alternative political voices remained subdued until the mid-1980s, when, after a period of conflict within the royal family over the succession, Mswati III became king in 1986. This conflict, coupled with parliamentary elections in 1987, prompted the emergence of a militant political opposition led by the People's United Democratic Movement (PUDEMO), which was formed in 1983. Strongly influenced by parallel processes then underway in neighboring South Africa, PUDEMO developed strong links with the Swaziland Federation of Trade Unions (SFTU). In the late 1980s, it appeared to Swazi social movement activists that the country was following the same road to democracy as South Africa. However, while in South Africa the United Democratic Front and its allied urban social movements played a central role in the successful struggle against apartheid (see chapter 4), PUDEMO failed to mobilize Swaziland's largely rural population against the monarchy. In 1990, PUDEMO leaders were arrested and were tried for treason the following year. PUDEMO responded by establishing the Swaziland Youth Congress (SWAYOCO). SWAYOCO's activist orientation sought to connect the demand for democracy to the poverty and unemployment affecting most Swazis.[59]

In the absence of legal party-based political expression, trade unions became the primary basis for opposition to the regime. This peaked in the mid-1990s, as political change elsewhere in Southern Africa created optimism for similar achievements at home. The incoming ANC government in South Africa was supportive of political change. In 1993, the SFTU launched its "27 Points" program of demands, backed by mass action and stayaways, under the leadership of Jan Sithole.[60] Limited political reform was granted in 1993 with some direct elections in that year's parliamentary poll, although the ban on parties remained in place. In 1995, the government responded to this wave of politically motivated strike action by temporarily banning trade unions. Following the lifting of the ban, unions called a general strike in 1996 that led to the detention of SFTU leaders. That year, PUDEMO sympathizers established the Swaziland Solidarity Network in Johannesburg, which remains an active and important part of regional civil society pressure on the royal regime. What had appeared to be an unstoppable political tide was stalled, and many opponents of the royal regime found themselves in exile in South Africa. PUDEMO leaders and activists remaining in Swaziland have been continually harassed and detained by the regime.

The movements of the mid-1990s, although heavily suppressed, did force the state into establishing a constitutional review process. In the late 1990s, a Constitutional Review Commission was established under the chairmanship of Prince Dlamini, the king's brother. It carried out an exhaustive consultative process which served in practice to delay the introduction of a more accountable political system for a decade. The commission presented its report to the king in 2001, who then appointed a new commission to draft the actual constitution, a draft of which was released in 2003. In the meantime, a new assembly was elected that year; the low turnout indicated the extent of popular dissatisfaction with the lack of democracy. Finally, the new constitution was approved in 2005 and came into effect in 2006. It ostensibly establishes a range of liberal rights such as gender equality which are at apparent odds with "traditional" practices hitherto defended by the royal elite. The constitution's most important progressive measure is to remove women's previous status as legal minors. More generally, however, the new constitution is an ambiguous compromise between internal and external pressure for democratic reform and the maintenance of the royal establishment's authority: for example, guaranteeing freedom of assembly while not specifically removing the ban on political parties.[61] Elections were held under the Tinkhundla system in 2008; political parties were not officially permitted to run for office, but some candidates linked to parties ran in the elections. However, PUDEMO and most other credible opposition parties opted to boycott these elections and press instead for full multi-party elections. PUDEMO, for its part, rejects calls to test the new constitution in practice by operating openly, demanding an explicit statement from the authorities that political parties are legal.[62]

During the last decade, social movement activists, effectively excluded from this top-down process of incremental and limited reform, have faced continual harassment and arrest in their efforts to achieve a more meaningful form of democratic government. In 2006, for example, Swazi activists blockaded the border with South Africa in an attempt to demand political reform; six members of opposition organizations were charged with sedition as a result. The following year, thousands of ordinary Swazis participated in a protest march in the country's second largest city, Manzini, demanding democratic reform. In 2008, following an explosion near the royal palace, PUDEMO leader Mario Masuku was detained on suspicion of involvement in a bomb attack. Masuku was released from prison the following year.

One effect of recent constitutional reform has been to accentuate the clear divide in Swazi civil society between more liberal reform-oriented organizations, internationally linked to bodies such as the Open Society Foundation, and those with more radical and socialist political orientation of the sort pioneered by PUDEMO and the SFTU. In the former category, Musa Hlophe, president of the Coalition of Concerned Civil Society Organisations, argues that a transition to democracy requires a focus on fighting corruption and greater fiscal discipline. Hlophe emphasizes the need for civic education on democracy, human rights, and constitutionalism. However, he recognizes that the centrality of such issues may not be foremost in the minds of the 70 percent of Swazis living below the poverty line.[63] While fully acknowledging its profound flaws, Hlophe's approach to the new constitutional dispensation is to seek to widen the "small window" it provides by testing the legalization of opposition activities (if not parties) in practice.[64] Participation in the somewhat-reformed political system is therefore the central question among social movements. SWAYOCO and PUDEMO continue to reject participation in a system which does not allow for political parties. Masuku notes that "freedom of association" under the new constitution must conform with the "security of the nation," giving the authorities the ability to legalize or ban any activity or organization they deem to undermine their vision of the nation.[65]

The lack of party political democracy means that, as in South Africa in the 1980s, the distinction between political organizations and social movements remains blurred: PUDEMO defines itself as a "national movement" rather than a political party.[66] Swazi social movements see their primary task as one of achieving political democracy and are willing to sublimate other concerns to that aim. But these issues of "political democracy" are complicated. Social movements are, to some degree, distinct from PUDEMO. The party subordinates struggle over "social issues" to the struggle to achieve political democracy, and the social movements generally follow this lead. But tensions remain; similarly, when the ANC was a party in exile, independent social movements often broke out, and the ANC scrambled to achieve hegemony over them. Within PUDEMO and the social movements in Swaziland, economic and social problems are, to a large extent, regarded as secondary issues that can only be adequately addressed by democratization and the establishment of legitimate, accountable government. Problems of economic mismanagement and donor relations tend to focus on the royal establishment's mismanagement, corruption, and waste. There is here an instructive comparison with other pre-transition countries such as Zambia under Kaunda and Zimbabwe under Mugabe, where opposition political and social movements claim that a single dictatorial leader is the primary cause of that nation's woes and that his removal is the key to addressing them. This tends to obscure the structural basis of socioeconomic problems in much of sub-Saharan Africa. It can also have the effect of distancing metropolitan civil society from the urban and rural poor, who, as in Swaziland, are more directly concerned with material problems that they may not directly associate with the lack of democracy.

Certainly, the Tinkhundla system of royal government is a massive drain on Swaziland's resources. Huge grants every month fund the lavish lifestyle of the king and his dozens of wives. The royal family and the parastatals its government controls dominate economic activity in the country.[67] Much of the best agricultural land is in private hands, with close cooperation between wealthy foreign investors and prominent royal figures in key state positions.[68] It is perhaps unsurprising, therefore, that some civil society activists believe that reform along largely neoliberal lines is a necessary first step toward an improved basis for economic development.[69] In some respects, their position resembles that of pro-democracy civil society activists elsewhere in Africa a decade ago, whose experience of personal economic accumulation by state-based elites led them to support aspects of economic liberalization. Members of the Socio-Economic Justice Foundation (SEJF), for example, argue that the economy needs to attract foreign investment and that, to do so, it needs to be run in a more "transparent" way.[70]

However, Swaziland is by no means immune to the negative impact of economic globalization. As across the continent as a whole, the introduction of the Multi-Fiber Agreement in 2005 increased imports of cheap, primarily Chinese-manufactured textiles and closed local textile plants, with the loss of thirty thousand jobs.[71] A similar decline is forecast when Swaziland's strategically important sugar industry loses its special export status with the demise of the EU's Lomé and Cotonou agreements. Hlophe forecasts that the proposed European Partnership Agreements could destroy the industry.[72] Despite this, some in civil society argue that external pressure for economic liberalization may produce effective pressure on the royal establishment for progressive reform. The IFIs, however, are noticeably unwilling to publicly criticize the waste or corruption of the royal system of governance in Swaziland. Although international donors have demanded substantial cuts in government spending, they appear to support this being done not by any obvious pressure for cutbacks in royal consumption, but instead by cuts in the civil service, which will reduce civil service employment by half, from twenty thousand to ten thousand.[73] These figures are massive given the country's population size and total employment. The lack of internal democracy substantially limits the capacity of civil society to effectively engage with international donors; there was until recently little or no contact between Swazi civil society and the IFIs, despite the IMF's annual review visits to the country.

Liberalization has had obvious negative effects. The reduction in public sector expenditure in recent years has led to significant job losses. Swazi Railways was conceded to South Africa's rail parastatal Spoornet, with the same result. The electricity, roads, and telecom sectors have been commercialized and liberalized, complete with the installation of pre-paid meters in Manzini.[74] SWAYOCO is working with the Swazi National Union of Unemployed People to mobilize unemployed youth.[75] In the context of marginal political changes and deepening economic problems, progressive civil society is seeking to mobilize rural Swazis to create a constituency for change in both areas. SWAYOCO, for example, organizes an annual National Cadreship School to provide political education to Swazi youth. Among more radical social movements, there is a desire to learn from Zimbabwe: Alex Langwenya of SWAYOCO points to the influence of capitalism over the MDC (see above) and is concerned that the Swazi labor movement might move in a similar direction.[76] Masuku similarly identifies the dangers of the pro-capitalist GEAR in South Africa, but also argues that a positive, non-corrupt environment should be created in Swaziland to encourage investment.[77]

The Swazi ruling elite has, like its Zimbabwean counterpart, long portrayed civil society activists as unrepresentative of the majority of the rural population, who are depicted as conservative, Christian, and accepting of royal authority. Activists strongly challenge such accusations, pointing to their efforts to mobilize the rural masses in unpropitious circumstances; SEJF works particularly closely with teachers based in rural areas, whose union membership also enables them to bridge the rural-urban divide.[78] However, there is profound ambiguity among educated Swazis active in civil society about the rural majority. Interviewees characterized the majority of their population as "docile" and "immature," for example.[79] Political repression has undoubtedly limited the extent to which the urban intelligentsia has been able to root its activities among the rural majority and seeks to articulate their concerns, but unless it does so, the royal establishment will be able to characterize it as unrepresentative of the Swazi people as a whole.

Conclusion: Withered hopes?

This chapter has shown us broad similarities between political outcomes in those countries that concluded the transition and those that saw their hopes frustrated. Whether new governments were installed (Senegal, Mali, Zambia, Malawi, South Africa) or old regimes revived (Cameroon, Zimbabwe, Swaziland, and in very different circumstances, the DRC), the tempo of resistance and social movement activism receded, often returning to "corporatist" and piecemeal demands or to the complete collapse of independent social movements. Corporatism (the notion that political change must focus on "economic" bread-and-butter demands rather than wider questions of democracy and regime change), as it appeared in social movement politics in the post-transition period, is symptomatic of a new and qualitatively different scale of protest, the experience of political defeat in the transitions, and state repression. Social movement activism—always complex and contradictory—tended to retreat into a routine of "economic" and factional contestation when wider popular and democratic movements in society declined or were frustrated.

In all these countries, already unpopular dictatorial and absolutist regimes generated increasingly active unrest when they implemented the economic liberalization policies demanded by the IFIs and other international donors. Social movements that mobilized around socioeconomic grievances made the link between the imposition of such policies and the lack of effective democratic accountability, so that material grievances fed into demands for political reform. Not unnaturally, activists reasoned that a government elected by and accountable to the people would be more likely to implement policies conducive to their needs and wishes. However, in an essentially post-ideological political context, this can lead to the belief that political transition is the sole or primary goal of social movements and that this will address many or most of the grievances of the African poor and working class. In addition, the experience of operating in corrupt or corporatist regimes, where problems are perceived to derive from a particularly autarkic or idiosyncratic political leadership, led some activists to believe that greater economic integration into global markets will help address or ameliorate the worst excesses of such comparatively closed systems. Such a stance, whether adopted by the MDC or by Swazi social movements, tends in practice to demobilize the mass base from which such parties or movements derive their support and make effective transition more difficult to bring about.

New governments that emerged from the "transition," or where the transition had been frustrated, resumed their commitment to implementing IMF and World Bank reforms. Although social movements in a number of countries managed to score some important victories against their governments (see chapter 5), these were small compared to the root and branch hopes for political transformations that the 1990s revolts momentarily offered. The predominance of neoliberalism across the continent ensured a quick death for the African renaissance and the movements that heralded it.

CHAPTER 7

SOCIAL FORUMS
AND THE WORLD SOCIAL FORUM
IN AFRICA

The growth and development of the anticapitalist movement since the late 1990s coincided with a period of increased activism among social movements in Africa. As we have argued in earlier chapters, political democratization in most of the region in the early 1990s significantly opened the political space available for civil society activity, while not generally translating into effective influence on governmental policy-making. In more repressive states, social movements played an important role in resisting dictatorship and authoritarianism (see chapter 6). Simultaneously, the debt crisis and the economic liberalization demanded by donors and international financial institutions reduced African nation-states' capacity for repressing social movement activism (compared to earlier phases of postcolonial nationalist rule) and increased the capacity of social movements to articulate economic and social injustices. Globalization has reduced the extent of autonomous national sovereign decision-making, but also opened up the potential for cross-border communication and cooperation between social movements to present alternatives to neoliberal globalization, including those generated by the international antiglobalization movement. This leads some observers to identify or assume a virtuous relationship and a coincidence of interests between the activities of both African social movements and the antiglobalization movement.

The key question addressed by this chapter is: To what extent are the assumptions at the heart of the anticapitalist movement accepted by social movements in these countries? Do they view the movement and its initiatives as relevant to them? Should the movement change to become more responsive to them? Viewed from an African perspective, what does this tell us about the underlying assumptions of the anticapitalist movement regarding the relative importance of political movements at a global and local level? Finally, how and in what ways are African social movements using the forum model to articulate their aims and aspirations at the local, national, and regional levels?

Globalization, anticapitalism, and transnational social movements

Transnational social movements are, of course, not new phenomena. The anti-slavery movement of the early nineteenth century, the feminist emancipation campaign, and the international peace movement of the inter-war period were all transnational to some degree. Nevertheless, social movements were generally constructed in relation to their (usually Western) national states during the twentieth century.[1] After the 1970s, however, environmental and peace movements placed an increasing emphasis on "transnational collective action" by a small minority of networked activists. The legacy of the direct action approach of organizations such as, for example, Greenpeace can be found in today's anticapitalist activism, much of which is based on highly visible direct action carried out by a self-selecting, voluntarist group of activists. It should be evident that, while such movements claim global reach and legitimacy, they are in practice organizations based in a handful of mostly Western states.

As outlined in chapter 2, Africa experienced many of the first protests against neoliberal economic policies in the mid-1980s, in the form of "bread riots" against structural adjustment policies imposed by the International Monetary Fund. However, the first self-conscious manifestation of the modern anticapitalist movement is generally agreed to be the Chiapas rising by the Mexican Zapatistas against the North American Free Trade Agreement (NAFTA) in January 1994. This appeared to herald the possibility of a global movement that, in the wake of the collapse of the Soviet bloc, could articulate a progressive, democratic model of socialism that would break from that movement's Eurocentric origins. Since the demonstrations in Cologne and Seattle in 1999, a wealth of literature has analyzed the positions and perspectives of the anticapitalist movement. The vast majority of this literature focuses on the inequities of globalized neoliberal capitalism rather than the nature of the movement itself. However, it is precisely from its analysis of the nature of twenty-first-century capitalism that the strategy and tactics of the movement flow. As Harvey describes, a new stage or phase of neoliberal globalized capitalism arose from the crisis in the international economic order in the mid-1970s, when the class compromise of the long post–World War II boom (predicated on steady and predictable global economic growth) broke down.[2] Since the late 1970s, neoliberal economic policies (such as privatizing state-owned companies, commercializing state services, removing barriers to international trade, and reducing state subsidies to businesses) have been implemented to a greater or lesser extent in almost every part of the world.

The result has been, for many anticapitalist activists, an apparent weakening of nation-states as instruments of effective policy-making and the construction of new mechanisms and institutions for political and economic decision-making at a transnational level. In the 1990s, a substantial shift of authority to indirectly elected or non-elected transnational institutions or policy frameworks such as the World Trade Organization (WTO) and, at a regional level, the European Union or NAFTA, suggested the need for opposing networks of transnational social movements. The logical culmination of these developments was the protests at Seattle in 1999 and the subsequent development of the anticapitalist movement. This movement, while lacking a single coherent identity or ideology, positions itself as a counter-hegemonic movement to neoliberal free-market capitalism in its various manifestations. Its advocates highlight its emphasis on diversity and claim that it represents a new and radical form of democracy.[3] The primary organizers of the World Social Forum (WSF) and the wider movement of Social Forums linked to it claim that it is designed to be a "space" in which the world's poor and marginalized can discuss their grievances and develop joint agendas for action to address them.[4] This movement posits that we are in a new era of Western-dominated, globalized neoliberal capitalism in which both multinational corporations and IFIs are undermining democracy and accountability at the nation-state level. This necessitates a global "movement of movements" that resists such processes at a transnational level. Technological changes, in particular, have undoubtedly contributed to the development of networks of activists who have apparently used the internet to break from the shackles of local and national particularities and become global social movement activists.

The extent to which such activists are genuinely representative of specific movements is a major concern. In this chapter we take pains to make it clear that there is no such thing as a pre-formed radical social movement that is authentically "of the people." Rather, such movements exist along a spectrum that reflects their origins, sources of funding, links to particular nation-states, and ideological bases. It may be suggested that larger non-membership NGOs that are highly dependent on governmental or commercial funding occupy one end of this spectrum, while more grassroots, local, and/or membership-based groups with little or no outside funding exist at the other. In addition, however, many social movements within the anticapitalist movement seek to reflect what they view as "post-industrial" or "postmodern" societies, in which what might be termed "Fordist" models of civil society, rooted in local communities or workplaces and derived from processes of election and delegation, are rejected in favor of newer "post-Fordist" models of horizontal social movement organization in which each activist is supposedly free to represent and speak for him- or herself. For example, Fisher and Ponniah stress the way the new anticapitalist movements emerge without central institutions, organizing in networks with (assumed) shared values. This does not, they stress, make them free of power relations; indeed, the emerging transnational civil society is, they argue, itself "an arena of struggle, a fragmented and contested area."[5] There is, however, little empirical analysis of the extent to which transnational social movements utilizing such approaches enable—or exclude—the participation of activists from the global south; this is one area this chapter aims to address.

Africa and globalization

Given the particular poverty of sub-Saharan African countries, their experience of debt dependency, and their apparent loss of national sovereignty resulting from the impact of IFI conditionalities, one might hypothesize that the anticapitalist movement would be of particular relevance to social movements in such countries. The imposition of SAPs in debt-ridden countries by the IMF and World Bank since the late 1970s appears to be an obvious manifestation of the negative impact of the Washington consensus. The relatively uniform imposition of such policies regardless of local circumstances; their baneful effect on the lives and livelihoods of African peoples; the relative inability of African governments to resist their imposition; and the apparent ineffectiveness of local popular resistance to such measures: all these factors suggest the utility of transnational social movement alliances in opposing the imposition of such policies.

However, there are reasons to question the applicability of the assumptions underlying this analysis of neoliberalism, and the resultant anticapitalist discourse, in relation to much of sub-Saharan

Africa. The practical imposition of liberalization has been uneven in the countries under study. For example, a major constraint on the privatization of public services in Africa has been the lack of willing buyers—whereas European and American firms have competed to profit from privatized water and electricity supply companies in Latin America and parts of Asia, there is little money to be made from the poverty-stricken consumers of much of sub-Saharan Africa. Similarly, the indigenous pro-reform elite who promoted and benefited from their privileged role in privatization processes in the wider global south (often as junior partners of international companies) are limited in much of sub-Saharan Africa, both in terms of access to capital and in the extent of their effective political influence. There are obvious exceptions—the ruling classes in Nigeria and South Africa are highly integrated into global capitalist structures and, in many respects, operate as regional sub-imperial powers. For example, leading South Africa–based telecommunications and infrastructure corporations, supported by global investment, increasingly dominate Africa's cellular phone and transportation systems. In other countries, however, economic liberalization processes over the last twenty years have resulted in limited gains for the indigenous business class (even when, as in Zambia and Zimbabwe in the early 1990s, they were initially strongly supportive of such measures). Therefore, rather than Africa being swept by untrammeled forces of economic liberalization or "left behind" by globalization, it is rather that globalization takes a distinct form in some parts of the continent that is not always understood by movements, which at times adopt a monolithic view of globalization.

Such factors, albeit uneven in their particular impact, affect the development of social movements and shape their attitudes towards international capital, global institutions, and their national states. However, the particular experiences and perspectives of African social movements are not well reflected in transnational social movements. The primary reason for this, ironically, is that the global anticapitalist movement, while in many respects a diverse and egalitarian initiative, unwittingly (and evidently against the earnest desires of its organizers) reflects and reproduces through its particular *modus operandi* of decentralized and apparently egalitarian decision-making some aspects of the inequalities against which it positions itself.

The World Social Forums

The WSF was first held in 2001 in Porto Alegre, Brazil. It was imagined both as a counter-summit to the World Economic Forum held in Davos, Switzerland, and as a venue for the collective self-expression of the anticapitalist movement that emerged at and in the wake of the Seattle protest of 1999. In 2010, the WSF celebrated its tenth anniversary. Most WSF events have taken place in Porto Alegre; to date, only two WSFs have been held in Africa, in Nairobi in 2007 and in Dakar in 2011. The authors attended the Nairobi event and it is a major focus of this chapter.

The WSF has been the subject of extensive study and debate. Its advocates make great claims for its capacity to transcend traditional organizational models and achieve, in the words of Hardt and Negri, "a new democratic cosmopolitanism, a new anti-capitalist transnationalism, a new intellectual nomadism, a great movement of the multitude."[6] Many of the claims made for the WSF are rooted in its distinctively egalitarian approach, compared to older models of decision-making. For example, Wainright claims that its "egalitarian, decentred way of co-operating and sharing knowledge produces a greater common understanding than any top down summing up of dispersed fragments of knowledge."[7] Indeed, in many respects, the Forum model of organization was a step forward from more hierarchical forms of organization utilized by many on the global left during the twentieth century, which tended to authoritarian and anti-democratic practices.

Nevertheless, distinctive problems arise from apparently anti-hierarchical forms of organization. Trevor Ngwane, a leading South African activist, is critical of the Forum's "tyranny of nonleadership," in which the apparent lack of visible hierarchical organization masks a largely unaccountable decision-making clique. Callinicos and Nineham make a similar point in recalling that the women's movement identified the "tyranny of structurelessness" as resulting in the flow of effective control to informal elites.[8]

Forum activists acknowledge and have highlighted and sought to address such concerns; the movement is generally a venue of open and honest self-criticism. Indeed, since its foundation it has been riven with divisions and arguments about its direction and its role. Specific criticisms have been made regarding the domination of its central structure, the Organizing Committee, by a handful of Brazilian organizations with close ties to the ruling Workers' Party. Waterman offers a useful analysis of the deficiencies in democratic organization in the International Committee, the ninety to one hundred members of which appear to have been selected by the Organizing Committee with little or no democratic process.[9] He notes the "striking power and wealth differences, particularly visible, predictably, in the case of the South."[10] The WSF has been criticized for its tendency to become dominated by northern and Latin American NGOs—large, professionalized, and bureaucratic CSOs. The WSF's voluntarist approach, presented positively as a marketplace of ideas, contains the danger that its spaces can become dominated by organizations with disproportionate resources and personnel. While concerns have been continually expressed about the uneven attendance of WSFs, little practical progress has been made in addressing this.

The sheer scale and unwieldy nature of the global WSF contrasts with the thriving phenomenon of Forums globally; hundreds of geographically and sectorally specific events have been organized along Forum lines in the last decade, including in sub-Saharan Africa,[11] though few studies have been carried out on Forums outside Latin America and the West.

Social Forums in Africa

Although the Nairobi event was the first WSF to take place in Africa, national, regional, and continent-wide Social Forums have taken place on the continent since 2002. African Social Forums (ASFs) took place in Mali (ASF I) in 2002 and Ethiopia (ASF II) in 2003. These were primarily gatherings of senior officials of large African NGOs, many able to attend because of funding from their European counterparts and international donors. At ASF II, it was acknowledged that African social movements found it particularly difficult to meet the transport and communication costs involved in attending continental and global events. Having committed itself to "the development of the ASF based on the participation of grassroots social movements," the 2003 ASF agreed that this would be achieved in part by hosting more accessible Forums on a national and regional basis.[12]

The third ASF took place in December 2004 in Zambia. (Two more continent-wide events have subsequently taken place, the most recent being held in Niger in November 2008.) In addition, many regional Social Forums have taken place. The first Southern African Social Forum (SASF) took place in Lusaka in December 2003, the second in Harare in October 2005. Since then, three more SASFs have taken place: in Malawi in 2006; in Swaziland in 2008; and in Lesotho in 2009. Focusing on three of these events (all of which were attended by the authors), this chapter examines the degree to which these events reflected and facilitated the effective articulation of growing popular resistance to neoliberalism, economic injustice, and political repression in Africa. It questions whether these Forums have enabled African social movements to participate practically in the wider global social justice movement. It also assesses the impact of the Social Forums on the practice of CSOs and social movements on the continent. It suggests that the capacity of Africans to influence the *global* anticapitalist movement remains limited, as does the relevance of this movement to

Africans themselves. It finds, however, that African social movements have utilized the Social Forum model and adapted it to their local contexts to strengthen and generalize their growing struggles against neoliberal capitalism and their own governments.

The first Southern African Social Forum: Lusaka, 2003

The first SASF took place in Lusaka, Zambia, in November 2003. Four hundred activists from social movements, trade unions, NGOs, churches, women's organizations, and other groups attended the event. Most were from Zambia and Zimbabwe, with a significant presence from South Africa and smaller numbers from Namibia, Botswana, the Democratic Republic of Congo, Angola, Malawi, Mauritius, Swaziland, and other countries. It was obvious that the inexperience of many delegates in operating in the distinctive Social Forum culture was a significant impediment to their effective participation. The lack of clear direction from the Organizing Committee and the poor organization of workshops hosted by individual CSOs prevented many activists from fully engaging with the themes of the event. Some found the Forum confusing and even alienating.

Nevertheless, some plenary sessions and workshops were able to highlight major themes of social movement activity and popular discontent. Sub-Saharan Africa experienced some of the earliest and most brutal structural adjustment policies in the 1980s and 1990s. Their largely negative impact on employment, living standards, and public services created widespread disillusionment with economic liberalization. In much of the continent, this popular consensus stood in direct contrast to the consensus among virtually all political leaders that further liberalization was the only feasible economic policy. This vacuum of representation at the party political level enabled CSOs to take the lead in representing popular discontent with neoliberal capitalism, ensuring that such movements were grounded in local experience and organization well before the advent of the anticapitalist movement. That movement had, however, begun to convince many African activists that another world was not only imaginable, but actually possible. This spark of feasibility can be likened to that provided by the uprisings in Eastern Europe in 1989, which greatly encouraged many pro-democracy campaigns already mobilizing in Africa (see chapter 3). This brought about a shift in the approach of many CSOs, which in the 1990s tended to accept the hegemonic power of SAPs and sought simply to mitigate their impact by giving them a "human face." Many such organizations are now committed to the outright rejection of liberalization policies.

Zambia's experience served as an instructive example at SASF I. As a highly indebted country, Zambia agreed to a so-called Poverty Reduction Strategy Program (PRSP) in 1999, which promised to relieve 50 percent of Zambia's $6.7 billion debt (this relief was finally granted in 2005). The PRSP was differentiated from previous structural adjustment policies because, it was claimed, it was based on consultation with, and inputs from, CSOs (see chapter 5). Indeed, many such organizations sought to influence the content of Zambia's PRSP; they were commonly disillusioned with the lack of effective participation and their inability to influence the neoliberal substance of the program. At a trade and debt workshop at SASF I, Jack Jones Zulu of Jubilee Zambia exposed the PRSP as an effective continuation of earlier adjustment policies, imposing devastating cuts in public spending which have actually increased poverty in Zambia. As is shown in chapter 5, Zambians resisted these measures: the PRSP requirement to privatize strategic state-owned companies was postponed by the government after popular union-led demonstrations.

SASF I delegates resolved to reject PRSPs and the related Highly Indebted Poor Countries (HIPC) initiative. They endorsed demands not only for the immediate and unconditional cancellation of unpayable international debts, but for the World Bank and IMF to make reparations for the damage caused by their policies. However, the event brought the dilemma of "participation" in processes such as PRSP into sharp focus. The Forum delegates agreed that the IMF, World Bank, and WTO had no useful role to play in their countries and should "pack up and go." However, it transpired that some Zambian organizations present were due to meet with a visiting IMF team during the course of the Forum. It was agreed that they would instead boycott the event, attending only to deliver the message that the IFIs were not welcome in Southern Africa. This did not, however, bring a permanent end to such engagement with the IFIs by some of the same organizations, which are often under pressure to do so from their northern NGO funders. SASF I thereby reflected the tensions that have expressed themselves in the wider global social justice movement. There were noticeable divisions between CSOs, many of which seek to lessen the negative impact of neoliberalism, and more radical social movements that seek to challenge the structure of the global economy itself.

The uneven development of social movements *within* the region was also noticeable. While many important Zambian organizations were absent from an event held in their country, Zimbabwean participation was impressive, numerically and qualitatively. The high tempo of struggle against the repressive policies of the Mugabe regime since 1998 (see chapter 6) defined a generation of radical social movement activists, who shared their experience regarding strategy and tactics with their regional counterparts. In particular, Zimbabwean activists rejected an implicit counterposing of "African" interests against those of an equally monolithic "West," offering a critique of national governments whose policies advance the interests of multinational capital. Indeed, the relationship between social movements and the state, and between Africa and the wider world, was a central (if often unstated) theme in the debates. Many activists believe that African governments are more progressive than their Western counterparts; at SASF I, the cooperation between African governments (linked to the G22 group of countries) and NGOs in helping derail the WTO talks in Cancun earlier that year was presented as evidence in this regard. Others argued that such "alliances" resulted from rising popular opposition to the negative impact of free trade policies implemented by those very governments. If the Cancun campaign had indeed succeeded, at least temporarily, in de-railing the WTO's Doha round, the lesson was that pressure on African governments should be increased, not lessened.

Similarly, "Africanist" arguments were voiced, implying that social justice would be improved if multinationals were replaced by African-owned businesses. This argument was challenged at the SASF by criticism of the increasing dominance of the regional economy by South African capital, which many argued represented a form of sub-imperialism. Participants were united in their rejec-tion of the African Union's New Economic Plan for African Devel-opment (NEPAD), which they characterized as support by some African leaders for the global elite at the expense of Africans.

The final plenary of the SASF drafted and issued an official statement. However, many delegates were unclear how their resolu-tions would practically influence the agenda of the then-forthcoming WSF, held in Mumbai in January 2004. Certainly, Forum partici-pants in Mumbai expressed concern that African voices were not being adequately represented in the movement. African partici-pants committed themselves to the mobilization of mass and peo-ple's organizations. They also debated whether the struggle within the ASF between radicals and moderates needed to be decisively resolved, or whether the Forum functioned best as an arena in which the battle between such ideas could be continually articu-lated.[13] The Mumbai gathering reaffirmed both the importance of the ASF and the need to ensure that it was more representative of "mass movements that are active on the ground."

The third African Social Forum: Lusaka, 2004

Following this commitment, the third African Social Forum was held in Lusaka in December 2004. This event attracted approxi-mately 650 social movement activists from across sub-Saharan Africa. Attendees included trade unionists, church leaders, women activists, environmentalists, and NGO representatives. The largest delegation was from Zimbabwe; about a hundred Zimbabwean delegates traveled north by bus, buoyed by the success of their own national Social Forum, held the previous month despite significant state intimidation. There was significant representation from South Africa, Malawi, Zambia, Tanzania, Kenya, and Nigeria and smaller delegations from Ghana, Côte D'Ivoire, Senegal, and elsewhere. The Forum was significantly better organized and more accessible than the 2003 SASF. However, very few sessions featured representatives of grassroots campaigns. Many plenaries featured the same speakers, mostly from nationally based NGOs.

The dominant themes of the main plenaries and workshops followed an agenda set primarily by international NGOs: the week of action on international trade scheduled for April 2005; the campaign against the European Partnership Agreements (EPAs); and the call for the total cancellation of Africa's international debt in the run-up to the G8 meeting in July 2005.[14] Glossy publicity materials were distributed, along with requests to organize local actions to coincide with these events. While these are, of course, important issues that have the potential to improve or worsen the lives and livelihoods of millions of Africans, their dominance of the ASF agenda was a reflection of the global tempo of international development politics and the response of international civil society to it. African civil society had little opportunity to challenge or shape the campaign agendas or activities. Rather, there was a sense that African activists' role was to passively endorse the campaigns of the international global social justice movement, rather than defining and expressing their own agenda from the bottom up.

The hierarchical nature of the event was challenged most effectively by women activists. They organized activities in ways designed not only to encourage popular participation, but also to place the concerns of ordinary African women at the heart of the event. In particular, the African Court of Women, a day-long session in which women participants gave personal testimony about their experiences of violence and injustice, was an opportunity to understand the devastating impact of violence on the lives of individuals and communities.[15]

It was noticeable that those countries that had held their own national Social Forums in the run-up to the ASF (Zimbabwe, Kenya, Nigeria, Ghana, and Malawi) tended to contribute to the event in a more coherent and focused way. The capacity to hold African countries. Kenyan activists, still on the offensive following the ousting of the Moi regime in 2003 and pressing home their advantage with its successor, organized Community Social Forums in the poorest areas of Nairobi. In Nigeria, where a series of general strikes over gasoline subsidies had coincided with an increased radicalization of the struggle in the Niger Delta, three thousand delegates attended the national Social Forum. By enabling the unevenness and diversity of African social movements to be expressed in a forum that enables discussion and generalization based on these localized experiences, national and local Social Forums suggested the possibility of an Africa-wide social movement rooted in the lives of those it seeks to represent.

Ambiguous and contradictory perspectives towards the African state were again highlighted at ASF III. At one session, a prominent Nigerian speaker claimed (somewhat inaccurately) that African governments opposed EPAs, and argued that it was necessary "to support them in rejecting EPAs." While most African states were then committed to rejecting EPAs in their current form, it seemed likely that, without significant pressure (as opposed to "support") from civil society, most governments were set to agree to a version of the agreements. This was of course the result of pressure from richer, more powerful European governments and the European Union, but more radical delegates noted that it was precisely the apparently "weak" and "dependent" African governments that had previously forced through privatizations, approved laws legalizing the removal of trade tariffs, and suppressed strikes and demonstrations that expressed Africans' discontent with the effects of economic liberalization.

While the ASF unambiguously rejected any role for the IMF or World Bank in addressing Africa's problems, there was no doubt that many of the organizations present remained tied into consultative and "participatory" civil society processes that effectively legitimized dialogue with the IFIs. The ASF's most significant omission, a plan of action to practically address the injustices identified in discussion, allowed the Forum's organizers to evade the increasingly stark tactical choice facing the global social justice movement: between critical engagement with the IFIs and governments on the one hand and mass action and civil disobedience on the other.

On the final day of the Forum, South African activists initiated a debate about the role of the ASF: What was it trying to achieve? What were its practical results? This was an important attempt to bring some clarity to an event at which many activists, excited by sharing their experiences and initiatives with like-minded radicals, were simultaneously frustrated about their inability to fully realize the potential this created. The decision not to agree to a final statement (characteristically replicating the latest WSF practice rather than any decision made at the ASF itself) reduced the capacity of the Forum to initiate concrete social movement actions and the ability of delegates to influence the agenda of the global social justice movement. African social movements thus remained dependent on the goodwill of those (largely unaccountable) African representatives fortunate enough to attend the next WSF in Porto Alegre in January 2005.

The second Southern African Social Forum: Harare, 2005

The second SASF, held in Harare from October 13 to 15, 2005, was a significant improvement on the 2003 event. Its two thousand participants were significantly more representative of grassroots activist groupings than those two years earlier. There were fewer senior NGO officials—and virtually no direct representatives of the Western NGOs that had set much of the agenda of the 2004 ASF. SASF II, held in a series of noisy tents and open-air spaces in the center of Harare, was a world away from the air-conditioned atmosphere of Lusaka's Mulungushi Conference Centre. Some delegates spoke in vernacular languages, and the thematic groupings (on issues such as HIV/AIDS, labor, governance, gender, and trade) provided important opportunities for rank-and-file participation which were seized with enthusiasm.

The success of SASF II was built upon the increasing number of national and local Social Forums that had by that time taken place in the region. That year, Zambia and Tanzania held their first national Social Forums, Malawi its second. Zimbabwe, which had already held two national Social Forums, held a series of local Social Forums in the run-up to the SASF. Mozambique was scheduled to hold its first national Social Forum in December 2005. While attendance and representation at these events was highly uneven, they enabled greater participation by grassroots participants than regional or continental events and gave activists experience and confidence in "owning" wider Forum processes. They also led to a more coordinated national approach to participation in regional Forums. SASF II also demonstrated the relative radicalization of the region's social movements over the intervening two years. In heavily indebted African countries, the significant debt relief then underway made it increasingly difficult for ruling politicians to reject civil society demands on the basis that they had no choice but to follow economic liberalization strictures (what we have labeled the "handcuffs" position). At least half of the delegates were Zimbabwean, and the radicalized atmosphere was certainly heightened by the context of economic, social, and political crisis in the host country. Zimbabwean activists were disillusioned in triplicate: by the impossibility of lobbying their own dictatorial government; by the unwillingness of the opposition Movement for Democratic Change to actively confront the Mugabe regime; and by the retreat of many prominent civil society leaders into lucrative NGO positions, often overseas. Their emphasis on insurrectionary mass action undoubtedly influenced the mood of activists from elsewhere in the region. More general disillusionment with the subcontinent's "choiceless democracies" (see chapter 5) had fueled new social movements and radicalized existing ones. Two years before, the respectable churchgoing women who form the backbone of CSOs in these countries were still repeating the NGO discourse of development and partnership; in Harare, influenced by their direct experiences of activism and struggle, they waved their fists and shouted "*Viva* socialism, *viva!*" In Zambia, for example, the new constitutional movement then blossoming led to a series of demonstrations demanding the adoption of a new constitution by a constituent assembly that limited presidential powers, strengthened accountability, and increased popular participation in decision-making. Kenya's recent experience of constitutional change was increasingly cited at SASF II as an example of why mass activism, rather than reliance on elected political leaders, is more likely to meet popular aspirations. Constitutional reform was identified as a way to restrict the power of corrupt politicians to force through policies in an unaccountable way and to introduce freedoms that better enable people to fight for economic and social justice. However, it was made clear that constitutional change without popular participation would simply result in increased opportunities for politicians to feed at the top table, with no improvement in terms of popular participation or accountability.

Social movements were on the move elsewhere in the region. In Tanzania, on the IMF's sixtieth anniversary in April 2005, NGOs organized a march to call on it to "pack up and go." Starting in the Mabibo suburb of western Dar es Salaam, thousands of people spontaneously joined the demonstration, which numbered around thirty thousand by the time it reached the city center. In diverse ways, CSOs in Botswana, Namibia, and Swaziland were detaching themselves from the agendas of donors and political parties and developing more autonomous critiques of the practices of national governments and international capital. As in Zimbabwe and South Africa, the lack of credible opposition parties in these countries encouraged civil society to take the lead in many such campaigns. South Africa saw a significant increase in the number of "service delivery protests" (see chapter 4). Local communities, disillusioned with the failure of the ANC government to meet their expectations of post-apartheid social and economic change, took to the streets, utilizing forms of protest that consciously replicated the mass struggles of the 1980s.

This changed context was evident in the main areas of discussion at SASF II. In contrast to the ASF of 2004, the agenda was mostly set by Africans themselves. For example, a comparative analysis of privatization across the region, initiated by the Southern African People's Solidarity Network, led to demands for the renationalization of strategic public resources. Activists made fewer requests to the region's governments for action, indicating an increased skepticism that African states can be progressive partners in resisting the agenda of global capital; NEPAD and the African Union were notable only for their absence. SASF thematic clusters placed an increased emphasis on the self-activity of Africans and their popular organizations, in particular the need for region-wide coordination of organization and activity. In this spirit, the SASF endorsed calls for a series of regional days of action to support the demands of the Zimbabwe Congress of Trade Unions (ZCTU) regarding the economic and social crisis in that country. There was, however, little concrete discussion regarding what form regional solidarity action would take.

There was also uneven participation, and even tension, between trade unions and social movement activists. This is, in part, a divide of culture and norms; social movements tend toward constant mass participation, whereas the union culture of delegation meant that labor movement representation was in general limited to a small number of officials. There was a significant confrontation between representatives of the Congress of South African

Trade Unions (COSATU) and South African social movements, which at one point threatened to become physical. COSATU officials' characterization of some CSOs as "unrepresentative" and unsupportive of the "national democratic revolution" that the COSATU leadership claimed was taking place in South Africa was undeniably provocative. This provoked some social movement activists into a tit-for-tat response that only reinforced the prejudices of the union bureaucrats.

More positively, there was widespread recognition from unionists that they need to participate in organizing and mobilizing the unemployed and informally employed. The question of how this is done, however, remains open to debate. Some unionists tend toward a top-down approach, expecting to recruit the informal sector into a "union" under their auspices. Others understand that informal traders can and should define and control their own autonomous organizations. There was more encouragement in a fiery speech by the president of the Southern African Trade Union Coordinating Council (SATUCC), Zimbabwean Lucy Matibenga. Matibenga joined other delegates in calling for an Africa where labor can move freely across the region as capital already does and for an end to xenophobia against foreigners in South Africa and elsewhere.

None of this meant that the familiar tensions between NGOs and social movements were absent. Indeed, the increased confidence of radical social movements created significant conflict with the NGOs that dominate the regional Organizing Committee, as the latter sought to manipulate the Forum's agenda in the run-up to the event. Prior information about SASF II was, as in previous years, limited and difficult to access. There were also disturbingly centralized aspects of the Forum as it unfolded. On the last day, it was announced that the next SASF would be held in Malawi, a decision apparently made by the Organizing Committee with no participation from the delegates. It was again unclear how the discussions and decisions of the SASF would be fed into the subsequent World

Social Forum. Indeed, given the increased focus on local activism at this event, there was very little discussion of the role or relevance of the WSF whatsoever. The SASF's role seemed to increasingly be organizing local, national, and regional campaigns rather than participating as a regional element in a wider global movement.

The radicalization of the Harare SASF was primarily a reflection of increasingly militant and confident social justice movements in a number of countries in the region. This is not to suggest that there was a singular coherent wave of radicalized social movement thought and action sweeping the region. There was still tremendous unevenness in the development of social and political consciousness and organization between and within countries. While this unevenness may restrict the potential to develop coordinated region-wide initiatives, it should be understood as a reflection of the different experiences of peoples across Africa and not dismissed as an unhelpful obstruction to be overcome. Indeed, one strength of recent social movement activism is that it has become more reflective of variegated local discontents and aspirations. New movements of resistance grow not from a rejection of the often nebulous concept of "globalization" but from its everyday localized manifestations.

There are, nevertheless, significant gains to be achieved from closer coordination between African civil society and social movements on issues of region-wide relevance. Trade unionists facing the same multinational corporations (increasingly operating across the region from South Africa) have much to gain from coordinated negotiation strategies, particularly at the sectoral level. Campaigns for constitutional reform have learned from each other's successes and failures. Ongoing campaigns against the privatization of remaining state-owned corporations could do the same.

In addition, the international anticapitalist movement had much to gain from more effectively integrating local African social movements into its activities. What the Social Forums and their participants have to say regarding (for example) inequality,

HIV/AIDS, privatization, and debt should be rooted in the experiences and ideas of those at the sharpest end of their impact. However, until these problems of unequal access to the structures of the global anticapitalist movement are acknowledged and practically reduced, the claims of the WSF to speak on behalf of the world's poor and exploited remain questionable.

World Social Forum: Nairobi, 2007

The Nairobi WSF was a potent expression of the contradictions inherent in the anticapitalist movement. The fact that Kenyan social movements were able to organize and host such a large event was a major achievement, reflecting the scale of social movement activism in Kenya and across the continent—it was by far the largest continent-wide non-governmental event ever seen in sub-Saharan Africa, dwarfing earlier Pan-African Congresses, for example. Nevertheless, the debate as to whether the WSF is a space in which social movements of various persuasions come together or whether it is (or should be) an initiator of specific actions to address specific problems was at the heart of the Nairobi Forum. Africans in particular criticized the WSF as a "talk shop" in which issues are discussed but not resolved and lead to little action.

The Forum was in practice less than the sum of its different parts: at one level, it functioned as the "annual general meeting" of professional and semi-professional, mostly Western, campaigners in a range of sectors, for example in campaigns around particular multinational corporations, the campaign against the EPAs, and so on. At another level, national delegations of CSOs arrived to raise their particular national concerns; for example, organizations from the Democratic Republic of Congo demonstrated as a national bloc behind their national flag. Major assemblies of Catholic organizations and trade union officials gathered on a sectoral basis. Elsewhere, thousands of Kenyans, most but not all linked to at least one CSO, drew connections between the continental and global processes under discussion and their own local experience of globalization and activism. Other than in marches and rallies, at no point did the movements come together to address a common agenda. It was an often confusing and at times exhilarating event that constantly manifested the very inequalities and problems it seeks to overcome.

At times it seemed that most of the debate revolved around the event itself. Forty-six thousand people attended the WSF, well down from the 150,000 who attended the last event in Porto Alegre in 2006 (the vast majority of whom were Brazilian).[16] While the fact that the majority of the attendees in Nairobi were Kenyans fulfilled the organizers' goal that three-quarters of Forum attendees should be from the continent hosting the event, they were in practice far less visible than Forum regulars and did not generally play a leading role in most debates or actions. Researchers based at the Sorbonne found that Africans were a minority of participants in many workshops in Nairobi directly concerned with African issues.[17] The obvious lack of ordinary Kenyans present at many events was in part a reflection of the different levels of social movement organization in each country, but it also came down to access. Kenyan participants were charged five dollars (US) to attend: small in comparison to the $110 charge for Western participants, but much higher in relative income terms. A series of direct actions demanded free access to the WSF for Kenyans. The fee was first reduced and then, by the third day, waived, but by then a perception had been created that the event was not accessible to ordinary Kenyans. While Kenyan national coordinator Onyango Oloo apologized for this, global organizers from the WSF's International Committee attacked the demonstrators as an "unrepresentative minority," terms familiar to any police chief or multinational faced with an anticapitalist protest.[18]

Kenyan politics also came into the picture through protests over access to food. Within the WSF arena, marquees were erected to provide food, run by the Windsor Golf and Country Club. It came to the attention of delegates that the Windsor was owned by

Kenyan internal security minister John Michuki, notorious not only as the initiator of the raid on the *Standard* newspaper in 2006, but also as a loyalist during the colonial period who won his nickname of "Kimeendero" ("the Crusher") by torturing Land and Freedom Army (Mau Mau) detainees. The high price of the food and the background of its owner were clearly out of spirit with the event—on the penultimate day, protestors invaded the Windsor marquee with dozens of street children, liberating all the food available and closing the stand. A hawker told the *Daily Nation* newspaper: "We are harassed in town. We came here to present our problems, but we found the big bosses selling food at exorbitant prices, and yet this function is made for the poor."[19]

Commercialization was generally pervasive. This was the first WSF to have a primary commercial sponsor, namely CelTel, the Africa-wide cell phone company (now rebranded as Zain). Not only was CelTel marketing highly visible throughout the Forum, but Kenyan delegates who registered in advance had been forced to do so using a text message system that required the possession of a CelTel SIM card. Since many registered organizations did not take up their allocated stalls, these were occupied by traders marketing safaris and selling wooden giraffes to delegates—engraved elephant tusks were on sale around the corner from stands run by environmental NGOs. These specific examples were manifestations of a widening gap between the Organizing Committee and its critics during the course of the WSF; many social movement activists, for example from South Africa, actively challenged and criticized these occurrences during the event, turning the Forum itself into a site of struggle.

The Nairobi WSF certainly enabled little expression of the enthusiasm and grassroots participation witnessed at the Harare SASF sixteen months earlier. Most respondents were critical of aspects of the Forum. Malawian interviewees expressed their skepticism that the Forum was anything other than an NGO-dominated talk shop. Peter Chinoko of the Catholic Commission for Justice and Peace in

Lilongwe pointed out that "most of the issues being discussed . . . touch people at the grassroots, but are being discussed at the highest [level]. . . .The venue is Nairobi, Africa. But everything is Western. The presentations, the guest speakers, there wasn't that African touch. I think it's still not on the ground . . . the people who feel the structural injustices should be involved right from the onset . . . but I feel it's like a workshop that doesn't really have that impact."[20] Chinoko was himself sponsored by DanChurchAid to attend, commenting to the authors that "I am representing about twenty or thirty organizations from Malawi . . . there aren't more than about fifteen Malawians present," and these were the usual attendees from the main NGOs.[21] A coordinated Malawian presence was indeed lacking at the event—reinforcing the sense that the national movement was dominated by two or three individuals, particularly those employed by Action Aid.

Zambians were present in larger numbers; while some attended as representatives of larger NGOs, there was a concerted move to bring more grassroots Zambians to the event via a "caravan." This initiative was a direct response to criticisms that Social Forums tended to be events for NGO professionals. A lack of funding apparently promised by the African Social Forum Organizing Committee severely reduced its scale. However, a bus from Lusaka traveled through northern Zambia and Tanzania, meeting up with three more from Dar es Salaam. For the delegates, this was a positive experience, an attempt to turn the claim of grassroots participation into reality. Less positive was their reception at the Kenyan border—the Zambians were told that their coach was not registered in East Africa and could not therefore be brought into the country. While other delegates flew into Nairobi, the Zambians were marooned at the border until hasty arrangements were made to get them to Nairobi. Such difficulties were, they felt, emblematic of the restrictions faced by African social movement activists in making common cause across what they regard as colonial borders.

Zambian delegates had mixed views regarding the WSF itself. Those like Muyatawa Sitali of Jubilee Zambia who were part of established transnational civil society networks participated in scheduled meetings on debt and trade with their counterparts from across Africa and elsewhere. Sitali was critical of what he saw as an undue focus on Africa's problems, in meetings dominated by non-African speakers.[22] Humphrey Sikapizye of the Zambia Council for Social Development was more skeptical:

> If you look at the World Social Forum, by definition we are saying that it is space for reflective thinking and giving opportunity for people to speak out their mind. But when you look at it, you find that we tend to be having the same people, and these are the people who have accessed information. They know what the World Bank is, they know what the corporation is. But where I'm coming from, the common man on the street doesn't know . . . how are we measuring success, and what is our ultimate goal? Is it to come here, we talk, then we go back, we chat by the internet? If this is the purpose, I think it should not be the case. Because if we look at the resources we are putting in to come here, these are millions of dollars. We can use that money to build more schools, we will make an impact. We need to take the Social Forum to the grassroot . . . to let the people speak for themselves.[23]

Sikapizye suggested that the space for grassroots voices is actually being restricted by the professionalization of civil society and the Forum: "The Social Forum has become too academic, i t's a place for the middle class. It's like the World Bank is pushing the government into a corner. The government is pushing the NGOs, civil society into the corner. And the NGOs are pushing the grassroots into the corner."[24] Despite such experiences, there was significant enthusiasm among Zambian delegates for their national Social Forums. There appears to be a genuine belief that, while global events have a tendency to remoteness and abstraction, the Social Forum approach, applied at a local level, can be an impetus to popular mobilization around issues of national concern.

The well-established Zimbabwe Social Forum brought hundreds of people to Nairobi, seeking to raise specific concerns regarding their domestic political situation (see also chapter 6). However, Zimbabwean activists were faced with difficulties arising from the views of many attendees regarding President Mugabe. Mugabe's attacks on Western powers have endeared him to many anticapitalist activists, some of whom see Zimbabwe's land occupations as a progressive attack on white capitalism. Venezuelan president Hugo Chavez, a hero for many social justice activists, praised Mugabe as a "freedom fighter" in 2004. Tshumba Nkosi of the Crisis in Zimbabwe Coalition felt the consequences: he estimated that 90 percent of visitors to his organization's stall viewed Mugabe primarily as a liberator and hero and were therefore hostile to the pro-democracy message of the Crisis Coalition. They expressed a belief that "anybody who is an enemy of George Bush, anybody who is an enemy of Tony Blair, is a friend to the world."[25] Nkosi regarded the purpose of his presence at the WSF to be correcting this distortion and emphasizing that Mugabe's rule stands in direct contrast to the values of the movement.

Lucia Matibenga, vice president of the ZCTU, similarly argued that anticapitalist activists should support popular struggles against the ZANU-PF regime, but was keen to distance civil society from the neoliberal policies of the MDC.[26] Matibenga, president of SATUCC, argued that advocacy activities directed at the international trade union movement, particularly in her region, have created a clear anti-Mugabe consensus, but that sufficient lobbying has not yet been carried out among wider civil society.

Zimbabwean activists made common cause with their counterparts in Swaziland during the WSF; a daily demonstration called for the removal of the unlikely pairing of Mugabe and King Mswati III. If the Zimbabweans did not receive overwhelming support for their message, they at least found solace and solidarity with activists from one of Africa's other least democratic country. The two groups made plans for exchange visits to share their experiences.

Despite the fact that Swaziland's social movement activists are some of the least integrated into the global antiglobalization movement, they were among the most positive about their experiences in Nairobi. During the authors' in-country research visit in 2006, Swazi organizations had appeared divided and pessimistic (see chapter 6). Organizing for the WSF seemed to have generated a new unity in their efforts to raise awareness about Swaziland's problems to a wider African and global audience.[27] At the Swaziland Economic Justice Network's meeting, social movements were united as never before. Although the Swazi activists were highly critical of their country's new constitution, they recognized that it has created a complex new political situation to which they must respond. The Forum provided an opportunity for them to talk to each other about their differences, strategies, and tactics in a way that had apparently not been possible at home. There were disagreements about whether Swaziland should become a constitutional monarchy or a republic as well as criticism of PUDEMO's tendency to adopt positions on behalf of the Swazi people without internal consultation.

Although Swazi interviewees were critical of the WSF's confused organization and the lack of clear outcomes, they were generally positive about the opportunity it provided to break out of their relative isolation and learn from other African activists. This led directly to their commitment to host the SASF held in 2008. More generally, however, the Nairobi event did not stimulate a general growth in the scale or activity of Social Forums on the continent. The three SASF events which have subsequently taken place have not maintained the high tempo of the Harare event in 2005. Two thousand activists did attend the 2006 event in Malawi, but subsequent events have been smaller, and in all these cases there has been a sense of institutionalization of the regional Social Forum model, organized among a relatively closed circle of activists and civil society professionals. This reflects the decreased tempo of struggle in a number of African countries in the last few

years, but also the limited relevance of the wider anticapitalist
movement to the grassroots campaigns of social movement activists in the region.

The anticapitalist movement and Africa

Research on the Social Forums in general and the Nairobi WSF in
particular indicates that the anticapitalist movement, ostensibly an
arena for the expression of the aspirations and demands of the
poor and excluded, is generally accessible only to the most geographically mobile and technologically connected activists in
Africa. Both globalization and antiglobalization processes appear to
the majority of civil society practitioners as highly important but
largely outside their influence. The negative impact of globalization, for example the loss of jobs as a result of international trade
agreements and cheap imports, appears to have a significant impact
on civil society's constituents. A minority of experts is engaged in
lobbying processes directed at the WTO, but there is a significant
gap in comprehension and accountability between these civil society technocrats and the wider movements they ostensibly represent.

The anticapitalist movement has had two significant positive
influences on the ideas and practice of leading civil society advocacy
practitioners. First, it has provided an alternative pole of political
and economic analysis from what had been a hegemonic neoliberal
discourse in the early 1990s. Secondly, its *modus operandi* of mass-
based activism and inclusiveness in decision-making was undoubtedly a progressive step from the paternalism hitherto pervasive in
many northern and southern NGOs. Nevertheless, practical policy-
making remains, for most civil society activists, in the hands of national governments rather than global bodies. The state remains the
major implementing agency of economic policy and therefore a primary target of civil society activity. Although activists are sometimes
persuaded by government claims of powerlessness in the face of
globalization, they usually believe that it is the state's responsibility

to minimize the impact of globalization on the poor. In this sense, the empirical experience of African activists controverts the more extreme claims made for the processes of globalization by its advocates and its critics alike.[28]

Understanding the ambiguous attitude of African social movements toward their own states is key to making sense of the complex triangular relationship between international donors and the IFIs, African states, and indigenous civil society and social movements. While social movements in the north generally see their governments as a major opponent, many African activists still believe in the potential of the developmental state. While the authoritarian tendencies of such states are understood, the experience of economic liberalization, the consequent impact on state-based service delivery, and the perceived loss of national sovereignty to unaccountable foreign institutions lead some in civil society to seek allies within their states against the IFIs. This is sectorally specific: while human rights organizations often see their states as advocacy targets, trade justice bodies work increasingly closely with ministries of trade, for example, playing an important part in the partial derailing of the WTO's Doha round.[29] In general, however, African nationalism (or neo-nationalism) is a powerful and relevant alternative to neoliberalism for many African social movement activists.

The generally negative experience of economic liberalization in Africa over the past twenty years has created a "common sense" of opposition to the IFIs. However, in practice, there is regular dialogue between the IFIs and civil society in some countries. Indeed, it is often those organizations most engaged in progressive campaigns on privatization and trade justice that have the closest relationships with the IFIs. The participation debate is one of the clearest divides in the region. While radical movements, particularly in South Africa, identify the IFIs as a primary enemy that cannot be debated with, their counterparts in Malawi and Zambia are confident that their interaction with the IFIs, in particular through PRSPs, have not only led to gains for their constituents but also widened the space for civil society participation in decision-making.

Conclusion: Which way forward for African anticapitalism?

It now appears that the anticapitalist movement may have passed its peak, its brief turn-of-the-century heyday passing with the realization that globalization may not in practice have been as even and coherent as was imagined—and with its failure to develop meaningful alternatives to this "actually existing" globalization. The most recent WSFs and, in particular, ASFs and SASFs have been smaller and less popular events, resembling workshops of established networks of CSOs rather than enabling mass participation. Although many of the most pressing issues require coordinated global action, attempts to establish a new global organizational architecture have stagnated or even regressed. The global economic crisis that began in 2007 has severely reduced—perhaps even destroyed—the ideological basis of neoliberal free-market economic policies. The continued failure of the WTO's Doha round is just one manifestation of the failure of pro-marketeers to achieve effective policy reform in the last decade. US unilateralism has provided an excuse for other countries, including Zimbabwe, to reject the enforcement of "international" human rights and environmental standards. Latin America has found electoral alternatives to neoliberalism, while China provides both a different model and an increasingly important alternative pole of political attraction in Africa. In general, it appears that many post-Seattle social movement activists wrongly assumed the unproblematic progress of globalization and the concomitant antiglobalization with which they sought to counter it.

There is a certain common-sense appeal to the idea of building the widest possible unity among the global poor and marginalized; African historians are familiar, for example, with the ways in which segmentation and societal divisions prevented an effective unity against formal colonization in the 1890s, and the construction of nationalist coalitions to bring about national independence in the 1950s and 1960s. However, those who argue for such unity without recognizing the enormous diversity of opportunity or resources among social movements not only disregard the real impact of the global inequalities the antiglobalization movement claims to oppose, but tend to replicate some of its most insidious manifestations.

The divergent perspectives reported here are a clear sign that even African social movements have no shared vision of how globalization affects their region. There are some strong parallels between Malawi and Zambia—in both countries, the effective democratic space for social movements has substantially increased, but there are clear limits on the extent of grassroots mobilization for economic and social change. There are also substantial differences, particularly with regard to the old question of how mineral wealth influences political change in Zambia. In both countries, civil society activists have embraced policy participation and, in Zambia at least, believe they can point to genuine progress as a result, something that sets them apart from social movement activists in South Africa and the West.

Zimbabwe and Swaziland are of course very different, but civil society activists in the least democratic countries in the region are finding surprising elements of common cause which may aid them in the future. Social Forums have undoubtedly contributed to strengthening bilateral relations that might not otherwise have occurred. What this points to is the limited relevance of a global event such as the World Social Forum. The evident goodwill of global activists is not enough to create a space above the surface of the sea of inequality in which they all swim. The Nairobi WSF displayed an extreme version of the contradictions evident in a movement that claims equality of access but is both unable and philosophically unwilling to challenge the ways in which the structural injustices they loudly declaim unavoidably pervade the foundations of the movement they have built. Like the radical decolonization and militant nationalist movements of the late 1950s and early 1960s described in chapter 3, the capacity for African social movement activists to transform these movements into fully developed projects of social transformation was constrained by the inequality of experience and participation, as well as the constraints of political perspective that pervaded movements for national independence and that have similarly limited the development of the anticapitalist movement.

This is not to downplay the importance of globalization issues; rather, it is to suggest that, for most activists, the primary forum for advocacy is within the old-fashioned confines of the nation-state. Government policies matter, and African governments, after periods of neoliberal reform (during which it appeared that policymaking was dominated by the IFIs) are demonstrating significant particularities in their national policies. As this book demonstrates, African participation in these antiglobalization and anticapitalist initiatives reflects the high (albeit uneven) tempo of struggle in campaigns for more meaningful democracy and economic and social justice on the continent. Because these reflect the particular insertion of their nation-states into the global economy, the potential demonstrated by the anticapitalist movements for international cooperation in the construction of global political and economic alternatives has been tremendously important (even if the uneven nature of the movement has not always led to particularly appropriate alternatives emerging from Social Forums). We will return to this issue in the conclusion.

CHAPTER 8

CONCLUSION

This book has sought to explain the role of social movements in Africa, both historically and today. It argues that the role of popular movements has been neglected in most writing on political change in Africa. Although it is evidently true that both African elites and external forces (Western governments, global markets, and international financial institutions) have decisively influenced the contemporary realities of Africa, this should not blind us to Africans' struggles to overcome injustice and inequalities and to achieve the societies, economies, and polities they wish to see. The primary, modest aim of the authors has been to place in the public domain evidence of the activities and motivations of social movement activists in this regard, as a rejoinder to Afropessimists who see the continent as a hopeless place whose people are either unwilling or unable to improve their own circumstances.

We have also sought to explore the reasons why, despite their creative and often heroic efforts, African movements have often failed to achieve their aims. This has, of course, been the result of a global political and economic system that is structured to prevent the full realization of the aspirations of most Africans (and indeed most people around the world). Global capitalism, over the past five hundred years and more particularly the last 120 years, has utilized sub-Saharan Africa as a supplier of unfree and cheap labor, raw materials, and land, all of which it has sought to exploit in ways that are inimical not only to notions of social justice, but also to the model of free trade and exchange that the system's advocates claim are central to its nature. The achievement of political independence and the establishment of new African nation-states in the third quarter of the twentieth century, while a tremendous achievement in which ordinary Africans played a vital role, did not (for the reasons explained in chapter 3) lead to a qualitatively different political and economic order on the continent. The contradictory and ambiguous nature of the African nationalist project, which established indigenous governments on the continent that did not articulate or reflect the wishes of most of their peoples, did not ultimately challenge the subordinate integration of Africa into the global system that was the primary cause of its problems. State-led economic programs (often written by Westerners) that sought to engineer development from above and treated ordinary Africans as passive objects were resisted by Africans with their own ideas of how their economies should develop. African political leaders who imagined themselves as the liberators of their peoples ultimately became responsible for suppressing their movements for a more meaningful form of independence. With the onset of the global economic recession in the mid-1970s, they were responsible for overseeing the drastic cuts in living standards demanded by neoliberal economic models that were equally authored from without, and for policing and suppressing resistance to these cuts.

Postcolonial Africa has seen successive waves of protest against the immediate manifestations of the continually exploitative relationships between Africa and the leading elements in the capitalist system and between Africa's highly unequal economic and political classes. Africans have continually resisted reductions of their basic living standards and encroachments on their lives and liberties, and at particular times (and for particular reasons) their acts of resistance have coalesced into more coherent movements for change that linked the struggle for economic and social justice with the need for effective political accountability and representation. This book has sought to explain the dynamics of these struggles: why they should be taken more seriously than they commonly are; why they should be regarded as movements strongly influenced by popular and working-class forces; and why these movements, while sometimes achieving their immediate aims, have not ultimately achieved lasting gains for the African masses.

The majority of the book has focused on the experience of African social movements since the pro-democracy movements of the 1990s. It has sought to draw comparisons between the experiences of African countries that successfully moved to formal democracy (chapter 5) and those that, for various reasons, did not (chapter 6). Although the context in which social movements activists operate is clearly more difficult (and indeed dangerous) in the latter than the former, the study indicates that in neither context has the achievement of democracy enabled a qualitative improvement in material circumstances or an effective political articulation of popular aspirations or grievances. The pro-democracy movements, like their nationalist predecessors, contained within them more radical activists and ideas, but did not ultimately challenge Africa's global subordination and exploitation. However, despite difficult circumstances, particular social movements have been able to win particular reforms or advances that have improved the lives of their constituents or members.

What should be clear to any critical reader is that this study, which provides significant original empirical material on African social movements, the struggles they engage in, and the wider national and international context in which they do so, is that the efforts of the researchers have barely scratched the surface of the rich and diverse traditions, organizational forms, and complex ideas of organizations and activists across the continent. It is hoped that this book, along with the efforts of other researchers working in

similar fields in other parts of the continent, will stimulate new research projects and questions on the myriad social movements that
are constantly emerging and evolving in Africa.[1] In carrying out
this study, a number of important themes and issues have arisen
that need to be addressed in any such research, which the remainder of this conclusion will address.

Inequality, hierarchy, and contradiction

As has been made clear throughout this book, a major challenge to
any prospective analyst of social movement-ism is to achieve any
coherent notion of what does and does not fall within their frame
of analysis. The authors have rejected any preconceived notion of
what is and is not a social movement, preferring instead a Thomp-
sonian approach of studying movements in motion to make sense
of their dynamics, hierarchies, and problems. Non-governmental
organizations, civil society organizations, self-defined social movements, strikes and riots, the mob and the crowd—all have elements
of what constitutes social movement action and all must be con-
sidered, together with their engagement with political parties and
international agencies, in attempts to critically analyze the role of
popular social forces in African societies.

Social movements are *not* best understood as authentic and
unproblematic movements of the people, easily contrasted in a bi-
nary way to the powerful and exploitative elite in society. They are,
rather, an expression of the contradictions and hierarchies of the
societies in which they operate, whose debates and conflicts express inequalities of resources, education, influence, gender, and
ethnicity, among many others. This does not, as some might believe, make them "inauthentic" social movements—rather, it
makes them real, living articulations of political difference in societies marked by inequality and social conflict.

This means that any analysis of social movement thinking or
activity needs to focus not only on a particular movement, but

also on the wider context in which movements operate. Individual movements or organizations influence and are influenced by a wider social, political, and economic environment, the analysis of which is usually central to grasping the vital context in which that movement operates. An instructive example is that of trade unions: these cannot be understood simply in their institutional form, by analyzing their internal structures, elected officials, and adopted policies—rather, the actions of their rank-and-file members, their relations with the wider political environment, and their interaction with wider urban (and in Africa, rural) communities of the poor. This is particularly true in an era of economic liberalization and declining living standards; as large numbers of formal-sector jobs are eliminated, the relationship between labor organizations with shrinking memberships and social movements seeking to represent the wider urban poor—including many former union members—is an increasingly important one in explaining the extent of social movement activism. In a number of cases in southern Africa, former union activists have taken their organizational skills with them into new campaigns for the rights of laid-off workers, against the environmental impact of industry, or into new political campaigns and parties.

Secondly, social movement research must always examine tensions and conflicts, not only between particular movements, but also within them—the fight within a fight. Any study of a particular movement should analyze the relationships between a series of (usually unequal) actors: its leaders and officials; its paid employees (where relevant); those it seeks to directly represent and benefit; and those who are affected, directly or indirectly, by its activities. Unequal power relations—between the more and less educated, women and men, different ethnic groups, and a dozen other potential divisions, have the potential to shape social movement discourse or activity.[2] The presumption of research should be to assume the existence of such tensions, hierarchies, and inequalities, the better to enable analysis.

Globalization, extraversion, and commodification

African social movements, perhaps more than their Western counterparts that serve as the basis for most social movement theoretical
work, have always been influenced by their continent's long history
of globalization. That history was controlled largely by Western
powers, but African agency was always highly influential. Ideas of
individual and collective freedoms that inform social movement
thinking and activism have their origins in the decidedly ambiguous
legacy of the Western Enlightenment, which brought modern concepts of democracy and rights to Africa, inextricably tied to Western
imperialism and capitalism. Africans, of course, have their own traditions of political representation and change, and African political
and social movements in the twentieth century debated endlessly
the relationship between Western liberal or socialist universalisms
and their particular relevance or manifestations in Africa. African
social movements utilized notions and approaches such as self-government, democracy, collective organization, direct action, political
parties, and civil society, all of which were in many respects defined
in advance by Western thinkers and activists. Although Africans
have appropriated, rethought, and reworked such concepts, utilizing
them in their own interests and in hybrid forms, tension nevertheless often arises between such globalized forms of organization and
resistance and the particular context in which they are conceived of
and utilized in Africa. This, coupled with the continent's continued
poverty and subordination in the global context, militates against
the development of a specifically "African" form of social movements. Actually existing social movements in Africa are unavoidably
hybrid in nature, utilizing and adapting Western ideas, funding,
forms of organization, and methods of activism.

However, we do not want to restate a simple truism. We believe that all ideas and organizational forms that have a history are
going to be "hybrid" in character. All development is "combined"
development, making use of old and new, local and exogenous. It

is therefore important to speak of the *specific ways* Africans have adapted ideas and organizational forms that are (partly) borrowed from the West—as we have tried to highlight at different points in the book. Consequently, we prefer to talk of the *unevenness* of development. African events, then, are affected by *inequality* in international relations. In this case, the "hybrid" character of some African events—both ideas and organizational forms—reflects not only the ways *Africans* have adapted these things to their needs, but how they are shaped partly by Africans and partly by foreign parties according to *their* needs. The hybrid character that we describe is made up of inherently conflicted elements.

This is particularly important when one considers the role of African pro-democracy and reformist movements that are funded by and therefore partly dependent on Western agencies—governments, but also international NGOs, think tanks, and donors. The Western powers and IFIs have come to regard certain forms of popular mobilization or protest as useful ways to remove certain particularly corrupt or intransigent governments that have failed to successfully implement structural adjustment programs.[3] This should not be interpreted as an argument that sees all protest movements as manipulated by American or imperialist power, but rather an appeal for careful analysis of the specific social forces involved in national political change. The transitions in this study, frustrated and "successful," were part of these waves of change, but also subject to the same enormous contradictions.

In the 1990s and 2000s, popular struggles that have erupted as a consequence of neoliberal reforms and structural adjustment have often manifested themselves as liberal movements for democracy and human rights. This arises from the fact that governments implementing neoliberal reforms rely on increasingly draconian measures to suppress popular discontent. Chris Harman described these processes well: "The path that began with neoliberalism ends up in quasi-dictatorship . . . the effect is to turn social and economic issues into political struggles around demands for democracy and human rights. In the process people can lose sight of the social and economic roots of these political issues."[4] Unless this link is made, social movements seeking to alleviate the effects of economic liberalization can easily be convinced that the primary answer to their grievances is more formal political or constitutional reform, rather than a deepening of democratic culture and practice that encompasses popular scrutiny and ultimately control of the socioeconomic situation.

In very different ways, the early 1990s saw movements for social, political, and economic transformation across southern Africa mutate into movements led by an opposition elite for democratization and citizenship. In most cases, such elites resumed the imposition of neoliberalism in a new context, eventually setting off a new wave of protests against the effects of those policies. In some cases, the new, comparatively democratic context enabled the reversal or weakening of such neoliberal reforms. In other cases, the democratic gains were themselves rolled back or weakened. In many cases, social movements were politically disarmed and their popular supporters manipulated for set-piece confrontations with the government that did nothing to advance their interests. Some new governments successfully co-opted and corrupted leading activists. Social movement activism was often softened up by the carrot of "participatory democracy" and the stick of economic decline, deforming and distorting activism and agendas. In such circumstances, new waves and generations of activists, frustrated at the failures and compromises of their seniors and elders, came to the fore to seek new and old types of changes, often with little opportunity to grasp why their forerunners had failed to achieve their aims.

The role of ideology, organization, and the scale of protests

The differences between the case studies analyses in this book reveal some important features of social movements. The first, most striking difference is the scale of political mobilization. From 1995,

Zimbabwe saw what one activist described as a "sort of revolution," with urban (and rural) protests increasing year after year. With each new wave of protest new layers of society would be galvanized, deepening the political movement that was tightening around the government. As Brian Kagoro explained, by 1997 "you had an outright . . . rebellion on your hands."[5]

The crucial element during this period of "rebellion" was that it was generalized. By the late 1990s, social movement action often became dominated by trade unions. In many respects, the experiences of other countries during the transition—in Senegal, Nigeria, Zambia, Kenya, and Malawi, for example—could not have been more different. The period of the transitions in the 1990s was not marked by massive urban protest and ferment. On the contrary, most of the political decisions were made by a political elite that, although drawn from the ranks of the opposition, was not directly accountable to a wider movement. Although there was a popular groundswell of support for the transition, it did not operate in conditions of widespread political protest, let alone "rebellion." Activists did not, as a result, reach the level of political development experienced by activists in Zimbabwe.

As a consequence, there are striking differences between activists on the continent, notable particularly at the World Social Forum in 2007 in Kenya (see chapter 7). Zimbabwean social movement activists talked about the euphoria of having been involved in massive social mobilization. Often they conceptualized this activism in general terms of liberation and revolution, terms that do not seem transplanted onto their activism but are a product of the scale of the protests—and the period—in which they have been involved. Elsewhere, while activists might remember the excitement of the campaign and the exquisite joy and hope that were generated by election victories, their horizons were sometimes fixed on more limited possibilities.

Undoubtedly, one of the reasons why some movements on the continent are weaker than others, and why activists are animated less by broader ideologies, is what Cherif Ba, an activist from Senegal, described in 2004 as the failure of *la formation des militants*—training and education of activists: "Political parties must take responsibility for raising the political level of their activists. But what party does this? . . . Therefore activists don't get the basic training they must . . . political involvement is simply engaged in . . . to support the president or further the aims of a political party."[6]

However, most of the political left, disoriented after the collapse of Stalinism, have immersed themselves in a political circus of recycled elites. In this circus social movement activists are relegated to the status of cheerleaders, with no real responsibilities except as uncritical supporters of their political leaders. Colin Barker argues for a model of organization based on the desire "to win fellow-militants to a common framework of understanding and intervention. Far from promoting passivity, they encourage activism; instead of neglecting education . . . [it is] their very *métier,* their be-all-and-end-all."[7]

The vision and practice of many activists does *not* emphasize self-activity or collective decision-making. Discussions in meetings do not turn movements into "talk shops" but into places where decisions are reached through the democratic process of the majority and then acted on. The goal is to create activists who are able to link specific questions and perspectives to more general issues of neoliberalism and regional development. This is a "dialogical engagement" with the wider movement, a process of constant political debate and discussion with other movement militants.[8]

This phenomenon is linked to an important theme in the book. If social movements can act to bring about social change, they do so with the organizational and ideological tools at their disposal. These resources are fashioned by the movement and conditioned by inherited conditions that inform beliefs, loyalties, and activism. However, these ideas do not act by themselves—independent of social context—nor are they simple reflections of this context. The case studies show us that ideas and organizations (or their absence) can have a vital influence on events.

We have argued in this book that after the second wave of democratic struggles, new governments across the continent followed, more or less obediently, the advice of the IFIs. This common resumption of neoliberalism stemmed from a common failure linked to the inability of protest movements to develop independent organizational and ideological alternatives that could have offered a sufficient counterweight to the global momentum of neoliberal forces. We have argued, therefore, for the need to distinguish between the effectiveness of political activism, against the extreme relativism of much social theory. Some groups did attempt to question not only specific economic reforms but also (implicitly or explicitly) the prevailing worldview of the local and global order. Activists and scholars must extend, develop, and critique these emancipatory alternatives.

The transition confronts us with many paradoxes. We have seen movements led by popular classes challenge governments, unseat incumbent dictatorships, and win (more recently) important incremental reforms and concessions. But in the transitions, these movements frequently came under the leadership of contradictory social forces: ex-ministers, politicians alienated (and ejected) from government office, and NGO and middle-class professionals and bureaucrats. Popular social movements fell under the direction of an intelligentsia driven by its commitment to neoliberal governance. As in the 1950s and 1960s (see chapter 3), this same elite group, deprived of economic and political power by colonialism but with a coherent organizational home and identity in student associations and unions, became the champion of national liberation—but it was an inherently impoverished version of liberation. Frequently tied to the purse strings of the colonial metropolis, they sought a national freedom that would maintain and develop Western political and economic involvement in independence. The position of such elites was, however, undermined by the global economic crisis that arose in the mid-1970s, which undercut the model of development that depended on Western markets for raw African produce and minerals.

The subsequent process of neoliberalism unleashed a succession of protest waves in Africa that widened popular engagement, but elite leaders eventually shepherded and corralled these movements into the narrower and more limited objectives of "good governance" and "liberalization." Economic liberalization—with its devastating whirlwind of job losses and factory closures—has to a certain extent weakened the organizations and coherence of the African working class while strengthening the role of what Frantz Fanon described as an "avaricious caste."[9]

The political transitions in sub-Saharan Africa in the 1990s occurred in a world fundamentally altered by global geopolitics. Struggles in peripheral capitalist societies have been profoundly affected by the collapse of ideas of national liberation linked to state-led development. In the period following the collapse of the Berlin Wall—which signaled the apparent death of state-dominated strategies for development—ideological confusion consumed many of the social forces that had looked to progressive and left-wing political change. However, the evidence presented in this book shows that social movements continue to effect political change even in the absence of a coherent program for socioeconomic change. Nevertheless, the inherited circumstances and the structural constraints within which they operate inevitably curtail their ability to exercise *meaningful* agency.

The collapse of vibrant protest movements into limited liberal reformism reflects the limited impact of the protests and rebellions described in this study. These limitations typically derive from the same sources: first, the failure of organizations and social groups within the social movements to distinguish themselves clearly and independently from the political weaknesses of wider political forces, and second, the absence of effective, independent movements that organize in a broad political and social milieu (in townships, factories, and universities). In the presence of such organizations, more radical actions could lead to deeper and more sustained political transitions. Without them, social movements often remain isolated and easily manipulated, and make only a limited impression on the underlying political and economic fabric of the continent.

Neoliberalism, crisis, and revolt

For much of the period under study in this book, conventional social science has viewed Africa from a Western perspective, seeing its problems (and potential solutions to them) through a Eurocentric lens. Today, many of the problems arrogantly perceived as peculiarly African, have pervaded the wider capitalist world. Economic crisis, stagnation, and austerity, long the standard (and lazy) epithets applied to Africa's political economy, are now apt descriptions of European and North American capitalism. The collapse of market-oriented Western economic models and the need for huge state bailouts of financial institutions by Western governments since 2007, significantly challenge the neoliberal project implemented by the West in Africa (and promoted elsewhere) since the mid-1970s. Approximately eleven trillion dollars (US) was spent globally to shore up banks and insurance companies, principally in the United Kingdom and United States, but also in other G20 countries. Illusions of free markets unhampered by state intervention were dramatically shelved in an opportunistic resurgence of selective neo-Keynesianism. Of course, the reality of neoliberalism since the onset of the "counterrevolution" in the late 1970s involved the state heavily underpinning the financial sector and failing companies.[10] Nevertheless, the current crisis may, in David Harvey's words, demonstrate that there are "no effective long-run capitalist solutions (apart from reversion to fictitious capital manipulations) to this crisis of capitalism."[11]

The myth of neoliberalism as the harbinger of prosperity, development, and unparalleled economic growth has been singularly exposed. Instead Europe and America face economic contraction, decline, and (even in the long run) feeble and fragile growth. As we write, the state debt incurred by the bailouts and by the property

bubble that burst across Europe and North America is being utilized by politicians who promoted neoliberalism and bailed out
its failures to implement deep and prolonged cuts in public-
sector spending.[12]

Even for a casual observer of Africa's recent history, there are
evident parallels with the current global crisis. Debts across the developing world were largely incurred in the 1970s by easy loans
from private banks, underwritten by a surplus of petrodollars from
Middle Eastern oil. When those loans turned into debts in the late
1970s, the resultant crisis was used to force through structural adjustment programs that fundamentally refigured Africa's political
economy. Throughout the early phases of structural adjustment,
the World Bank and IMF spoke piously about profligate spending
and bloated budgets and insisted on reforms. Limited state welfare
was slashed, education and health budgets savaged, and jobs lost as
state support to national industries was withdrawn. The continent
would never be the same again.

Today, much of the Western world faces similar austerity that
threatens the survival of the postwar welfare state. This book's
analysis of the achievements and failures of Africa's social movements in response to that continent's crisis has a particular relevance here. Two decades of revolts were triggered by the debt crisis
in sub-Saharan Africa. As we have seen, social movements over-
threw governments and brought together coalitions of the poor
and the working class. It is important to learn from the successes of
these movements in challenging such attacks, but also from their
evident failure to generate political alternatives. The resistance that
lies ahead may see a vital convergence of movements in the global
north and south.

However, the burden of global economic turbulence and speculation continues to fall unevenly—in particular on Africa. The recent rise in financial speculation, an attempt to make profitable bets
in the context of a relative squeeze on industrial and manufacturing
profits, has seen a massive expansions of bets on "softs"—rice, grain,

and other staple foods. The result was spectacular increases in the price of staple foodstuffs, to the particular detriment of the global poor. Food price rises between 2007 and 2009 led to food riots, general strikes, and protests in thirty-five countries across the world, twenty-four of which were in Africa. Eleven uprisings occurred on the continent in that two-year period, directly linked to increases in the price of cooking oil, bread, and rice.[13] Any attempt to draw out commonalities and collective action between African and Western social movements in response to the global economic crisis, welcome though that would be, should be alert to the particularly acute African experience of that crisis and responsive to African social movements' analyses.

The nature of political change

This brings us to the central question of the nature and degree of political change to which social movements can contribute. Progressive Western analysts of African political history have tended over the last fifty years to seek to identify particular social forces or movements that can form the basis of overarching, self-conscious projects of radical political transformation, usually of the kind that they themselves have already preconceived. Social democrats and liberals saw African nationalism as the answer to the continent's problems, believing that self-rule in the hands of wise indigenous leaders (whose ideas, developed in Western universities and missions, closely resembled their own) would enable steady and controlled change of the sort appropriate to the continent's level of (as they saw it) education and civilization. Development advisors eager to implement their blueprints for economic "take-off" and "catch-up" sought to identify indigenous agents of such changes and were constantly disappointed by the inability or unwillingness of the African people to play the role prescribed to them. More radical socialists argued about whether the urban working class, the rural peasantry, or the Westernized intelligentsia would be in

the vanguard of socialist or communist revolution on the continent, and were equally disappointed by the dismal results of such
vanguardist attempts at radical change. We believe that many of
these debates took place away from real struggles in social movements. The discussions in this book show a preference for self-
activity of the poor, workers, or the "grassroots." This is not a moral
preference, but it reflects our understanding of the likely agents of
major social change—the working class and poor on the continent.

Anticapitalist activists, in theory more open to diverse forms of
political expression and organization, have in our experience been
similarly disappointed with the failure of African social movements
to sound, look, and act like their counterparts in the West or in
Latin America. Western observers of many political hues (and their
allies among Africa's elites) have been periodically seized with enthusiasm about Africa's decade, century, moment, or renaissance—
and been rapidly disillusioned with the continent's enduring failure
to meet their expectations in a timely manner.

Meanwhile, Africans—individually but also collectively—have
gone about the difficult and often dangerous business of organizing
actions and organizations to improve the particular circumstances of
sections of their society, of the sort that we have attempted to depict
in this book. At times, these movements have coalesced into broader
movements for social change that carried within them the potential
for a radical transformation of society, a genuine revolutionary
change. Whether this potential was achieved or not, it has normally
been the case that Western observers have been unable to see past
their own expectations and norms to understand the real extent of
these social movements' achievements. We invite radical observers of
the continent to see the importance of counter-hegemonic forces
that will provide the answer to the continent's exploitation, marginalization, and suffering, as well as focusing on the myriad day-to-day
struggles for change that are Africa's true story of struggle.[14] It is only
out of these highly complex and differentiated movements that the
organizations and political alternatives to capitalism's uneven and

brutal global hegemony will emerge. Messy, ideologically confused, and inherently contradictory, such struggles and movements never-theless contain within them genuinely organic seeds of revolutionary change, the only sort that have any chance to take root and blossom on the continent's fertile soil.

We urge activists not only to focus on these day-to-day strug-gles, but to discover how they relate to broader issues and bigger struggles to come. It is true that the organizations and political alternatives to capitalism's hegemony will emerge from today's struggles, but activists need to *make* them emerge in ways that will advance their hopes for radical political change. To do that, ac-tivists need to learn where to focus their energies, where to build social bases, how to form tactical alliances, and when to break them—in short, activists need to develop a strategic outlook for a longer-term struggle to overthrow capitalism. That does not mean that they need to create a fixed template or to find a single social sector that can provide all the crucial strategic wisdom and social leverage for revolution. While we reject the idea of finding a single counter-hegemonic force that will provide the answer, we refuse to retreat into a focus only on concrete "day-to-day struggle." Neither posture is genuinely strategic.

This book, we believe, has provided such a strategic position. Our focus has been on the self-activity of the grassroots—and the broadly-conceived working class we have outlined in chapter 2—to combat and ultimately overturn exploitation and oppression glob-ally. We have also asserted the special capacities of urban wage workers within the broad movement of this class. We have stated explicitly the necessity of a militant leadership within this broad movement, one that is able to link specific questions and perspec-tives to more general issues and that strives to win fellow militants to a common framework of understanding and intervention. We also argue that militants must maintain independence from West-ern donors and local exploiters to protect themselves against becoming mere cheerleaders in a political circus of recycled elites—

while providing a nuanced view of how, under real conditions of capitalism, independence is often a matter of degree.

Our strategic position is clearly one that belongs on the revolutionary socialist and anti-Stalinist left. We hope that activists who read this book—both African and Western—will see struggles and movements as messy, ideologically confused, and inherently contradictory—but that the book will also help them navigate through the mess, clear up confusion, and expose contradiction. While our contribution has necessarily been modest, we are, nevertheless, trying to make a contribution. We *do not* believe that African liberation will spring only from "indigenous seeds," because in our globalized world seeds get blown in from everywhere—as we have already stated, all development is "combined" development. Our book may contain ideas that answer some people's needs in Africa; if it does, these ideas may take root there. Then, if they get passed on and developed and become further "naturalized," they will be as authentically "African" as any other ideas that any region or group may have. The key point about self-determination will still stand—that Africans will figure out which ideas work best.

LIST OF ACRONYMS

ABM	Abahlali baseMjondolo (Shack Dwellers Movement)
ADMARC	Agricultural Development and Marketing Corporation
AEC	Anti-Eviction Campaign
AMEC	African Methodist Episcopal Church
ANC	African National Congress
APF	Anti-Privatization Forum
ASF	African Social Forum
BLA	Black Local Authority (South Africa)
CCJDP	Catholic Commission for Justice, Development and Peace
CONGOMA	Coalition of Non-Governmental Organizations of Malawi
COSATU	Congress of South African Trade Unions (South Africa)
CSANET	Civil Society Agricultural Network
CSOs	Civil society organizations
CSPR	Civil Society for Poverty Reduction (Zambia)
DPP	Democratic Progressive Party (Zambia)
DRC	Democratic Republic of Congo
DUF	Democratic United Front for a People-Driven Constitution (Zimbabwe)
EPAs	European Partnership Agreements
ESAP	Economic and Structural Adjustment Program (Zimbabwe)
FEANF	Fédération des Étudiants d'Afrique Noire en France (Federation of Black African Students in France)
FFTUZ	Federation of Free Trade Unions of Zambia

FIS	Front Islamique du Salut (Islamic Salvation Front) (Algeria)
FLN	Front de Libération Nationale (National Liberation Front) (Algeria)
FODEP	Foundation for Democratic Process (Zambia)
FOSATU	Federation of South African Trade Unions
GDP	Gross Domestic Product
GEAR	Growth and Employment and Redistribution Programme (South Africa)
GNU	Government of National Unity
HIPC	Highly Indebted Poor Countries
IFIs	International financial institutions
IMF	International Monetary Fund
ISO	International Socialist Organisation (Zimbabwe)
JMPR	Jeneusse du Mouvement Populaire de la Révolution (Youth of the Popular Movement of the Revolution)
KANU	Kenya African National Union
MCTU	Malawi Congress of Trade Unions
MDC	Movement for Democratic Change (Zimbabwe)
MEJN	Malawi Economic Justice Network
MK	Umkhonto we Sizwe (Spear of the Nation) (South Africa)
MMD	Movement for Multi-Party Democracy
NAFTA	North American Free Trade Agreement
NCA	National Constitutional Assembly (Zimbabwe)
NCC	National Constitutional Conference (Zambia)
NCNC	National Council of Nigeria and the Cameroons
NDR	National Democratic Revolution
NEPAD	New Economic Plan for African Development
NGO	Non-governmental Organization
NGOCC	Non-Governmental Organizations Coordinating Committee (Zambia)
NP	National Party (South Africa)
NUCIZ	National Union of the Clothing Industry of Zimbabwe
PRSP	Poverty Reduction Strategy Program

PUDEMO	People's United Democratic Movement (Swaziland)
RDP	Reconstruction and Development Programme (South Africa)
SACP	South African Communist Party
SACTU	South African Congress of Trade Unions
SAP	Structural adjustment program
SASF	Southern African Social Forum
SATUCC	Southern African Trade Union Coordinating Council
SEJF	Socio-Economic Justice Foundation
SFTU	Swaziland Federation of Trade Unions
SMI	Social Movements Indaba (South Africa)
SWAYOCO	Swaziland Youth Congress
TAC	Treatment Action Campaign
TANGO	Tanzania Association of Non-Governmental Organizations
TANU	Tanganyika African National Union
UDF	United Democratic Front (South Africa); also United Democratic Front (Malawi)
UDPS	Union pour la Démocratie et le Progrès Social (Union for Democracy and Social Progress) (DRC)
UNIP	United National Independence Party (Zambia)
UWT	Umoja wa Wanawake wa Tanganyika (Women's Unity of Tanganyika) (Tanzania)
WETUM	Water Employees' Trade Union of Malawi
WOZA	Women of Zimbabwe Arise
WSF	World Social Forum
WTO	World Trade Organization
ZANU-PF	Zimbabwe African National Union–Patriotic Front
ZCC	Zimbabwe Council of Churches
ZCTU	Zimbabwe Congress of Trade Unions; also Zambia Congress of Trade Unions
ZESN	Zimbabwe Election Support Network
ZINASU	Zimbabwe National Student Union
ZNCB	Zambia National Commercial Bank
ZSF	Zimbabwe Social Forum

NOTES

Chapter 1: Introduction

1. This very general definition of "social movements" will be elaborated upon in this chapter and in chapter 2.
2. See Martin Meredith, *The State of Africa: A History of Fifty Years of Independence* (London: Free Press, 2006) and John Reader, *Africa: A Biography of the Continent* (London: Penguin, 1998).
3. E. P. Thompson, *The Making of the English Working Class* (London: Penguin, 1991), 11–12.
4. Charles van Onselen, *Chibaro: African Mine Labour in Southern Rhodesia, 1900–1933* (Johannesburg: Ravan Press, 1980); Shula Marks and Richard Rathbone, eds., *Industrialisation and Social Change in South Africa: African Class Formation, Culture, and Consciousness, 1870–1930* (Harlow: Longman, 1982). More recently, some excellent work has followed a similar trajectory. See George Nzongola-Ntalaja, *The Congo: From Leopold to Kabila: A People's History* (London: Zed Books, 2002).
5. See, for example, Peter Waterman, *Division and Unity amongst Nigerian Workers: Lagos Port Unionism, 1940s–60s,* (The Hague: Institute of Social Studies, 1982); Michael Burawoy, *A Comparison of Strikes among Zambian Workers in a Clothing Factory and the Mining Industry* (Lusaka: University of Zambia, 1974).
6. In Zimbabwe, an excellent example of history from below is Brian Raftopoulos and Ian Phimister, eds., *Keep on Knocking: A History of the Labour Movement in Zimbabwe, 1900–1997* (Harare: Baobab Books: 1997).
7. David Renton, David Seddon, and Leo Zeilig, *The Congo: Plunder and Resistance* (London: Zed Books, 2007).
8. Karl Marx and Friedrich Engels, *The Communist Manifesto* (London: Penguin, 1964), 58.

9. Chris Harman, "The Rise of Capitalism," *International Socialism Journal* 2:102 (2004), 82, available at http://www.isj.org.uk/?id=21.
10. Ibid., 80.
11. Ibid., 82.
12. Otherwise we would all, presumably, *choose* much more favorable circumstances!
13. This, of course, implies a further importance to the struggles in periphery capitalist societies. As relatively "weak" links in the global hierarchy, it is perhaps in these areas that the chains of capitalist society can be the first to be prized apart. See Leon Trotsky, *The History of the Russian Revolution* (Chicago: Haymarket Books, 2008).
14. Harman, "Rise of Capitalism," 81.
15. We will see the same kind of argument about the pro-democracy movements of the 1990s—that their unity was achieved on a "negative" basis as different sectors desired the removal of the dictatorships but differed in their "positive" social goals.
16. John Bomba, interview by Leo Zeilig, May 23, 2003.
17. Karl Marx, *The Eighteenth Brumaire of Louis Bonaparte*, available at http://www.marxists.org/archive/marx/works/1852/18th-brumaire/ch01.htm.
18. Thompson, *Making of the English Working Class*, 8.
19. Asse Lilombo, interview with the authors, Kinshasa, November 20, 2006.
20. Peter Dwyer and David Seddon, "The New Wave? A Global Perspective on Popular Protest," paper presented at the 8th International Conference on Alternative Futures and Popular Protest, April 2–4 2002, Manchester Metropolitan University, Manchester, UK.

Chapter 2: Social Movements and the Working Class in Africa

1. Inspiration for many ideas in this chapter came from the work of Colin Barker. While we have been influenced by his writing on social movements and Marxism for more than two decades, it is his recent elaboration of the "social movement in general" that informs our work here: "Class Struggle and Social Movement—An Effort at Untangling," conference paper presented at *Alternative Futures and Popular Protests*, Manchester Metropolitan University, March 29–31, 2010, as well as Barker's brilliant critique of recent writings on revolutions, "Looking in the Wrong Direction? Reflection on Revolutionary Possibility in the 21st Century," unpublished working paper. See also Colin Barker, Alan Johnson, and Michael Lavalette, eds., *Leadership and Social Movements* (Manchester: Manchester University Press, 2001).
2. See Charles Tilly, "Social Movements as Historically Specific Clusters of Political Performances," *Berkeley Journal of Sociology* 38 (1994), 1–30. Social movements occupied a space outside the state for most of the nineteenth

century. However, in the last decades of the century, this began to change as capitalist states incorporated "movements" of contestation. Suffrage was widened, trade unionism legalized, and social-democratic parties born. A new phenomenon developed in the shape of semi-permanent movement organizations embodied in left-wing political parties, trade union structures, and cooperatives.

3. For a basic statement of this proposition, see Marx and Engels, *Communist Manifesto*.

4. See Friedrich Engels, "The Revolt in India 1858," in *Karl Marx and Friedrich Engels, Collected Works,* vol.15 (London: Lawrence and Wishart, 1986), 607–11.

5. Aijaz Ahmad, *In Theory* (London: Verso, 1991), 229.

6. Barker, "Class Struggle and Social Movement," 28.

7. Jeff Goodwin, *No Other Way Out: States and Revolutionary Movements, 1945–1991* (Cambridge: Cambridge University Press, 2001), 44.

8. Dan Georgakas and Marvin Surkin, *Detroit, I Do Mind Dying: A Study in Urban Revolution* (New York: South End Press, 1998).

9. Thompson, *Making of the English Working Class*, 8.

10. Barker, "Class Struggle and Social Movement," 27–30.

11. Sidney Tarrow, *Power in Movements: Social Movement, Collective Action and Politics* (Cambridge: Cambridge University Press, 1994).

12. This is no more than Thomas Paine's statement during the French Revolution that in humanity there is a "mass of sense laying in a dormant state, and which, unless something excites it to action . . . all that extent of capacity . . . never fails to appear in revolutions." See "The Rights of Man," available from the University of Virginia at http://xroads.virginia.edu/~hyper2/CDFinal/Paine/contents.html.

13. These are not abstract statements. This vision illuminated the popular democracies and workers' councils in the revolutionary movements in Germany (1918–23), Spain (1936), and Budapest (1956), but also in peripheral capitalist countries such as Senegal (1968) and Iran (1979), for example.

14. Thomas Hodgkin, *Nationalism in Colonial Africa*, (London: Frederick Muller, 1956), 25.

15. Frederick Cooper, "The Dialectics of Decolonization: Nationalism and Labor Movements in Post-War French Africa," in Frederick Cooper and Ann Laura Stoler, eds., *Tensions of Empire: Colonial Cultures in a Bourgeois World* (Berkeley: University of California Press, 1997), 406. Cited in Joseph Mtisi, Munyaradzi Nyakudya, and Teresa Barnes, "War in Rhodesia, 1965–1980," in Brian Raftopoulos and Alois Mlambo, eds., *Becoming Zimbabwe: A History from the Pre-Colonial Period to 2008* (Harare: Weaver Press, 2009), 150–51.

16. Lilombo, interview, November 20, 2006.

17. Kwame Nkrumah, *Africa Must Unite* (London: Panaf, 1985), 166–67.

18. For a good introductory overview of the origin and initial consequences of this policy, see Duncan Hallas, *The Comintern* (Chicago: Haymarket Books, 2007).

19. For a classic statement of the labor aristocracy in Africa, see Giovanni Arrighi

and John Saul, "Socialism and Economic Development in Tropical Africa," *Journal of Modern African Studies* vol. 6, no. 2 (1968), 141–69. For a number of effective challenges to such arguments, see Richard Sandbrook and Robin Cohen, eds., *The Development of an African Working Class* (London: Longman, 1976). Joan Davies cites at least one African labor leader who believed revolutionary socialist change was possible at this time: *African Trade Unions* (New York: Penguin, 1966), 143–47.

20. Frantz Fanon, *The Wretched of the Earth* (London: Penguin Books, 1963).

21. Ibid., 174.

22. Basil Davidson, *Africa in Modern History: The Search for a New Society* (London: Pelican, 1977).

23. Amílcar Cabral, *Revolution in Guinea* (London: Stage 1, 1969), 83.

24. Ibid., 87.

25. Amílcar Cabral, *Return to the Source: Selected Speeches of Amílcar Cabral* (New York: Monthly Review Press, 1973), 83–84.

26. See Patrick Chabal and Jean-Pascal Daloz, *Africa Works: Disorder as Political Instrument* (Oxford: James Currey, 1999).

27. Jill Natrass, *The South African Economy: Its Growth And Change* (Oxford University Press, 1988), 27.

28. Miles Larmer, *Mineworkers in Zambia* (New York: I.B. Tauris, 2007), 149–50.

29. Patrick Bond and Mzwanele Mayekiso, "Toward the Integration of Urban Social Movements at the World Scale," *Journal of World Systems Research* 2:2 (1996), 1–11.

30. James Petras and Denis Engbarth, "Third World Industrialization and Trade Union Struggles," in Roger Southall, ed., *Trade Unions and the New Industrialization of the Third World* (London: Zed Books, 1988). John Saul was also doubtful about the progressive nature of these movements; see John Saul and Colin Leys, "Sub-Saharan Africa in Global Capitalism," *Monthly Review* 51:3, (1999).

31. Patrick Chabal, "Political Transitions and Civil Society in Africa," in Nuno Vidal and Patrick Chabal, eds., *Southern Africa: Civil Society, Politics and Donor Strategies* (Luanda: Media XXI & Firmamento, 2009).

32. Ousseina Alidou, George Caffentzis, and Silvia Federici, eds., *A Thousand Flowers. Social Struggles against Structural Adjustment in African Universities* (New York: Africa World Press, 2000).

33. John A. Wiseman, *The New Struggle for Democracy in Africa* (Aldershot: Avebury, 1996), 49.

34. David Harvey, *A Brief History of Neoliberalism* (London: Oxford University Press, 2005).

35. Gareth Dale, "A Short Autumn of Utopia: The East German Revolution of 1989," *International Socialism Journal* 124 (2009).

36. Joseph Iranola Akinlaja, the former general secretary of the National Union of Petroleum and Natural Gas Workers in Nigeria, explained in 2002 that the collapse of the Soviet Union "weakened our belief in Marxist resistance in

Africa." Personal communication, February 2002.

37. But much happened in the 1990s, including the Zapatista uprisings in 1994, the struggles of social movements in South America, and the slow revival of radical left politics in France after the "winter of discontent" in 1995.

38. For an early example, see Emma Bircham and John Charlton, eds., *Anti-Capitalism: A Guide to the Movement* (London: Bookmarks, 2001).

39. See Achille Mbembe, *On the Postcolony* (Berkeley: University of California Press, 2001); Jean-François Bayart, *The State in Africa: The Politics of the Belly* (London: Longman, 1993).

40. See Richard Werbner, "Multiple Identities, Plural Arenas," in Richard Werbner and Terence Ranger, eds., *Postcolonial Identities in Africa* (London: Zed Books, 1996), and James Manor, ed., *Rethinking Third World Politics* (London: Longman, 1991).

41. Manor, *Rethinking Third World Politics*, 2.

42. Eboe Hutchful, "Eastern Europe: Consequences for Africa," *Review of African Political Economy* vol. 18, no. 50 (1991), 51–59.

43. Graham Harrison, *Issues in the Contemporary Politics of Sub-Saharan Africa: The Dynamics of Struggle and Resistance* (New York: Palgrave, 2002), 107. Two important studies are illustrative of these trends. One edited collection, Werbner and Ranger, *Postcolonial Identities in Africa*, and Manor, *Rethinking Third World Politics*. These texts look at specific examples within states, concentrating on detailed case studies to avoid large-scale categorization. This, they argue, allows the researcher to delve into the localized complexity of social formations. The emphasis is on anthropological and cultural enquiry that brings out the symbolic and linguistic significance in a social practice.

44. "Afropessismism" was a fashionable term in the 1990s, and in academic circles became attached to the work of Jean-François Bayart. It was linked to the general pessimism, as we have seen, that followed the collapse of the Berlin Wall.

45. Bayart, *The State in Africa*, 57–58.

46. Achille Mbembe, interview by Christian Höller, "Africa in Motion," *Springerin*, 2001, available at http://www.springerin.at/dyn/heft_text.php?textid=1195&lang=en.

47. Achille Mbembe, "Power and Obscenity in the Post-Colonial Period: The Case of Cameroon," in Manor, ed., *Rethinking Third World Politics*, 171. It is an unfortunate fact for Mbembe that as he was describing the "performance" of people in Cameroon involved in perpetuating their own oppression, there was a popular upheaval that almost bought the government down.

48. Pascal Bianchini, "Le Mouvement Étudiant Sénégalais: Un Essai d'Interprétation (The Student Movement in Senegal: An Interpretive Essay)" in M.C. Diop, *La Société Sénégalaise entre le Local et le Global (Senegalese Society between the Local and the Global)* (Paris: Karthala, 2002).

49. Harrison, *Issues*, 109–10.

50. Piet Konings, "University Students' Revolt, Ethnic Militia, and Violence during Political Liberalization in Cameroon," *African Studies Review* 45:2

(2002), 179–204.

51. Hal Draper, *Karl Marx's Theory of Revolution: The Politics of Social Classes* (New York: Monthly Review Press, 1977), 38.

52. Karl Marx, "First Draft of the *Civil War in France*," in *Karl Marx and Friedrich Engels, Collected Works*, vol. 22 (Moscow: Progress Publishers, 1986), 495.

53. Leo Zeilig and Claire Ceruti, "Slums, Resistance and the African Working Class," *International Socialism Journal* 117 (2007), available at http://www.isj.org.uk/index.php4?id=398&issue=117.

54. Leo Zeilig and David Seddon, "Class and Protest in Africa: New Waves," *Review of African Political Economy* 32:103 (2005), 12.

55. Therefore we refuse to dissolve the working class into the amorphous "multitude" described in most academic accounts of sub-Saharan Africa. The working class on the continent, together with other popular forces, has both agency and organization. See Antonio Negri and Michael Hardt, *Multitude: War and Democracy in the Age of Empire* (London: Hamish Hamilton, 2005).

56. Thompson, *Making of the English Working Class*, 9.

57. Mike Davis, *Planet of Slums* (London: Verso, 2006), 7.

58. Ibid., 201.

59. The heterogeneity of classes has never been the reason for their political decay—rather, a factor of their real condition. As Lenin argued in 1920: "Capitalism would not be capitalism if the 'pure' proletariat were not surrounded by a large number of exceedingly motley types intermediate between the proletarian and the semi-proletarian (who earns his livelihood in part by the sale of his labor power), between the semi-proletarian and the small peasant (and petty artisan, handicraft worker, and small master in general), between the small peasant and the middle peasant, and so on, and if the proletariat itself were not divided . . . according to territorial origin, trade, sometimes according to religion, and so on." Vladimir Lenin, "Left Wing Communism, an Infantile Disorder," (1920) in *Selected Works* (Progress Press: London 1969), available at http://www.marxists.org/archive/lenin/works/1920/lwc/.

60. For an example of this research, see Zeilig and Ceruti, "Slums, Resistance and the African Working Class."

61. Karl Marx, *Capital* vol. 1, emphasis added, available at http://www.marxists.org/archive/marx/works/1867-c1/ch28.htm.

62. Leo Zeilig, "Tony Cliff and Deflected Permanent Revolution in Africa," *International Socialism Journal* 126 (2010), available at http://www.isj.org.uk/?id=641.

Chapter 3: An Epoch of Uprisings

1. Ruth First, *The Barrel of a Gun: Political Power in Africa and the Coup d'État* (London: Allen Lane, 1970), 57–58.

2. Davidson, *Africa in Modern History*, 284.
3. Dwyer and Seddon, "The New Wave?"
4. Michael Bratton and Nicholas van de Walle, *Democratic Experiments in Africa: Regime Transitions in Comparative Perspective* (Cambridge: Cambridge University Press, 1997), 5.
5. Mbembe, "Power and Obscenity in the Post-Colonial Period," 166–82.
6. Quoted in Isaac Deutscher, *Stalin: A Political Biography* (London: Penguin Books, 1966), 328.
7. For an overview of some of the working-class-led movements, see Leo Zeilig, ed., *Class Struggle and Resistance in Africa* (Chicago: Haymarket, 2009).
8. The best summary of labor organization and political change during this period is Frederick Cooper, *Decolonization and African Society: The Labor Question in French and British Africa* (Cambridge: Cambridge University Press, 1996).
9. Ibid., 408–52.
10. Leo Zeilig and David Seddon, "Marxism, Class and Resistance in Africa," in Zeilig, ed., *Class Struggle and Resistance in Africa*, 14–28.
11. For example, Julius Nyerere's "Ujamaa" socialism: see Julius Nyerere, *Ujamaa: Essays on Socialism* (Dar es Salaam: Oxford University Press, 1968).
12. For an example of these ideas, see Nkrumah, *Africa Must Unite*.
13. For Nigeria, see Robin Cohen, *Labour and Politics in Nigeria, 1945–71* (Heinemann: London, 1974). For Zambia, see Larmer, *Mineworkers in Zambia*.
14. Fanon, *Wretched of the Earth*.
15. Shula Marks, "Southern and Central Africa, 1886–1910," in Roland Oliver and G.N. Sanderson, eds., *The Cambridge History of Africa: Volume 6, 1870 to 1905* (Cambridge: Cambridge University Press, 1985), 431.
16. George Shepperson, *Independent African: John Chilembwe and the Origins, Setting and Significance of the Native Rising of 1915* (Edinburgh: Edinburgh University Press, 1987).
17. Robert I. Rotberg, *The Rise of Nationalism in Central Africa: The Making of Malawi and Zambia, 1873–1964,* (Cambridge, MA: Harvard University Press, 1966), 67–72.
18. Adrian Hastings, *A History of African Christianity, 1950–1975* (Cambridge: Cambridge University Press, 1979), 101.
19. On Aladura, see J.D.Y. Peel, *Aladura: A Religious Movement among the Yoruba* (London: Oxford University Press, 1968).
20. David M. Gordon, "A Community of Suffering: Narratives of War and Exile in the Zambian Lumpa Church," in Derek Peterson and Giacomo Macola, eds., *Recasting the Past: History Writing and Political Work in Modern Africa* (Athens: Ohio University Press, 2009), 191–211.
21. Jeff Haynes, *Religion and Politics in Africa* (London and New Jersey: Zed Books, 1996), 79.
22. Quoted in Hastings, *History of African Christianity,* 185.
23. Haynes, *Religion and Politics in Africa,* 112.

24. Quotes in Hastings, *History of African Christianity*, 150.
25. Catherine Coquery-Vidrovitch, *African Women: a Modern History* (Boulder, CO: Westview Press, 1997), 166–67.
26. Ifi Amadiume, *Re-Inventing Africa: Matriarchy, Religion, and Culture* (London: Zed Books, 1997), 168–69.
27. Ibid, 170–73.
28. Susan Geiger, *TANU Women: Gender and Culture in the Making of Tanganyikan Nationalism* (Portsmouth, NH: Heinemann, 1997).
29. Coquery-Vidrovitch, *African Women*, 181.
30. Geiger, *TANU Women*, 165–67.
31. D.A. Low and J.M. Lonsdale, "Introduction: Towards the New Order, 1945–1963," in D.A. Low and Alison Smith, eds., *History of East Africa*, vol. 3 (Oxford: Oxford University Press, 1976), 12.
32. John Iliffe, *A Modern History of Tanganyika* (Cambridge: Cambridge University Press, 1994), 440–41.
33. Quoted in ibid., 443.
34. Quoted in ibid., 502.
35. Henrietta Moore and Megan Vaughan, *Cutting Down Trees: Gender, Nutrition and Agricultural Change in the Northern Province of Zambia, 1890–1990* (Portsmouth, NH, Heinemann, 1994), 132–36.
36. Terence Ranger, *Peasant Consciousness and Guerrilla War in Zimbabwe,* (London: James Currey, 1985), 300–14.
37. Norma Kriger, *Zimbabwe's Guerrilla War: Peasant Voices* (Cambridge: Cambridge University Press, 1991).
38. Moore and Vaughan, *Cutting Down Trees*, 138.
39. James Scott, *Seeing like a State: How Certain Schemes to Improve the Human Condition Have Failed* (New Haven, CT: Yale University Press, 1998), 223–61.
40. Merle L. Bowen, *The State against the Peasantry: Rural Struggles in Colonial and Postcolonial Mozambique* (Charlottesville: University Press of Virginia, 2000), 2.
41. Harrison, *Issues in the Contemporary Politics of Sub-Saharan Africa*, 46.
42. Tony Cliff, *Marxism at the Millennium* (London: Bookmarks, 2000), 48.
43. Mahmood Mamdani, "The Intelligentsia, the State and Social Movements in Africa," in Mamadou Diouf and Mahmood Mamdani, eds., *Academic Freedom in Africa* (Dakar: Council for the Development of Social Science Research in Africa, 1995), 253–55.
44. Silvia Federici, "The New Student Movement," in Ousseina Alidou, George Caffentzis, and Silvia Federici, eds., *A Thousand Flowers: Social Struggles against Structural Adjustment in African Universities* (New York: Africa World Press, 2000), 90.
45. M.E. Chambrier Rahandi, "Introduction," in Charles Diané, *La FEANF et les Grandes Heures du Mouvement Syndical Étudiant Noir* (Paris: Chaka, 1990), 16. Interestingly, FEANF stood at the summit of approximately fourteen African student organizations in France from 1947 to 1956.
46. It is hard to exaggerate the role played by Nkrumah as an exemplary radical

nationalist and model to a generation of African students in the 1950s. Diané writes that for students active in FEANF, "Nkrumah is an older brother, a precursor and a sort of mirror to the new class of engaged intellectuals." Ibid., 29.

47. Panaf, *Patrice Lumumba* (London: Panaf, 1973), 196.

48. This was the opinion of many African socialists, but also of those who had no socialist inclinations. So Lumumba stated in 1956, "Let poor Belgium keep its ideological squabbles. The Congo needs something other than petty wranglings. Let us all unite, Catholics, Liberals, Socialist, Christians, Protestants, Atheists, to achieve real peace in this country.... Our country has much greater need of 'builders' than of squabblers, pamphleteers and purveyors of communist slogans." Cited in Leo Zeilig, *Patrice Lumumba: Africa's Lost Leader* (London: Haus Publishing, 2008), 81–82.

49. Robert Biel, *The New Imperialism: Crisis and Contradictions in North/South Relations* (London: Zed Books, 2000), 91.

50. Kofi Buenor Hadjor, *Nkrumah and Ghana* (London: Kegan Paul, 1988), 23.

51. Phil Marfleet, "Globalisation and the Third World," *International Socialism Journal*, 2, 81 (1998), available at http://pubs.socialistreviewindex.org.uk/isj81/marfleet.htm.

52. Abdelkader Zghal, "The 'Bread Riot' and the Crisis of the One-Party System in Tunisia," in Mahmood Mamdani and Ernest Wamba-dia-Wamba, eds., *African Studies in Social Movements and Democracy* (Dakar: Council for the Development of Social Science Research in Africa, 1995), 99–129.

53. *Times of Zambia*, April 4, 1987, cited in Larmer, *Mineworkers in Zambia*, 52.

54. Christopher, Colcough, *The Labour Market & Economic Stabilisation in Zambia,* World Bank Country Economics Department WPS 222 (Washington: World Bank, 1989), vol. 1, available at http://go.worldbank.org/4HOIL5ANJ0.

55. See also Munyaradzi Gwisai, *Revolutionaries, Resistance and Crisis in Zimbabwe: Anti-Neoliberal Struggles in Periphery Capitalism* (Harare: International Socialist Organization, 2002).

56. Zeilig and Seddon, "Marxism, Class and Resistance in Africa."

57. Jeremiah Dibua, "Students and the Struggle against Authoritarianism in University Governance in Nigeria," in Paul Tiyambe Zeleza and Adebayo Olukoshi, eds., *African Universities in the Twenty-First Century,* vol. 2 (Dakar: Council for the Development of Social Science Research in Africa, 2004), 473.

58. Federici, "The New Student Movement," 88.

59. This useful phrase was coined by Thandika Mkandawire: "Crisis Management and the Making of 'Choiceless Democracies' in Africa," in Richard Joseph, ed., *The State, Conflict and Democracy in Africa* (Boulder, CO: Lynne Rienner, 1999), 119–36.

60. Bratton and van de Walle, *Democratic Experiments in Africa*, 5.

61. Theodore Trefon, Saskia Van Hoyweghen and Stefaan Smis, "State Failure in the Congo: Perceptions and Realities," *Review of African Political Economy*, vol.29 no. 93/94 (September–December 2002), 379–88.

62. M. Ngalamlume Nkongolo, *Le Campus Martyr* (Paris: L'Harmattan, 2000),

96–98.

63. Blaine Harden, *Africa: Dispatches from a Fragile Continent* (London: Harper Collins, 1993), 53.

64. Renton, Seddon, and Zeilig, *Congo.*

65. Zeilig and Seddon, "Marxism, Class and Resistance in Africa," 48.

66. John A. Wiseman, *The New Struggle for Democracy in Africa* (Aldershot: Avebury, 1996), 49.

67. Quoted in D. Throup, "'Render unto Caesar the Things that Are Caesar's': The Politics of Church-State Conflict in Kenya, 1978–1990," in Holger Bernt Hansen and Michael Twaddle, eds., *Religion and Politics in East Africa: The Period Since Independence* (London: James Currey, 1995),143–76.

68. Ibid, 143.

69. Norbert Tengende, "Workers, Students and the Struggles for Democracy: State-Civil Society Relations in Zimbabwe," Ph.D. dissertation, Roskilde University, Denmark (1994), 389–92.

70. Gwisai, *Revolutionaries, Resistance and Crisis.*

71. Tengende, "Workers, Students and the Struggles for Democracy," 427.

72. Arthur Mutambara, interview by the authors, Harare, July 7, 2003.

73. Ludo Martens, *Kabila et la Révolution Congolais: Panafricanisme ou Néocolonialisme?* vol.1 (Brussels: EPO, 2002),115.

74. Thomas Hodgkin, "The Revolutionary Tradition in Islam," *Race and Class* vol. 21, no. 3 (1980), 221–30.

75. Harrison, *Issues in the Contemporary Politics of Sub-Saharan Africa,* 100.

76. John Saul and Colin Leys, "Sub-Saharan Africa in Global Capitalism," *Monthly Review* vol. 51, no. 3 (1999), 25, available at http://monthlyreview.org/1999/07/01/sub-saharan-africa-in-global-capitalism.

77. Ibid.

78. John Saul, "Africa: The Next Liberation Struggle,"*Review of African Political Economy* vol. 30, no. 96 (2003), 187–202.

79. Saul and Leys, "Sub-Saharan Africa in Global Capitalism," 26.

Chapter 4: Cracks in the Monolith

1. Events since 1994 have resulted in a wide range of books on the social changes underway. Those not familiar with the country will find the following of use. On the initial years after 1994: Patrick Bond, *The Elite Transition: From Apartheid to Neoliberalism in South Africa,* 2nd ed. (Scottsville, South Africa: University of KwaZulu-Natal Press, 2000) and Hein Marais, *South Africa: Limits To Change: The Political Economy of Transition* (London: Zed Books, 1999). On the changes to the ANC, see William Mervin Gumede, *Thabo Mbeki and the Battle for the Soul of the ANC* (London, Zed Books, 2007); for the rise of the new social movements, see Richard Ballard, Adam Habib, and Imraan Valodia, eds., *Voices of Protest: Social Movements in Post-Apartheid South*

Africa (Pietermaritzburg, South Africa: University of KwaZulu-Natal Press, 2006); and for the labor movement, see Sakhela Buhlungu, ed., *Trade Unions and Democracy* (Pretoria:Human Sciences Research Council Press, 2006). The best single overview is Hein Marais, *South Africa Pushed to the Limit: The Political Economy of Change* (London: Zed Books, 2011).

2. During apartheid (1948–1994), people were divided into four racial classifications, in descending order of population: Africans, Coloureds, Whites, and Indians. "Africans" are indigenous people whose ancestors' presence in the region predated the arrival of European settlers. "Coloured" legally referred to persons of "mixed blood," often, but not always, meaning white and African. "Indian" refers to people descended from South Asians, and "White" to descendants of European settlers. Political activists rejected this classification as racist. The term "Black" has progressive political connotations and is an all-inclusive term referring to all South Africans who are not "white." We will use this term, although, at times, it will be necessary to use terms such as "African."

3. See chapter 2. The text of the Bill of Rights is available at http://www.info .gov.za/documents/constitution/1996/96cons2.htm (accessed May 30, 2010).

4. Ibid.

5. Moeletsi Mbeki, "The curse of South Africa," *New Statesman*, January 17, 2008, available at http://www.newstatesman.com/world-affairs/2008/01/south-africa -anc-zuma (accessed May 30, 2010).

6. Constituted on May 9, 1990, the Alliance is headed by the ruling ANC and includes the Congress of South African Trade Unions (COSATU) and the South African Communist Party (SACP—formerly known as the Communist Party).

7. Sher Verick, *Unravelling the Impact of the Global Financial Crisis on the South African Labor Market*, International Labor Office, Economic and Labor Market Analysis Department, Employment Sector (Geneva: ILO, 2010), available at http://www.ilo.org/wcmsp5/groups/public/@ed_emp/documents/publication /wcms_122402.pdf (accessed May 30, 2010). In South Africa, two unemployment rates are widely used: a narrow rate that includes only those who have actively searched for a job in the last fourteen days and a broad definition that includes individuals who say that they want a job but who have not actively searched for work in the last fourteen days. This figure is based on the broad definition.

8. Approximately 19 percent of adults between ages fifteen and forty-nine are infected, with prevalence rates of up to 40 percent among women aged twenty-five to twenty-nine. South African National AIDS Council, *HIV and AIDS and STI National Strategic Plan 2007–2011* (Pretoria: SANAC, 2007), available at http://www.info.gov.za/otherdocs/2007/aidsplan2007/ (accessed May 30, 2010).

9. Donwald Pressly, "Study finds SA now falls below Brazil," *Business Report*, September 28, 2009. The Gini coefficient is the most commonly used measure of inequality and measures equality across society. The higher the value on a

range of zero to one, the more unequal a society is. If income is shared equally (perfect equality), the Gini coefficient would be zero.

10. Murray Leibbrandt, Ingrid Woolard, Arden Finn, and Jonathan Argent, "Trends in South African Income Distribution and Poverty since the Fall of Apartheid," OECD Social, Employment and Migration Working Papers, No. 101, OECD Publishing, Organisation for Economic Co-operation and Development, 2010, 18.

11. Seven South Africa rand equals approximately one US dollar.

12. Leibbrandt et al., "Trends in South African Income Distribution," 14–20, 26.

13. William Gumede, in William Gumede and Leslie Dikeni, eds., *The Poverty of Ideas: South African Democracy and the Retreat of Intellectuals* (Auckland Park, South Africa: Jacana Media, 2009), 3.

14. Political analyst Susan Booysen, quoted in Michael Georgy, "S. Africa Riots Press Zuma to Live Up to Promises," Reuters, July 24, 2009, available at http://www.reuters.com/article/idUSLO185274 (accessed May 30, 2010).

15. For example, one union activist estimated that in the 1980s there were up to 150 union meetings taking place on any one night across the country. See Steven Friedman, *Building Tomorrow Today: African Workers in Trade Unions, 1970–1984* (Johannesburg: Ravan Press, 1987).

16. The non-party political sections of which are now commonly referred to as "civil society."

17. A popular ANC slogan from the 1994 elections that is still commonly referred to in government and among social movements.

18. This is a process of industrialization whereby a large part of imports are substituted by domestic production. The theorization of ISI, an already existing practice in many developed and developing countries, by development economists such as Raul Prebisch carried enormous intellectual currency. South Africa, together with countries such as India and Brazil, embarked on a state capitalist directed industrialization program very similar to ISI.

19. Marais, *Limits To Change.*

20. Between 1965 and 1973, the average growth rates for sub-Saharan Africa, East Asia, and Latin America were 3 percent, 5.4 percent, and 4.1 percent respectively. For the OECD countries, it was 3.5 percent. See World Bank, *World Development Report* (Washington, D.C.: Oxford University Press, 1990) and William Beinart and Saul Dubow, eds., *Segregation and Apartheid in Twentieth Century South Africa* (London: Routledge, 1995), 165.

21. Police shot sixty-nine African protestors dead and wounded 227 at Sharpeville, triggering nineteen days of mass nationwide strikes and protests. The killings were condemned internationally and domestically by white South African business leaders and media. This prompted organizations like the ANC to reject previous methods based on pacifism and turn to armed struggle.

22. The Freedom Charter was created by leaders of the Congress Alliance to unite and mobilize people. It was ambiguous enough to appeal to people on the basis of social class, ethnicity, and nation; the three constituencies repeatedly

drew upon under the rubric of a national identity by the ANC as the liberation struggle developed.

23. Monetarism was a global response to the inability of Keynesian economics to explain or cure the seemingly contradictory problems of rising unemployment and inflation ("stagflation") as a result of the collapse of the Bretton Woods system in 1972 and the oil shocks of 1973. Many of its ideas and policies formed the basis of what today is known as neoliberalism.

24. Gramsci notes: "A crisis occurs, sometimes lasting for decades. This exceptional duration means that incurable structural contradictions have revealed themselves (reached maturity), and that despite this, the political forces that are struggling to conserve and defend the existing structure itself are making every effort to cure them, within certain limits, and to overcome them . . . and it is upon this terrain that the forces of opposition organize." Antonio Gramsci, *Selections from the Prison Notebooks*, Quintin Hoare and Geoffrey Nowell Smith, eds. and trans.(London: Lawrence and Wishart, 1998), 178.

25. Between 1969 and 1977, the number of skilled jobs grew by 30 percent and the proportion of jobs filled by Africans went from 9.3 percent to 23.2 percent. See Helene Perold and Dawn Butler, eds., *The Right To Learn* (Johannesburg: Sached Trust/Ravan Press 1986).

26. Anthony W. Marx, *Lessons of Struggle: South African Internal Opposition, 1960–1990* (New York: Oxford University Press, 1992).

27. In Soweto on June 16, fifteen thousand schoolchildren gathered to protest a government announcement that half of all classes must be taught in Afrikaans. Police opened fire and shot dead unarmed children. Anger at the killings sparked protests in other townships; six days later, 130 people had been officially recorded as dead. The single best coverage and analysis of the events surrounding Soweto and its political consequences can be found in Baruch Hirson, *Year of Fire, Year of Ash: The Soweto Revolt: Roots of a Revolution?* (London; Zed, 1979).

28. The Soweto uprisings boosted the exiled wing of the social movements as approximately six thousand people went into exile and joined the ANC between 1975 and 1980. As the best equipped and organized in exile, with funding and support from Moscow through its ties with the SACP, the ANC attracted many of those who fled the country. The ANC population in exile went from one thousand to nine thousand, with the average age dropping from thirty-five in 1975 to twenty-eight in 1976. See Stephen Davis quoted in ibid., 93. Inspired by the rebellions and flushed with external recruits, but not centrally involved and thus worried about being marginalized, the exiled and imprisoned ANC leadership made moves to set up structures, recruit, and circulate propaganda more purposefully inside the country. See Dale McKinley, *The ANC and the Liberation Struggle* (London: Pluto, 1997), 48.

29. See Alex Callinicos, *Southern Africa After Zimbabwe* (London: Pluto Press, 1981), 119 and Merle Lipton, *Capitalism and Apartheid: South Africa*

1910–1986 (Aldershot: Gower/Maurice Temple Smith, 1985), 381–82.

30. For example, in Katlehong, near Germiston, the number of shacks increased from three thousand in 1979 to forty-four thousand by 1983. See Beinart and Dubow, *Segregation and Apartheid*, 239.

31. The ANC related to its mass support base by setting up the UDF, through which they could internally popularize their politics. The UDF played an important role in the ANC's turn to "people's war" and its declared intention to make the country "ungovernable." For a detailed but uncritical account of the UDF, see Jeremy Seekings, *The UDF: A History of the United Democratic Front in South Africa, 1983–1991* (Cape Town: David Phillip, 2000).

32. Popo Molefe, former general secretary of the UDF and former premier of North West province, now executive chairman of Lereko Investments, quoted in Seekings, *UDF*, 17.

33. Quoted in Marx, *Lessons of Struggle,*134.

34. Replicated by communist parties elsewhere in the Third World, this theory argued that "capitalism was not the enemy in such countries," more "local interests and the US imperialism that supported them," and the way forward was "a broad popular or national front in which 'national' bourgeoisie or petty-bourgeoisie were allies." See Eric J. Hobsbawm, *Age of Extremes: The Short Twentieth Century*, 1914–1991 (London: Abacus, 1995), 436. Detaching racial oppression from its material roots in capitalist exploitation, it also implies that a "normal" capitalist society was hidden under "apartheid capitalism." Politically and organizationally, this meant relegating the struggle for socialism to that of the "national democratic revolution" through building a national alliance of social groups.

35. See Seekings, *UDF*, 321. After meeting the ANC leadership in exile in 1986, the COSATU leadership agreed that the question of the NDR could not be "resolved without the full participation of the ANC, which is regarded by the majority of the people of South Africa as the overall leader and genuine representative." Quoted in Robert Fine and Dennis Davis, *Beyond Apartheid: Labour and Liberation in South Africa* (London: Pluto Press, 1991), 265. Practically the majority of COSATU's first national executive committee, elected at its founding congress, were ANC members or supporters. See Jeremy Baskin, *Striking Back: A History of COSATU* (London: Verso, 1991). [1]

36. McKinley, *ANC and the Liberation Struggle,* 33.

37. See also Martin Legassick, "Myth and Reality in the Struggle against Apartheid," *Journal of Southern African Studies*, vol. 24, no. 2 (June 1998), and references therein. Mandela notes that a letter read out by his daughter at a rally in February 1985 signaled a willingness to negotiate. Nelson Mandela, *Long Walk to Freedom: The Autobiography of Nelson Mandela* (London: Abacus, 1996), 623. Such duplicity echoes Frantz Fanon, who warned against nationalist leaders making "a show of force" while seeking conciliatory means.

38. More details about the period from 1984 to1986 can be found in Baskin, *Striking Back*; Marx, *Lessons of Struggle;* McKinley, *ANC and the Liberation*

Struggle; and Seekings, *UDF.*

39. See the *South African Labour Bulletin*, May 6, 1985, 74–100.

40. Gerald Kraak, *Breaking the Chains: Labour in South Africa in the 1970s and 1980s* (London: Pluto Press, 1993), 236.

41. See Beinart and Dubow, *Segregation and Apartheid*, 246.

42. This united the independent union, FOSATU, with those unions with much closer ties to the ANC; this majority argued that COSATU should be aligned with the ANC. This represented a weakening of the independent left in the labor and liberation movement; in 1987, the National Union of Mineworkers of South Africa, a stronghold of the independent left, adopted the Freedom Charter.

43. Beinart and Dubow, *Segregation and Apartheid*, 246–47.

44. "If the emergency had not been introduced the economy would have been finished. There was no way we could have continued to do business while people were burning down schools and murdering one another." Donald Mason, former president of the Afrikaanse Handelsinstituut, quoted in Baskin, *Striking Back,*137.

45. Kraak, *Breaking the Chains,*129, table 6.1.

46. Seekings, *UDF*, 3.

47. Kraak, *Breaking the Chains,*129.

48. Ibid., 245–46.

49. Martin J. Murray, *The Revolution Deferred: The Painful Birth of Post-Apartheid South Africa* (London: Verso, 1994), 142.

50. Ibid., 169. Today this area comes under the provinces of Gauteng, Limpopo, Mpumalanga, and the North West province.

51. *Financial Times*, December 28, 1989.

52. Mac Maharaja (now presidential spokesperson), quoted in Heribert Adam, Frederik van Zyl Slabbert, and Kogila Moodley, *Comrades in Business: Post-Liberation Politics in South Africa* (Cape Town: Tafleberg, 1998), 69.

53. Fine and Davis, *Beyond Apartheid*, and Callinicos, *Southern Africa After Zimbabwe,* suggest this. In July 1990, when the SACP announced its leadership, it included former leading FOSATU activists and critics of the ANC-SACP Moses Mayekiso and John Gomomo. Other leading activists soon followed.

54. Quoted in Baskin, *Striking Back*, 420–21.

55. Mandela, *Long Walk*, 724.

56. *Star*, June 30, 1993.

57. African National Congress, *The Reconstruction and Development Programme* (Johannesburg: Umanyano Publications, 1994), 5.

58. *Star*, March 4, 1994.

59. *Financial Times*, May 7, 1994.

60. *Financial Times*, May 2, 1995.

61. Quoted in Adam et al, *Comrades in Business,*151.

62. *Sunday Times*, June 16, 1996.

63. At the time, official unemployment was approximately 30 percent and the economy had to grow by between 8 and 10 percent per annum to accommodate

new entrants into the labor market, according to then-labor minister Tito Mboweni. Quoted in *Financial Times*, May 2, 1995.

64. *Economist,* October 12, 1996.

65. See Jonathan Michie, "South Africa's Transition: The Policy Agenda," in Jonathan Michie and Vishnu Padayachee, eds.,*The Political Economy of South Africa's Transition* (London: Dryden Press, 1997), 50 and Oupa Lehulere, "The Political Significance of GEAR," *Debate*, no. 3 (1997), 74.

66. *Business Day*, March 1, 2000.

67. See, for example, *South African Labour Bulletin*, vol. 22, no. 3 (June 1998), 94.

68. See the "Declaration on Gear" in *Shopsteward*, October/November 1997, 20 and 40.

69. Bond, *Elite Transition,* 193–94.

70. *Business Report*, September 9, 1998, and *Business Day*, March 29, 2000.

71. *Citizen*, September 8, 1999.

72. For more on TAC, see Steven Friedmanin Ballard et al.,*Voices of Protest.*

73. *The Star*, July 9, 1999. A much-heralded success at election time was the electrification of three hundred thousand new households each year between 1994 and 1996. Others estimate that at some point or other since 1994, a total of ten million people have been disconnected from water and electricity and two million evicted from their homes because they could not afford their municipal bills. See David McDonald, "The Bell Tolls for Thee," and David McDonald and Laila Smith, "Privatizing Cape Town," Municipal Services project paper, 2002.

74. In this election, four million fewer people voted than in 1994. The Democratic Party emerged with 9.58 percent of the vote, up from 1994—a "recycled" white vote from the NP, now the New National Party (NNP), which got 6.87 percent and later merged with the ANC. See Tom Lodge, *Consolidating Democracy: South Africa's Second Popular Election* (Johannesburg: Witwatersrand University Press, 1999), available at http://tinyurl.com/ct69myp.

75. At an ANC Women's League election rally, attended by one of us in Gugulethu Township near Cape Town, May 1999.

76. Quoted in Edward Cottle, "ANC Elections Manifesto is a Decoy," *South African Labour Bulletin*, vol. 23, no. 4 (August 1999), 80.

77. *Business Day*, May 11, 1999.

78. *Business Day*, March 1, 2000.

79. In South Africa the term "social movements" has taken on a particular narrow meaning as opposed to to how the term is more widely understood. Here it refers to a group of mainly community-based organizations that are largely independent and, to varying degrees, critical of the policies and practices of the ANC government and the ANC-led Alliance.

80. For an extensive discussion of the origins, characteristics, and history of these groups, see the specific chapters in Ballard et al.,*Voices of Protest.*

81. For an overview of the role of civil society at these events see Ashwin Desai and Peter Dwyer, "Civil society, the United Nations and WCAR" and "The World

$ummit on $ustainable Development," in Patrick Bond and Ashwin Desai, eds., *Foreign Policy Bottom Up: South African Civil Society and the Globalisation of Popular Solidarity* (Durban: University of KwaZulu-Natal Centre for Civil Society, 2008), available at http://tinyurl.com/c4fz9vf (accessed April 27, 2012).

82. The SMI was a split from the broader Civil Society Indaba set up to facilitate participation in parallel events of the World Summit on Sustainable Development. In the process, differences emerged with organizations such as COSATU over the role of those groups critical of the government.

83. Labour Research Service, *Labour Research Service Annual Report 2004-2005*, available at http://www.lrs.org.za/docs/Annual_Report2004-5.pdf (accessed May 30, 2011).

84. *Business Day*, February 26,2004.

85. *Financial Mail*, May 28, 2004, 20.

86. *This Day*, June 4, 2004.

87. For more on the ABM, see its website: www.abm.co.za.

88. The fractious and fragmented nature of post-apartheid social movements is evidenced by the divisions between ABM and other groups in the SMI. An example was their disruption, along with the AEC, of the SMI national meeting in Durban in December 2006.

89. This is what one social movement activist initially argued. See Ashwin Desai, *We are the Poors: Community Struggles in Post-Apartheid South Africa* (New York: Monthly Review Press, 2002), 124, and Dale McKinley and Prishani Naidoo, "New Social Movements in South Africa," *Development Update*, vol. 5, no. 2 (2004), 14–15.

90. Interestingly, this was also the year of the first serious reflective critique of the social movements by one of its key activists. See Ashwin Desai, "Vans, Autos, Kombis and the Drivers of Social Movements," Centre for Civil Society, University of KwaZulu-Natal, paper presented at the Harold Wolpe Memorial Lecture Series, July 28, 2006, International Convention Centre, Durban, available at http://ccs.ukzn.ac.za/files/dn072006desai_paper.pdf (accessed May 30, 2011).

91. This is argued by social movement activist Oupa Lehulere in "The New Social Movements, COSATU, and the 'New UDF,'" in *Khanya*, No. 11 (December 2005), available at http://amadlandawonye.wikispaces.com/file/view/New+social+movements%2C+COSATU+and+New+UDF%2C+Oupa+Lehulere.pdf (accessed May 30, 2011).

92. See the talk by a key SMI organizer: Mondli Hlatshwayo, "The Genesis of the Social Movements Indaba," lecture delivered at UKZN Centre for Civil Society, November 22, 2007, available at http://tinyurl.com/bue3vno (accessed May 30, 2011).

93. It is all the more tragic that such a respected militant as Oupa Lehulere should reduce this to COSATU getting involved in "internal squabbles with the ruling class" (ibid.).

94. Clearly many social movements are in a very serious malaise and have yet to recover from what Lehulere called "a lull, a temporary retreat" in 2005. A recent

example of this was evident at the protest held at the COP17 United Nations Climate Change conference in Durban in December 2011. Ten years after WCAR, the coming-out party of the social movements, only five thousand people marched.

95. Desai, *We Are the Poors*, 49.

Chapter 5: Social Movements after the Transition

1. For example, Larry Diamond, "Towards Democratic Consolidation," *Journal of Democracy*, vol. 5, no. 3 (1994), 4–17; John W. Harbeson, Donald Rothchild, and Naomi Chazan, eds., *Civil Society and the State in Africa* (Boulder, CO: Lynne Rienner, 1994).

2. The term is commonly associated with Bayart, *The State in Africa*.

3. Interview, Fr. Joe Komakoma, secretary general, Zambia Episcopal Conference, Lusaka, April 5, 2006.

4. Harri Englund, *Prisoners of Freedom: Human Rights and the African Poor* (Berkeley: University of California Press, 2006).

5. Interview, Undule Mwakasungule, Centre for Human Rights and Rehabilitation, Lilongwe, June 8, 2006.

6. Harri Englund, ed., "Introduction," in *A Democracy of Chameleons: Politics and Culture in the New Malawi* (Uppsala, Sweden: Nordic Africa Institute, 2002), 12.

7. Interview, Lucy Muyoyeta, chairperson of Women for Change, chief executive of NGO Coordinating Committee, Lusaka, April 6, 2006.

8. David M.C. Bartlett, "Civil Society and Democracy: A Zambian Case Study," *Journal of Southern African Studies*, vol. 26, no. 3 (2000), 429–46.

9. Miles Larmer, *Mineworkers in Zambia: Labor and Political Change in Post-Colonial Africa, 1964—1991* (London: I.B. Tauris, 2007), 172.

10. Interview, Jack Jones Zulu, Jubilee Zambia, Lusaka, April 4, 2006.

11. Muyoyeta interview.

12. Interview, Elijah Rubvuta, executive director of Foundation for Democratic Process (FODEP), Lusaka, April 6, 2006.

13. Englund, *Prisoners of Freedom*, 74.

14. Interview, Peter Ngulube Chinoko, coordinator, Catholic Commission for Justice, Development, and Peace—Lilongwe Diocese, Lilongwe, June 5, 2006.

15. Interview, Desmond Kaunda, director, Malawi Human Rights and Rehabilitation Centre, Lilongwe, June 8, 2006.

16. Ibid.

17. Mwakasungule interview.

18. Interview, Andrew Mushi, advocacy officer, Tanzania Association of NGOs (TANGO), Dar es Salaam, August 29, 2005.

19. Lise Rakner, *Political and Economic Liberalisation in Zambia, 1991–2001* (Uppsala, Sweden: Nordic Africa Institute, 2003); Miles Larmer, "Reaction

and Resistance to Neo-Liberalism in Zambia," *Review of African Political Economy* vol. 32, no. 103 (2005), 29–45.

20. Larmer, "Reaction and Resistance," 39.
21. Englund, *Prisoners of Freedom*, 126–27.
22. Ibid., 127.
23. Rubvuta interview.
24. Muyoyeta interview.
25. Interview, Limbani Nsapato, coordinator, Civil Society Coalition for Quality Basic Education, Lilongwe, June 9, 2006.
26. Kaunda interview.
27. Interview, John Njunga, national coordinator, Malawi Health Equity Network, Lilongwe, June 9, 2006.
28. Interview, Mabvuto Bamusi, director, Malawi Economic Justice Network, Lilongwe, June 7, 2006.
29. Interview, Deus Kibamba, Tanzania Gender Networking Programme (TGNP), Dar es Salaam, August 29, 2005.
30. Interview, Rev. Japhet Ndhlovu, Council of Churches (CCZ) and executive director of Oasis Forum, Lusaka, April 7, 2006.
31. Mwakasungule interview.
32. Chinoko interview.
33. Englund, *Prisoners of Freedom*, 197–98; Kaunda interview.
34. Mwakasungule interview.
35. Chinoko interview.
36. Englund, *Prisoners of Freedom*, 43.
37. Interview, Rev. Malawo Matyola, Zambia Council for Social Development, Lusaka, April 5, 2006.
38. Interview, Fr. Peter Henriot, Jesuit Centre for Theological Reflection, Lusaka, April 10, 2006.
39. Ndhlovu interview.
40. Rakner, *Political and Economic Liberalisation*, 78–79.
41. Central Statistical Office, "Formal Sector Employment Trends in Zambia, 1985–2005," (Lusaka: Central Statistical Office, 2006).
42. Central Statistical Office, *Zambia Demographic and Health Survey (DHS) EdData Survey*, (Lusaka: Central Statistical Office, 2002).
43. Central Statistics Office, "National Trends in Poverty, 1991—2004," (Lusaka: Central Statistical Office, 2005).We should note at this point that progress (or lack of progress) in democratization is not just a function of the interaction of the state and social movements, but is also affected by the performance of the economy.
44. Blessings Chinsinga, "The Politics of Poverty Alleviation in Malawi: A Critical Review," in Harri Englund, ed., *A Democracy of Chameleons: Politics and Culture in the New Malawi* (Uppsala, Sweden: Nordic Africa Institute, 2002), 25–42, 26.
45. Inter-African Network for Human Rights & Development (AFRONET), Citizens for a Better Environment, and Rights and Accountability in

Development (RAID), "Zambia: Deregulation and The Denial of Human Rights," Submission to the OECD Committee on Economic, Social and Cultural Rights (Lusaka, Kitwe, Oxford: March 2000).

46. Interview, Joyce Nonde, president, Federation of Free Trade Unions of Zambia (FFTUZ), Lusaka, March 13, 2003.
47. *Sunday Post*, January 25, 2003.
48. *The Post*, December 19, 2002.
49. World Bank Public-Private Infrastructure Advisory Facility, quoted in Corporate Europe Observatory report, "Case Study on Malawi," May 2007, available at http://www.corporateeurope.org/water-justice/content/2007/11/ppiaf-case-study-malawi (accessed February 11, 2010).
50. Interview, Olivia Kunje, vice–general secretary, Water Employees Trade Union of Malawi (WETUM), Lilongwe, June 8, 2006.
51. Corporate Europe Observatory report, "Case Study on Malawi."
52. Interview, Joyce Nonde, president, Federation of Free Trade Unions of Zambia (FFTUZ), Lusaka, March 28, 2006.
53. Interview, Joyce Nonde, president, Federation of Free Trade Unions of Zambia (FFTUZ), Lusaka, May 11, 2008.
54. Miles Larmer and Alastair Fraser, "Of Cabbages and King Cobra: Populist Politics and Zambia's 2006 Elections," *African Affairs*, vol. 106, no. 425 (2007), 611–37, 627–29.
55. Alastair Fraser and John Lungu, *For Whom the Windfalls? Winners and Losers in the Privatization of Zambia's Copper Mines* (Lusaka: CSTNZ, 2006).
56. All PRSPs are available at http://www.imf.org/external/np/prsp.aspx.
57. Jeremy Gould, ed., *The New Conditionality: The Politics of Poverty Reduction Strategies* (London: Zed Books, 2005).
58. Chinoko interview.
59. Interview, Besinati Mpepo, executive director, Civil Society for Poverty Reduction, Lusaka, April 3, 2006.
60. Bamusi interview.
61. Ibid.
62. Ibid.
63. Mpepo interview.
64. Mushi interview.
65. Ibid.
66. Interview, Peter Sinkamba, executive director, Citizens for a Better Environment, Kitwe, May 27, 2008.
67. African Forum and Network on Debt and Development (AFRODAD), "The Impact of Economic Reform Programs on Social Services: The Case of Malawi" (Harare: AFRODAD, 2007), available at http://www.afrodad.org/downloads/Malawi%20FTA.pdf (accessed January 28, 2010).
68. Zulu interview.
69. Interview, Victor Mhoni, coordinator, Civil Society Agriculture Network (CSANet), Lilongwe, June 7, 2006.

70. Ibid.
71. The full CRC report is available at http://www.ncczambia.org/media/final_report_of_the_constitution_review_commission.pdf.
72. Episcopal Conference of Malawi, "Choose Life: Preparing for 2009 Elections During Lent: Sunday Reflections and Guiding Principles from our Bishops," Lilongwe, 2009, available at http://www.fides.org/eng/documents/LENT_english_2009.pdf (accessed November 29, 2009).
73. Matyola interview.
74. Joint interview, Oscar Tembo (program officer) and Theresa Chewe (administrator), Southern Africa Centre for Constructive Resolution of Disputes (SACCORD), Lusaka, March 28, 2006.
75. Ndhlovu interview.
76. Komakoma interview.
77. Muyoyeta interview.
78. Komakoma interview.
79. Mushi interview.
80. Kibamba interview.
81. Chinoko interview.
82. Bamusi interview.
83. Ibid.
84. Kaunda interview.
85. Mwakasungule interview.
86. Chinoko interview.
87. Englund, *Prisoners of Freedom*, 195.

Chapter 6: Frustrated Transitions

1. See Renton, Zeilig, and Seddon, *Congo*.
2. Cited in Martins, *Kabila*, 115.
3. Harden, *Africa*, 54.
4. Stephen Riley and Trevor Parfitt, "Economic Adjustment and Democratization in Africa" in John Walton and David Seddon, eds., *Free Markets and Food Riots: The Politics of Global Adjustment* (Oxford: Blackwell, 1994), 136.
5. Trefon, Van Hoyweghen, and Smis, "State Failure in the Congo," 381.
6. Nkongolo, *Campus Martyr*, 182.
7. Nzongola-Ntalaja, *Congo*, 155–56.
8. Walton and Seddon, eds., *Free Markets and Food Rights*, 163.
9. Nzongola-Ntalaja, *Congo*,188.
10. Martins, *Kabila*, 78.
11. Nzongola-Ntalaja, *Congo*, 190.
12. Martins gives a good description of the demonstration and the risks that were involved. Martins, *Kabila*, 83–84.

13. An important collection of eyewitness accounts from the demonstration published two years later provides a unique insight into the nature of the popular struggles that were sweeping the Congo. Philippe de Dorlodot, *Marche d'Espoir: Kinshasa 16 Février 1992 Non-violence pour la Démocratie au Zaire* (Paris: l'Harmattan, 1994).

14. Ibid., 25–26.

15. Ibid., 28.

16. Ibid., 30.

17. Gauthier de Villers and J. Omasombo Tshonda, "When Kinois Take to the Street," in Theodore Trefon, ed., *Reinventing Order in the Congo* (London: Zed Books, 2004), 144.

18. Riley and Parfitt, "Economic Adjustment and Democratization in Africa," 165.

19. Nzongola-Ntalaja, *Congo*, 195.

20. Ibid., 197.

21. Gauthier de Villers and J. Omasombo Tshonda, "An Intransitive Transition," *Review of African Political Economy* vol. 93, vol. 4 (2002), 403.

22. Martins, *Kabila*, 83.

23. Cited in ibid., 115.

24. Cited in ibid., 115.

25. United Nations Security Council, *Report of the Panel of Experts on the Illegal Exploitation of Natural Resources* (New York: UNSC, May 2002), 19.

26. The international community raised $450 million to hold the elections. Problematic as this funding maybe, it is some achievement that in a country devastated by war, twenty-five million Congolese were encouraged to vote in fifty thousand polling stations. In general, the elections were held without major incident. Francois Manga-Agoa, ed., *Republique Democratique du Congo* (Paris: l'Harmattan, 2008).

27. George Ngonzola-Ntalaja, "DRC's Potential: Lighting the Continent from Cape to Cairo," *Pambazuka,* July 21, 2006, available at http://www.pambazuka.org/en/category/features/35486.

28. For a recent account of a massacre in Makombo in the Haute Uele district of the Congo, see Human Rights Watch, "Trail of Death: LRA Atrocities in the Northeastern DRC," March 2010, available at http://www.hrw.org/en/reports/2010/03/29/trail-death (accessed April 30, 2012).

29. Amnesty International, "End Persecution of Human Rights Defenders in the Democratic Republic of Congo," press release, February 17, 2010, available at http://www.amnesty.org/en/news-and-updates/report/democratic-republic-congo-must-end-persecution-human-rights-defenders-201 (accessed April 30, 2012).

30. Ibid.

31. Joseph Tanyanyiwa, "Country report at the ITGLWU's 10th World Congress," speech delivered in Frankfurt, Germany, December 2–4, 2009.

32. Interview, Joseph Tanyanyiwa, general secretary, NUCIZ, Harare, March 20, 2010.

33. Interview, Brian Kagoro, civil society activist, Harare, June 23, 2003.
34. Leo Zeilig, "Crisis in Zimbabwe," *International Socialism Journal* 94 (2002).
35. Interview, Job Sikhala, MDC MP, July 30, 2003.
36. *Financial Gazette* (Zimbabwe), March 12, 1999.
37. Elinor Sisulu, Pascal Richards, and Steve Kibble "Where To for Zimbabwean Churches and Civil Society?," in Vidal and Chabal, eds., *Southern Africa*, 243.
38. Though there has been no recent audit of civil society organizations in Zimbabwe, a study in 2006 reported an impressive array of diverse organizations with a national spread of members and affiliate groups. As a snapshot of the Zimbabwean political scene it remains important today. "Despite a shrinking membership, the trade unions also retain a national infrastructure [including] a network of 21 offices with 45 full-time officers. . . . The National Constitutional Assembly (NCA) network [consists] of approximately 480 formal and informal committees. . . . The Bulawayo Agenda is made up of 36 active civil society organizations in Bulawayo. . . . The Zimbabwe Civic Education Trust (Zimcet), with its infrastructure of five regional offices, has established 57 peace committees across the country." The research concludes that "Zimbabwe retains a wealth of community-based organizations [with] more than 50,000 members in 50 districts." Zimbabwe Human Rights NGO Forum, *Exploring Transitional Justice Options in Contemporary Zimbabwe* (Harare: Zimbabwe Human Rights NGO Forum, 2006), available at http://www.hrforumzim.org/reports/special-reports/exploring-transitional-justice-options-in-contemporary-zimbabwe/ (accessed April 30, 2012).
39. Rejoice Shumba, "Social Identities in the National Youth Service of Zimbabwe," MA dissertation, University of Johannesburg, 2006.
40. Munyaradzi Gwisai, *Revolutionaries, Resistance and Crisis in Zimbabwe* (Harare: International Socialist Organisation, 2002), 32.
41. For an overview, see Leo Zeilig, "Zimbabwe: Imperialism, Hypocrisy and Fake Nationalism," in *International Socialism* 119 (2008), available at http://www.isj.org.uk/index.php4?id=458&issue=119.
42. Ibid.
43. Ibid.
44. Bomba interview.
45. Interview, Tella Barangwe, March 21, 2010.
46. Zimbabwe Human Rights NGO Forum, *Exploring Transitional Justice Options.*
47. Sisulu, Richards, and Kibble, "Where to for Zimbabwean Churches and Civil Society?," 246–47.
48. Zimbabwe Human Rights NGO Forum, *Exploring Transitional Justice Options.*
49. Interview, Tinashe Chisaira, March 19, 2010.
50. Ibid.
51. Interview, Mike Sambo, March 12, 2012.
52. Interview, Tafadzwa Choto, March 13, 2010.
53. Chisaira interview.

54. Interview, Munyaradzi Gwisai, March 20, 2010.
55. Patrick Bond, "Vultures Circle Zimbabwe," *Counterpunch*, April 5–7, 2008, available at www.counterpunch.org/bond04052008.html (accessed April 30, 2012).
56. Tanyanyiwa interview.
57. See Brian Raftopoulos's conclusion on the recent period in Zimbabwean history in Brian Raftopoulos and Alois Mlambo, eds., *Becoming Zimbabwe: A History from the Pre-Colonial Period to 2008* (Harare: Weaver Press, 2009).
58. Sisulu, Richards, and Kibble, "Where to for Zimbabwean Churches and Civil Society?," 255.
59. Interview, Alex Langwenya, SWAYOCO, Mbabane, February 25, 2006.
60. Interview, Vincent Dlamini, Mbabane, February 25, 2006.
61. Interview, Joyce Vilikati, Women's Resource Centre, Manzini, Swaziland, February 24, 2006.
62. Interview, Mario Masuku, PUDEMO, Manzini, February 27, 2006.
63. Interview, Musa Hlophe, Coalition of Concerned Civil Society Organisations, Manzini, Swaziland, February 28, 2006.
64. Ibid.
65. Masuku interview.
66. Ibid.
67. Discussions with Socio-Economic Justice Foundation (SEJF), Simunye, Swaziland, February 27, 2006.
68. Langwenya interview.
69. SEJF discussions.
70. Ibid.
71. Hlophe interview.
72. Ibid.
73. International Monetary Fund, *Kingdom of Swaziland Article IV Consultation—Staff Report* (Washington, D.C.: IMF, 2006), available at http://www.imf .org/external/pubs/ft/scr/2006/cr06106.pdf (accessed April 30, 2012). See also *Government Gazette* vol. XLIV, no. 8 (February 6, 2006); interview, Quinto Dlamini, Swaziland National Association of Civil Servants, Manzini, Swaziland, February 28, 2006.
74. Vincent Dlamini interview.
75. Langwenya interview.
76. Ibid.
77. Masuku interview.
78. SEJF discussions.
79. Vincent Dlamini interview; SEJF discussions.

Chapter 7: Social Forums
and the World Social Forum in Africa

1. Donatella Della Porta and Sidney Tarrow, *Transnational Protest and Social Activism* (Lanham, MD: Rowman & Littlefield, 2005), 1–21.
2. David Harvey, *A Brief History of Neoliberalism* (Oxford: Oxford University Press, 2005), 15.
3. William F. Fisher and Thomas Ponniah, eds., *Another World is Possible: Popular Alternatives to Globalization at the World Social Forum* (London: Zed Books, 2003); Boaventura de Sousa Santos, *The Rise of the Global Left: The World Social Forum and Beyond* (London: Zed Books, 2006).
4. A useful summary of these arguments is provided by Focus on the Global South, "Focus on Trade No. 136" (Bangkok: Focus on the Global South, 2008), available at http://www.focusweb.org/node/1327 (accessed November 20, 2009).
5. Fisher and Ponniah, *Another World is Possible*, 3.
6. Michael Hardt and Antonio Negri, "Foreword," in Fisher and Ponniah, *Another World is Possible*, xvi–xix.
7. Hilary Wainright, "The Forum as Jazz," in Jai Sen, Anita Anand, Arturo Escobar, and Peter Waterman, eds., *The World Social Forum: Challenging Empires* (Montreal: Black Rose Books, 2004), xviii–xix.
8. Alex Callinicos and Chris Nineham, "At an Impasse?: Anti-Capitalism and the Social Forums Today," *International Socialism* 115 (2007), 69–110.
9. Peter Waterman, "The Secret of Fire," in Sen et al., *The World Social Forum*, 148–60.
10. Ibid., 153.
11. Michael Albert, "'The WSF: Where to Now?,'" in ibid., 323–28.
12. African Social Forum 2003 Addis Ababa Consensus, "Another Africa is Possible!" (Addis Ababa: ASF, 2003), available at http://www.sarpn.org.za/documents/d0000167/P163_ASF_consensus.pdf (accessed December 12, 2006).
13. Thomas Deve, "Africa in Search of a Deeper Dialogue beyond Addis and Bamako: Reflections on Africa and the Mumbai 2004 World Social Forum" (2004), available at http://www.sarpn.org.za/documents/d0000699/WSF_Deve.pdf (accessed March 12, 2006).
14. EPAs are the European Union's aid-trade partnership agreements. Replacing the Lomé and Cotonou Agreements, they effectively impose free-trade policies on African (and Caribbean and Pacific) countries, opening their domestic markets to greater access for highly subsidized European agricultural producers and further undermining local producers.
15. Amanda Alexander and Mandisa Mbali, "Have the Slaves Left the Master's House? A Report on the Africa Social Forum," *Journal of Asian and African Studies* vol. 39, no. 5 (2005), 407–16.
16. Callinicos and Nineham, "At an Impasse?," 72.
17. Marie-Emmanuelle Pommerolle and Joanna Siméant, "African Voices and Activists at the WSF in Nairobi: The Uncertain Ways of Transnational African

Activism," paper presented to the Africa-Europe Group for Interdisciplinary Studies (AEGIS) European Conference on African Studies, Leiden, Netherlands, July 11–14, 2007. See also Marie-Emmanuelle Pommerolle and Joanna Siméant, *Un Autre Monde à Nairobi: Le Forum Social Mondial 2007, Entre Extraversions et Causes Africaines* (Paris: Karthala, 2008).

18. Quoted in *Terra Viva*, World Social Forum newspaper, January 24 and 25, 2007.
19. Quoted in *Daily Nation* (Nairobi), January 25, 2007.
20. Interview, Peter Ngulube Chinoko, coordinator, Catholic Commission for Justice, Development, and Peace, Lilongwe Diocese, Nairobi, January 23, 2007.
21. Ibid.
22. Interview, Mutawaya Sitali, Jesuit Centre for Theological Reflection Zambia, Nairobi, January 22, 2007.
23. Interview, Humphrey Sikapizye, Zambia Council for Social Development, Nairobi, January 23, 2007.
24. Ibid.
25. Interview, Tshumba Nkosi, Crisis in Zimbabwe Coalition, Nairobi, January 23, 2007.
26. Interview, Lucia Matibenga, vice president, Zimbabwe Congress of Trade Unions, Nairobi, January 24, 2007.
27. Discussion with Swazi activists, Nairobi, January 22–24, 2007.
28. For a powerful argument regarding the continued relevance of the nation-state, see Linda Weiss, *The Myth of the Powerless State: Governing the Economy in a Global Era* (Cambridge: Polity Press, 1998).
29. Interviews with Mabvuto Bamusi, director, Malawi Economic Justice Network, Lilongwe, June 7, 2006, and Andrew Mushi, advocacy officer, Tanzania Association of NGOs, Dar es Salaam, August 29, 2005.

Chapter 8: Conclusion

1. See, for example, the recent special issue of *Review of African Political Economy* 125 (September 2010), on "Social Movements and Struggles in Africa," available at http://www.roape.org/125/ (accessed May 2, 2012).
2. For an exemplary study of such inequalities and power relationships, see Nadine Beckmann and Janet Bujra, "The 'Politics of the Queue': PLHA Politicisation and AIDS Activism in Tanzania," paper presented at the University of Leeds conference Democratization in Africa: Retrospective and Future Prospects, December 4–5, 2009.
3. Alex Callinicos, "Ukraine: is the Future Orange?" *Socialist Worker* (UK), December 11, 2004.
4. Chris Harman, "Are You Being Served?," *Socialist Review* 286 (2004).
5. Kagoro interview.
6. Interview, Cherif Ba, Université Cheikh Anta Diop, Dakar, February 12, 2004.
7. Colin Barker, "Robert Michels and the 'Cruel Game'" in Barker, Johnson, and Lavalette, eds., *Leadership and Social Movements*, 42.

8. Gwisai, *Revolutionaries, Resistance and Crisis in Zimbabwe*, 27.

9. See Leo Zeilig, "Tony Cliff: Deflected Revolution in Africa," *International Socialism Journal* 126 (2010), available at http://www.isj.org.uk/?id=641 (accessed May 2, 2012).

10. See Ben Fine and Dimitris Milonakis, *From Economics Imperialism to Freakonomics: The Shifting Boundaries Between Economics and Other Social Sciences* (London: Routledge, 2009).

11. David Harvey, "Organising for the Anti-Capitalist Transition," speech delivered at the World Social Forum, Porto Alegre, Brazil, January 26, 2010, available at http://davidharvey.org/2009/12/organizing-for-the-anti-capitalist -transition/ (accessed May 2, 2012).

12. For example, the UK's previous prime minister, Gordon Brown, boasted before the financial crash that he had ended, singlehandedly, capitalism's tendency to boom and bust: Deborah Summers, "No Return to Boom and Bust; What Brown Said When He Was Chancellor," *Guardian*, September 11, 2008, available at http://www.guardian.co.uk/politics/2008/sep/11/gordonbrown .economy (accessed April 30, 2012).

13. Afrique 21, "2007–2009 Crise Alimentaire: Révoltes et Résistances" in *Afriques 213* (Spring 2010), available at http://www.scribd.com/doc/29323136/Afriques -21-n%C2%B03-6-pages (accessed May 2, 2012); Makama Bawa Oumarou and Bénédicte Maccatory, "Des Mobilisations à Caractère Socio-économique mais aussi Politique," paper presented at *Lutters dans les Afriques* conference, Université Paris I Panthéon, January 22–23, 2010.

14. See, for example, John Saul, "African Studies in Canada," speech delivered at the Annual Conference of the Canadian Association of African Studies, Ottawa, May 5–7, 2010.

INDEX

Abahlali baseMjondolo (ABM) (South Africa), 121, 126, 255, 274
Abekouta Women's Union, 65
Aborisade, Femi, x, 57
Action Aid, 228
Africa Synod House, 184
African Court of Women, 217
African Forum and Network on Debt and Development, 160, 277
African Methodist Episcopal Church (AMEC), 60, 255
African Mineworkers' Union, 56
African National Congress (ANC) (South Africa), 56, 92–98, 100–01, 103–28, 196, 199, 222, 255, 272
See also Congress Alliance
African Social Forums (ASF), 158, 212–22, 228, 234, 255, 257
African Union, 216, 222
See also New Economic Plan for African Development (NEPAD)
Agence Nationale de Renseignements, 180
Agricultural Development and Marketing Corporation (ADMARC), 145, 152–52, 255
AIDS. see HIV/AIDS
Akosombo Dam, 75
Aladura church (Nigeria), 61
Alexandra township, 106–07

Algeria, 32, 76, 83, 256
Amin, Samir, 6
Amis de Nelson Mandela pour la Defénse des Droits de l'Homme (Congo), 181
Amnesty International, 181, 279
Anglo-American Corporation, 151
Angola, 52, 68, 108, 213
Anti-Eviction Campaign (AEC), 120, 123, 255, 274
Anti-Privatization Forum (APF), 120, 123, 125, 126, 255
Arab Maghreb Union, 76
Arab Spring, 15, 16, 192
Arusha Declaration of 1967, 63
Association Africaine de Défense des Droits de l'Homme (Congo), 181

Ba, Cherif, 246, 283
Bamba, Cheikh Ahmadou, 61
Bamusi, Mabvuto, 151
Banda, Hastings Kamuzu, 132, 133, 137, 139, 170
Banda, Rupiah, 154, 156
Barker, Colin, x, 21, 23, 246, 259
Bas-Congo, 181
Bashir, Omar al-, 83
Basic Conditions of Employment Act (South Africa), 116
Bayart, Jean-François, 41, 262, 275

Belgian Congo, 61
  See also Democratic Republic
    of Congo
Belgium, 61, 171, 266
Bemba peoples, 68
Bemba, Jean-Pierre, 180
Benin, 57, 84
Bianchini, Pascal, 42
Biel, Robert, 75
Biko, Steve, 100
Bill of Rights (Malawi), 155
Bill of Rights (South Africa), 93
Bill of Rights (Zambia), 153
Bissau, 33
Biti, Tendai, 191
Black Local Authority (BLA), 102, 255
Blair, Tony, 230
Boipatong, South Africa, 111
Bophuthatswana, South Africa, 113
"Bop" Uprising, 113
Botha, P. W. , 35, 102
Botswana, 190, 213, 221
Bourguiba, Habib, 77
Bowen, Merle L., 71, 265
Brazil, 82, 94, 210, 269
British Communist Party, 73
Brown, Gordon, 284
Bukavu, Congo, 172, 174
Bulawayo, 55, 193, 280
Burkina Faso, 84
Burundi, 84
Bush, George W., 230
Business Day, 118

Cabral, Amílcar, 32–34, 73
Callinicos, Alex, x, 211
Cameroon, 42, 84, 202, 262
Cancun, Mexico, 215, 216
Cape of Good Hope, 96
Cape Town, South Africa, 101, 106, 273
Cape Verde, 34
Caritas Zambia, 158
Catholic Church, 60–63, 85, 132, 155,
    173–76, 181, 225, 255
Catholic Commission for Justice and
    Peace, 227
Catholic Commission for Justice,

Development and Peace (CCJDP),
    146, 154, 158, 161, 255
Ceauşescu, Nicolae, 171
CelTel, 158, 227
Central African Federation, 56
Central African Republic, 84
Ceruti, Claire, 44
Chabal, Patrick, 34, 36
Chad, 76, 84
Chambishi, Zambia, 145
Chancellor College, 132
Chavez, Hugo, 230
Chiapas, Mexico, 206
Chicago, 46
Chihana, Chakufwa, 133
Chilembwe, John, 60
Chiluba, Frederick, 133, 135, 137, 140,
    141, 149
China, 6, 68, 114, 122, 145, 146, 200, 234
Chinoko, Peter, 161, 227, 228
Chinsali, Northern Rhodesia, 68
Chisaira, Tinashe, 190
Chitungwiza, Zimbabwe, 193
Choto, Tafadzwa, x
Christian Aid, 146
Christianity, 60, 61, 88, 103
Citizens for a Better Environment, 151
Citizens Forum, 154
Civil Society Agriculture Network
    (CSANet), 152, 255
Civil Society for Poverty Reduction
    (CSPR), 150, 255
Civil Society Trade Network of Zambia, 146
Cliff, Tony, 71
Coalition of Concerned Civil Society
    Organisations, 198
Coalition of Non-Governmental Organi-
    sations of Malawi (CONGOMA),
    138, 139, 255
Cold War, 15, 169
Cologne, Germany, 206
Comintern, 31, 260
Comité Laïc de Co-ordination, 174
Commission for Conciliation, Mediation,
    and Arbitration, 116
Communist Parties, 54, 74, 271
Communist Party (South Africa), *see* South

African Communist Party (SACP)
Community Social Forums, 218
Comoros, 84
Concerned Citizens Forum, 120
Conference for a Democratic Future, 108
Congo, see Democratic Republic of Congo
Congress Alliance (South Africa), 93, 95,
     103–06, 110, 113, 115, 119–27, 133
Congress of Malawi Trade Unions, 136
Congress of South African Trade Unions
     (COSATU), ix, 101, 104–07, 110–19,
     123–27, 223, 255, 268, 271, 272, 274
Congress of the People in Kliptown, 98
Constitution of the Republic of South
     Africa, 93
Constitutional Review Commission, 153,
     196
Constitutional Women's Coalition, 183
Convention People's Party, 65
Cooper, Frederick, 29, 264
Copperbelt region of Zambia, 36, 55, 78, 147
Côte d'Ivoire, 84, 217
Cotonou, Benin, 84
Cotonou agreement, 200, 282
Crisis in Zimbabwe Coalition, 230
Crossroads, 106
Cuba, 32, 68, 108
Cuito Cuanavale, Angola, 108

Daily Nation, 227
Dakar, vii, 210
DanChurchAid, 228
Dar es Salaam, Tanzania, 160, 221, 228
Davidson, Basil, 52
Davis, Mike, 45, 48
Davos, Switzerland, 210
Defiance Campaign against Unjust Laws,
     98, 108
Democratic Republic of Congo (DRC), 5,
     29, 63, 73–74, 82–83, 87, 166–82 pas-
     sim, 202, 213, 225, 255, 257, 266, 279
Democratic Progressive Party (DPP),
     149, 155, 255
Democratic United Front for a People-
     Driven Constitution (DUF), 192, 255
Desai, Ashwin, 127
Destour party (Tunisia), 77

Development of Malawi Traders' Trust, 141
Dibua, Jeremiah, 80
Dlamini, Prince Cedza, 196
Doha, Qatar, 216, 233, 234
Draper, Hal, 43
Durban, South Africa, 120, 121, 274, 275
Durban Social Forum, 120
Dutch East India Company, 96

Economic and Structural Adjustment
     Programs (ESAP), 182–84, 255
Economic Association of Zambia, 147
Economic Justice Network, 150, 231, 256
Economist, 114, 149
Egypt, 52, 54, 76
Employment Act of 1999 (Malawi), 136
Employment Equity Act (South Africa), 116
Engels, Friedrich, 20
Englund, Harri, 132, 134, 136, 139, 163
Environmental Protection Fund, 151
Eskom, 121
European Partnership Agreements
     (EPAs), 200, 217–18, 225 255, 282
European Union (EU), 200, 206, 218, 282

Fanon, Frantz, 32–34, 47, 59, 248, 271
Fédération des Étudiants d'Afrique Noire
     en France (FEANF), 73, 255, 265, 266
Federation of Free Trade Unions of
     Zambia (FFTUZ), 136, 142, 146, 255
Federation of South African Trade
     Unions (FOSATU), 100, 101, 104,
     110, 256, 272
Federation of South African Women, 98
Financial Mail, 121
Financial Times, 109
First, Ruth, 52
For Whom the Windfalls?, 146
Foster, Joe, 110
Foundation for Democratic Process
     (FODEP), 134, 137, 256, 275
France, 73, 255, 260, 262, 265
Freedom Charter, 98, 105, 269, 272
French West Africa, 56, 57, 61, 65
Front de Libération Nationale (FLN), 83,
     256
Front Islamique du Salut (FIS), 83, 256

Gabon, 84
Gandhi, 8, 175
Gauteng, South Africa, 105, 112, 120, 122, 272
Ghana, 4, 65, 73, 75, 76, 84, 217, 218
Godongwana, Enoch, 111
Goma, Congo, 174
Gondwe, Goodall, 153
Gono, Gideon, 187
Goodwin, Jeff, 21, 25
Government of National Unity (GNU), 191, 256
Greenpeace, 205, 249
Growth Africa, 121
Growth and Employment and Redistribution Programme (GEAR), 42, 110, 114–16, 118–21, 201, 256
Guinea, 33, 56, 64, 73, 76, 84
Guinea-Bissau, 34, 52
Gwisai, Munyaradzi, 186

Hani, Chris, 112
Harare, Zimbabwe, 186, 193, 212, 227, 231
    Southern African Social Forum in, 219–24
Harare Declaration, 109
Harman, Chris, 5, 243
Harrison, Graham, 41, 90
Harvey, David, 38, 206, 249
Highly Indebted Poor Countries (HIPC), 148, 157, 214, 256
HIV/AIDS, 89, 93–95, 117, 135, 141, 192, 220, 225, 268
Hlophe, Musa, 198, 200
Hodgkin, Thomas, 28
Housing Act of 1997 (South Africa), 115
Human Development Index, 141
Human Rights Watch, 181

Ilunga, Robert, 181
Imbokodvo party (Swaziland), 195
India, 8, 20, 269
Indian Revolt of 1857, 20
Indigenization Bill, 192
Inkatha Freedom Party, 111
International Human Rights Day, 117
International Labor Organization, 118

International Monetary Fund, 13, 27, 35–39, 82, 186, 203, 206, 221, 250, 256
    "IMF riots", 36, 76
    1977 revolt in Egypt and, 52
    African Social Forums and, 214–15, 219
    Poverty Reduction and Growth Facility, 152
    in Swaziland, 200
    in Zambia, 78-79, 142-143
    in Zimbabwe, 85
    second wave of revolts against, 52
    United States policy and, 208
International Socialist Organisation (ISO) (Zimbabwe), 191, 193, 256
Islam, 88
Islamism, 83, 88

Jehovah's Witnesses, 60, 62, 64
Jeneusse du Mouvement Populaire de la Révolution (JMPR), 82, 83, 256
Johannesburg, iv, ix, 46, 98, 105, 106, 111, 117, 196
Jubilee movement, 35, 148
Jubilee Zambia, 152, 214, 229, 275
Justice and Peace Department of the Catholic Secretariat, 160

Kabila, Laurent, 168, 179–82
Kagoro, Brian, 183, 245
Kamwana, Elliott, 60–61
Kananga, Congo, 174
Karl-i-Bond, Jean Nguza, 172, 177
Kaunda, Kenneth, 62, 78, 133, 135, 137, 199
Keita, Aoua, 65
Kennedy, John F. , 75, 121
Kenya, 4, 56, 84, 155, 217–218, 221, 245, 256
    see also Mau Mau movement, 61
    World Social Forum in, 16, 225–32, 245
Kenya African National Union (KANU), 85, 256
Kérékou, Mathieu, 84
Keynesianism, 13, 112, 270
Keys, Derek, 113
Khutsong, South Africa, 122
Kibamba, Deus, 160
Kigali, Rwanda, 63
Kimbangu, Simon, 61

King, Martin Luther, Jr., 175
Kingis, Pastor Alphonse, 64
Kinshasa, Congo, 170–73, 175, 177, 179–81
Kisangani, Congo, 64, 174, 175
Kitawala movement (Congo), 63, 64
Kitwe, Zambia, 147
Kitwit, Congo, 174
Klerk, F. W. de, 107, 108
Komakoma, Father Joe, 131, 160
Kongo, Loka Ne, 87, 169, 178, 179
Kuti, Fummilayo Anikulapo-, 65
KwaZulu-Natal, 112, 120

Labor Relations Act (South Africa), 115
Labor Research Services, 121
Labour Relations Act (Zambia), 146
Labour Relations Act of 1996 (Malawi), 136
Lagos, Nigeria, 64
Lagos Market Women's Association, 64
Land and Freedom Army, see Mau Mau
    movement
Langwenya, Alex, 201
Larmer, Miles, x
Law Association of Zambia, 140
Law Commission of Malawi, 155
Lehulere, Oupa, 125, 274, 275
Lenshina, Alice, 61, 62
Lesotho, 84, 212
Leys, Colin, 90
Liberation Front of Mozambique
    (FRELIMO), 71
Lilombo, Asse, 12, 29
Lilongwe, Malawi, 228
Limpopo River, 126, 272
Lobunda, Gustave, 175
Lomé agreement, 200, 282
London, x, 65, 73
London Metal Exchange, 35
Lubumbashi (Congo), 171, 172
Lumpa Church, 61, 62
Lumumba, Patrice, 83, 180, 266
Lusaka, Zambia, 140, 143, 228
    Southern African Social Forums in,
        213–16, 216–19

M'membe, Fred, 137
Madagascar, 84

Madzikzela-Mandela, Winnie, 118
Making of the English Working Class, The, 4
Malawi, 60, 64, 132, 136–63, 170, 202,
    233, 235, 255–57
    Social Forums and, 212–13, 217–18,
        220, 223, 227–28, 231
Malawi Congress of Trade Unions
    (MCTU), 136, 143, 256
Malawi Congress Party, 132
Malawi Economic Justice Network
    (MEJN), 150, 151, 256
Malawi Growth and Development
    Strategy, 152
Malawi Human Rights and
    Rehabilitation Centre, 139
Mali, 76, 84, 202, 212
Mamdani, Mahmood, 72
Manchester, England, 46
Mandela, Nelson, 92, 96, 103, 109, 111,
    113, 116, 271
Manzini, Swaziland, 197, 200
Maoism, 32, 68
Martins, Ludo, 178
Marx, Karl, x, 11, 20, 43–44, 259–60, 263,
    270–71
Marxism, 73
Masuku, Mario, 197, 198, 201
Matibenga, Lucia, 223, 230
Mau Mau movement, 61, 227
Mauritania, 76, 84
Mauritius, 213
Mayekiso, Moses, 110, 111, 272
Mbeki, Thabo, 96, 114, 116, 118, 121–25
Mbembe, Achille, 42, 262
Mboya, Tom, 56
Mbuji Mayi, Congo, 172–74
McKinley, Dale, 125–26
Meru, Tanganyika (Tanzania), 67
Michuki, John, 227
Misabiko, Golden, 181
Mobutists, 178
Mobutu Sese Seko, Joseph, 82–83, 87,
    167–73, 176–79
Mohammed, Bibi Titi, 65, 66
Moi, Daniel Arap, 85, 218
Moore, Henrietta, 68, 70
Morocco, 76

Moscow, USSR, 74, 103, 270
Motsepe, Patrice, 121
Mouvement Populaire de la Révolution
    (Congo), 170
Mouvement Républicain National pour la
    Démocratie et le Développement
    (Zaire), 63
Movement for Democratic Change
    (MDC) (Zimbabwe), 86–87, 167,
    182–94, 201, 203, 220, 230, 256
Movement for Multi-Party Democracy
    (MMD) (Zimbabwe), 131, 133–35,
    139, 141, 145–47, 149, 256
Mozambique, 52, 68, 71, 220
Mpundu, José, 175
Mswati III, King, 195, 230
Mugabe, Robert, 86–87, 186–87, 190–91,
    199, 215, 220, 230
Muge, Bishop, 85
Multi-Fiber Agreement, 200
Mulumba, Étienne Tshisekedi, 171
Muluzi, Bakili, 132, 136–37, 139, 141, 143,
    149, 155
Mumbai, India, 216
Mung'omba, Wila, 153
Musokotwane, Kebby, 78
Mutambara, Arthur, 86, 186
Mutharika, Bingu wa, 149, 155
Mwanakatwe Commission, 137, 153–54
Mwanawasa, Levy, 149, 153–54, 156
Mwonzora, Douglas, 192

Nairobi, 16, 56, 218
    World Social Forum in, 210, 212,
        225–32, 235
Namibia, 108, 213, 221
National Association of Nigerian
    Students, 80
National Association of Small Business
    Women (Malawi), 141
National Cadreship School (Swaziland),
    201
National Conference (Congo), 173–78
National Conference of Active Forces
    (Benin), 84
National Constitutional Assembly (NCA)
    (Zimbabwe), 183, 184, 191, 256, 280

National Constitutional Conference
    (NCC) (Zambia), 154, 256
National Council of Nigeria and the
    Cameroons (NCNC), 65, 256
National Economic Development and
    Labour Council, 116
National Federation of Workers' Unions
    of Benin, 84
National Party (NP) (South Africa), 35,
    97, 107, 256
National Union of Metalworkers of South
    Africa, 101, 110
National Union of Mineworkers (South
    Africa), 102, 272
National Union of Tanganyika, 57
National Union of Textile Workers
    (South Africa), 100
National Union of the Clothing Industry
    of Zimbabwe (NUCIZ), 183, 194, 256
National Women's Lobby (Zambia), 133
National Youth Service (Zimbabwe), 185,
    280
Native Land Act (South Africa), 97
Neo-Keynesianism, 249
Netherlands, 143
New Economic Plan for African Develop-
    ment (NEPAD), 216, 222, 256
New National Party (South Africa), 273
NGO Act (Malawi), 139, 156, 164
NGO Bill (Zambia), 139
NGO Bill (Zimbabwe), 189
Ngwane National Liberatory Congress
    (Swaziland), 195
Ngwane, Trevor, 210
Nicaragua, 169
Niger, 212
Niger Delta, 46, 218
Nigeria, 4, 58, 61, 73, 80, 84, 209, 245, 261
    general strikes in, 55, 218
    Social Forums in, 217–18
    women's movement in, 64–65
Nigerian Union of Young Democrats, 64
Nigerian Women's Party, 64
Nigerian Women's Union, 65
Nimeiri, Gaafar, 36, 83
Nineham, Chris, 211
Nixon, Richard, 75

Nkomo, Joshua, 56
Nkosi, Tshumba, 230
Nkrumah, Kwame, 30, 64, 65, 73–75,
    265–66
Non-Governmental Organizations
    Coordinating Committee
    (NGOCC), 134, 140, 256
Nonde, Joyce, 142, 146
North American Free Trade Agreement
    (NAFTA), 206, 256
Nyasaland, 60
    See also Malawi
Nyerere, Julius, 57, 63, 66, 74, 264
Nzongola-Ntalaja, George, 173–74, 180

Oasis Forum, 140
Oates, Stephen B., 175
Okello, Bishop, 85
Oloo, Onyango, 226
Open Society Foundation, 198
Organisation for Economic Co-operation
    and Development (OECD), 94, 269

Pan-African Congresses, 225
Paris, France, 73
Paris Commune, 20
Partido Africano da Independência da
    Guiné e Cabo Verde, 32
Patriotic Front party (Zambia), 146
People's Revolutionary Party (Benin), 84
People's United Democratic Movement
    (PUDEMO) (Swaziland), 195–99,
    231, 257
Pijiguiti, Guinea-Bissau, 33
Planet of Slums, 45, 48
Poland, 82
Polokwane, South Africa, 123
Poni, Mzonke, 124
Porto Alegre, Brazil, 210, 219, 226
Portugal, 33, 34, 52, 71, 73
Poverty Reduction and Growth Facility, 152
Poverty Reduction Strategy Programs,
    (PRSPs), 143, 148–49, 150–53,
    156–57, 160, 164, 214, 233, 256
Prebisch, Raul, 269
Pretoria, 108, 112
Public Services International, 144

Rabobank, 143
Rainbow Nation, 92, 118, 120
Rassemblement Démocratique Africain, 65
Reconstruction and Development
    Programme, 112–15, 117, 257
Rhodesia, 55, 56, 61, 68
    See also Zambia
Romania, 171
Rosa Luxemburg Foundation, 192
Russia (post-Soviet), 117, 161
Rwanda, 63, 179

Sambo, Mike, 191
Sata, Michael, 146, 147, 156
Saul, John, 90, 261
Scott, James, 71
Seattle WTO protests, 15, 39, 40, 119, 206,
    207, 210, 234
Seddon, David, x
Senegal, vii, 5, 55, 202, 217, 245–46, 260
Senghor, Leopold, 73, 74
Sexwale, Tokyo, 112
Sharpeville massacre, 98, 101
Shinkolobwe, 181
Sichone, Lucy, 137
Sierra Leone, 64
Sikapizye, Humphrey, 229
Sikhala, Job, 184, 186
Sisulu, Walter, 103, 111
Sitali, Muyatawa, 229
Sobhuza II, King, 195
Social Movements Indaba Council (SMI)
    (South Africa), 120, 123, 257, 274
Social Movements United, 120
Socio-Economic Justice Foundation
    (SEJF), 199, 201, 257, 281
South African Communist Party (SACP),
    98, 100, 103–04, 106, 110–14 passim,
    122–26 passim, 257, 268
South African Congress of Trade Unions
    (SACTU), 98, 100, 101, 257
South African Council of Churches, 117
South African Students Organization, 100
Southern Africa Centre for Constructive
    Resolution of Disputes, 156, 278
Southern Africa Centre for Economic
    Justice, ix

Southern African People's Solidarity Network, 160, 222
Southern African Social Forum (SASF), 158, 212–24, 227, 231, 234, 257
   See also Harare, Lusaka
Southern African Trade Union Coordinating Council (SATUCC), 223, 230, 257
Soviet Union, 30, 55, 73, 74, 109, 270
   collapse of, 53, 87, 178, 206, 261
   See also Russia
Sow, Aissata, 65
Soweto, South Africa, 46, 47, 100, 270
Soweto Electricity Crisis Committee, 120
Soweto Uprising, 100
Sparks, Alistair, 92
Spoornet, 200
Sputnik, 30
Stalin, Joseph, 55
Stalinism, 31, 54, 127, 254
Standard, 227
Students and Academics' International Assistance Fund, 188
Sudan, 83
Swazi National Union of Unemployed People, 201
Swazi Railways, 200
Swaziland, 84, 166–67, 195–96, 199–201, 195–203, 221, 230–31, 235, 257
   Social Forums in, 212–13
Swaziland Federation of Trade Unions (SFTU), 195, 196, 198, 257
Swaziland Solidarity Network, 196
Swaziland Youth Congress (SWAYOCO), 196, 198, 200, 201, 257
Switzerland, 210

Tambo, Oliver, 103
Tanganyika, 64, 66, 67, 68, 257
   See also Tanzania
Tanganyika African National Union (TANU), 57, 65, 67, 257
   Women's Section, 65–66
Tanganyikan African Association, 67
Tanyanyiwa, Joesph, 183, 194
Tanzania, 63, 66–67, 71, 148, 257
   debt relief in, 151
   Social Forums and, 217, 220, 228

social movements in, 64, 131, 135, 138, 160, 221
Tanzania Association of Non-Governmental Organizations (TANGO), 151, 160, 257
Tarrow, Sidney, 26
Telkom, 121
Thompson, E. P., 4, 11, 23, 44–45, 240
Tilly, Charles, 19, 20, 25
Tinkhundla system, 195, 197, 199
Tomorrow is Another Country, 92
Toure, Sekou, 56, 57, 64
Trade Union Council of South Africa, 98
Transvaal, 108
Treatment Action Campaign (TAC), 117, 126, 257
Tripartite Alliance (South Africa), 93, 95
Tripartite Labour Consultative Council (Zambia), 146
Tshisekedi, Étienne, 87, 171, 173, 176–78, 181
Tshonda, J. Omasombo, 177
Tsvangirai, Morgan, 86, 184, 190–91
Tunisia, 76–78

Uganda, 132, 179
Ujamaa, 71
Umkhonto we Sizwe (MK) (South Africa), 105, 108, 256
Unilever, 67
Union des Fédéralistes et Républicans Indépendants (Congo), 172
Union pour la Démocratie et le Progrès Social (UDPS) (Congo), 87, 170–72, 177–78, 181, 257
Union Sacrée de l'Opposition Radicale (Congo), 172
UNISON, 144
United Democratic Front (UDF) (South Africa), 102–04, 106–07 132–33, 137, 149, 195, 257, 271
United Kingdom, 4, 8, 20, 65–69 passim, 73, 139, 195, 249, 284
United Nations World Conference against Racism, 120
United National Independence Party (UNIP) (Zambia), 62, 68, 78–79, 133,

135, 257
University of Dakar, 42
University of Kinshasa, 171
University of Lubumbashi, 5, 82, 171
University of the Witwatersrand, 4
University of Yaoundé, 42
University of Zimbabwe, 184, 190

Vaughan, Megan, 68, 70
Vereeniging. *See* Gauteng
Vietnam, 22, 68
Villers, Gautheir de, 177
Volta River, 75
Vorster, John, 35

Wabo, Willy, 181
Wainright, Hillary, 210
Wakeford, Kevin, 121
Wanawake, Umoja wa, 66, 257
Watchtower Society, 60
Water Boards (Malawi), 143, 144
Water Employees' Trade Union of Malawi
    (WETUM), 143–44, 257
Waterman, Peter, 211
West African Student Union, 73
Witwatersrand, 112
Women for Change (Zambia), 134, 158
Women of Zimbabwe Arise (WOZA),
    188–89, 257
Women's Leagues, 54, 65, 66
Women's Unity of Tanganyika (UWT),
    66, 257
World Bank, 35, 39, 55, 76, 82, 203, 250
    ͏eria, 80

͏2–43

͏44
͏219, 229

͏59,

World Trade Organization (WTO), 206,
    214–16, 232, 257
Doha round, 233–34
Seattle summit in 1999, 15, 27, 28, 39,
    64–65, 119, 206
World War I, 67
Wynne, Andy, x

Zaire, 63, 82–84, 168–71, 174–75
    See also Democratic Republic of Congo
Zambia Council for Social Development,
    156, 229
Zambia Election Monitoring and
    Coordination Committee, 134
Zambia National Commercial Bank
    (ZNCB), 143, 257
Zambia's Fifth National Development
    Plan, 151
Zambia's Poverty Reduction Strategy
    Program, 143
Zapatistas, 206
Zeilig, Leo, 44
Zghal, Abdelkader, 77
Zikist Movement, 55
Zimbabwe African National
    Union–Patriotic Front (ZANU-PF),
    85, 167, 182, 184–94, 230, 257
Zimbabwe Catholic Bishops' Conference,
    184
Zimbabwe Congress of Trade Unions
    (ZCTU), 86, 133, 136, 140, 184–85,
    222, 230, 257
Zimbabwe Council of Churches (ZCC),
    184, 257
Zimbabwe Election Support Network
    (ZESN), 184, 189, 257
Zimbabwe Human Rights NGO Forum,
    184, 189, 280
Zimbabwe National Student Union (ZI-
    NASU), 188, 191, 257
Zimbabwe Social Forum (ZSF), 188, 191,
    192, 229, 257
Zimbabwe Youth Democracy Trust, 188
Zionism, 61
͏ulu, Jack Jones, 214
͏na, Jacob, 96, 118, 124, 125, 127

About Haymarket Books

Haymarket Books is a nonprofit, progressive book distributor and publisher, a project of the Center for Economic Research and Social Change. We believe that activists need to take ideas, history, and politics into the many struggles for social justice today. Learning the lessons of past victories, as well as defeats, can arm a new generation of fighters for a better world. As Karl Marx said, "The philosophers have merely interpreted the world; the point, however, is to change it."

We take inspiration and courage from our namesakes, the Haymarket Martyrs, who gave their lives fighting for a better world. Their 1886 struggle for the eight-hour day reminds workers around the world that ordinary people can organize and struggle for their own liberation.

For more information and to shop our complete catalog of titles, visit us online at www.haymarketbooks.org.

Also from Haymarket Books

Class Struggle and Resistance in Africa
Edited by Leo Zeilig

Civil Rights in Peril
The Targeting of Arabs and Muslims, Elaine C. Hagopian

American Insurgents
A Brief History of American Anti-Imperialism, Richard

Boycott, Divestment, Sanctions
The Global Struggle for Palestinian Rights, On

The Democrats
A Critical History (updated edition), L

Field Notes on Democracy
Listening to Grasshoppers, Aru

The Meek and the Mil
Religion and Power across